Mystical Numerology

The Creative Power of Sounds and Numbers

Published by Eltanin Publishing, 95 Spear St., Charlotte, Vermont 05445. First edition.

For more resources, visit www.eltaninpublishing.com

ISBN 978-0615859552 (paperback)

Cover art and design by Sean P. Pehrson

Mystical Numerology

The Creative Power of Sounds and Numbers

John B. Pehrson

Dedication

This book is dedicated to my lovely wife,

Jeanne White Eagle

and to the five children we have between us:

Ryan, Sean, Alan, Jenny and John

with love.

Contents   Page

Foreword ....

Introduction: How Mystical Numerology Came About xi

Chapter One: Mystical Numerology: Getting Started 17

    The Vowel Sounds 20

    Working with the Vowel Sounds 24

Chapter Two: Working With Names: Vowel Sound Readings 26

    The First Name Vowel Sound 36

    Missing Vowels 39

Chapter Three: The Consonants & Number Paths 42

    Basic Number Meanings Chart 47

Chapter Four: First Letter & Personality 52

Chapter Five: Going Deeper With Names 59

    Life Purpose, Inner Urge, Legacy & Drive 60

Chapter Six: The 13-Month Mystical Numerology Calendar .73

    13-Month Calendar Conversion Charts 73

Chapter Seven: Working With Dates 77

Chapter Eight: Attainment Cycles, Year-Month-Day Cycles .. 99

Chapter Nine: Life Challenges 135

    Life Challenge Descriptions 139

Chapter Ten: Number Meanings – Going Deeper.................157

Chapter Eleven: Putting it All Together.....................................261

Chapter Twelve: Conclusion 275

Appendix A: Medicine Wheel Map 277

Appendix B: Traditional Systems of Numerology 283

Foreword

Dear Reader,

Some time ago, I asked my friend and mentor Joseph Rael, Beautiful Painted Arrow, to write a Foreword for my book on Mystical Numerology. And, he said yes! It was a natural choice as it was Joseph who taught me about the power and importance of the vowels sounds, a teaching that became the catalyst for looking at the ancient science of numerology in an entirely different way.

His teaching shifted and expanded my thinking, and helped me realize that the power of names, and of the very words we use to communicate, is rooted in sound. When we speak, the vibrations of our names and the words we use sing our reality into existence. Indeed, this realization became the cornerstone for the foundation upon which I built a new system of numerology.

One of Joseph's primary teachings is not to get stuck in form. Accordingly, Joseph rarely does exactly what you expect. Still, when I received a gorgeous 16" x 21" painting in the mail from Joseph instead of a written foreword, I have to admit I was puzzled. Then, my lovely wife, Jeanne White Eagle, reminded me about something Joseph said years ago. If you keep looking at a painting of his, the Spirit faces and symbols will talk to you. The painting will teach you.

And so it is with this painting, dear reader. It is an activator of the ancient wisdom that is within you. Call it a fore-knowledge instead of a fore-word. Indeed, if you will study Joseph's painting, *Fires of Enlightenment or New Knowledge*, it will prepare you to read on. You will find that it acts as a key to the doorway of new knowledge and the teachings embodied in this new system of numerology. Use the key. Open the door. And enter into a world of wonder and beauty and unbounded potential possibilities.

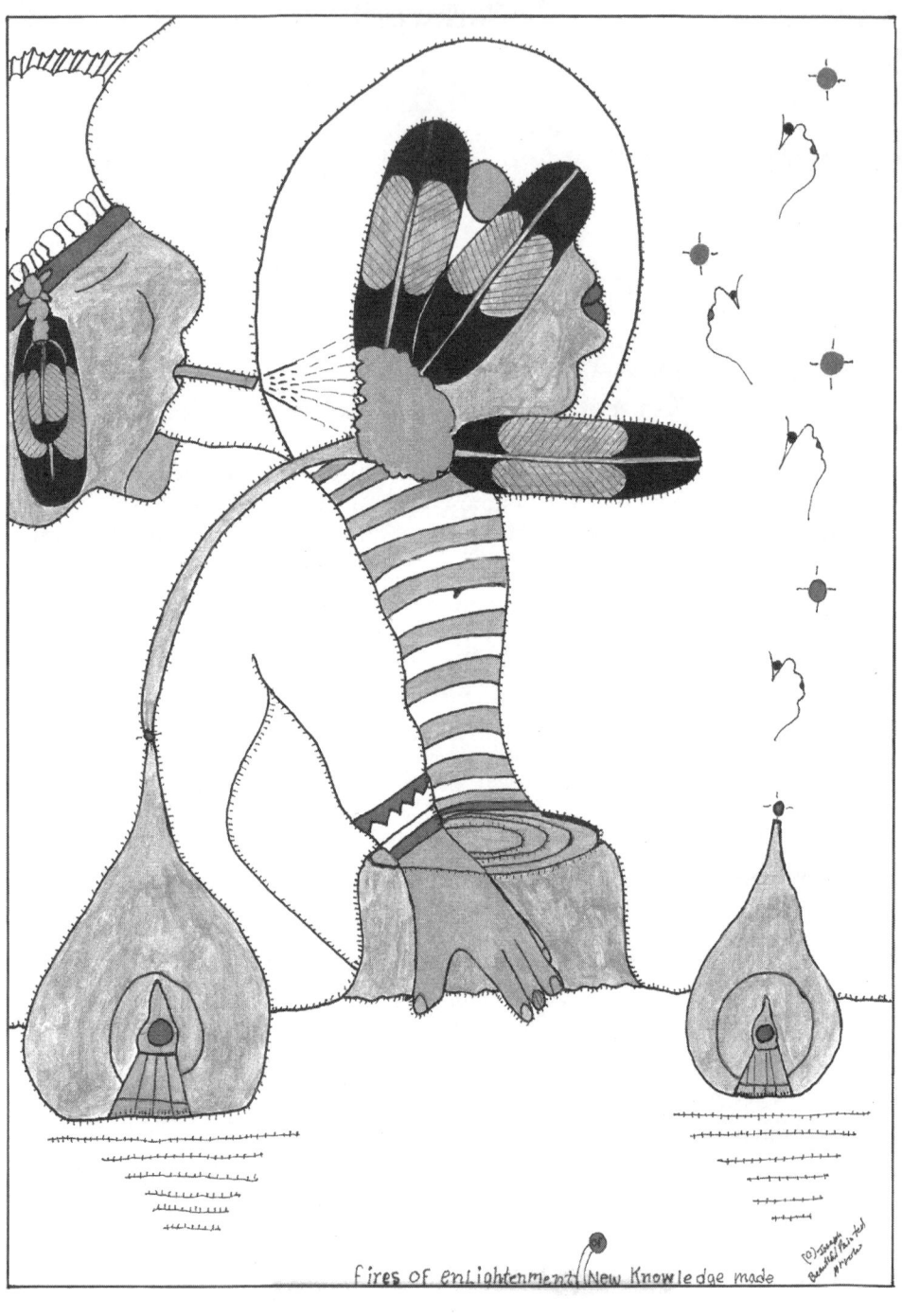

fires of enlightenment (New Knowledge made

If, at any time you feel lost, come back to the painting. Let its power re-activate ancient wisdom within you. Then, read on again. And, enjoy the journey.

John Pehrson

Waterbury, Vermont

January 2013

Note: The original painting is gorgeous in turquoise, brilliant gold, and splashes of red. But, it is expensive to reproduce. We will do so in limited edition, signed copies. Contact the publisher if you are interested in purchasing one of these.

Introduction

How Mystical Numerology Came About

I like to think of my system of Mystical Numerology as numerology for the Shift in Ages that is now upon us. It is a new system that is different from traditional western numerology in several significant ways, including a new 13-month calendar. But, before I describe more of the particulars of *what* Mystical Numerology is, perhaps it would be instructive to say something of how it came about.

My father was an Electrical Engineer, with quite an analytical and linear view of the world. He grew up on a farm, so he was also very practical and knew how to apply his engineering knowledge to the real world. My mother was an elementary school teacher and loved books. From her, I inherited a love for reading and writing. From my father, I inherited a love for numbers and for all things scientific.

Even when I was six years old, my favorite books were ones with scientific facts. I loved collecting and memorizing data: the distance from earth to the sun and moon, the speed of light, the circumference of the earth at the equator, the speed of sound, and so on. I also had a facility with numbers. They spoke to me. Math was always relatively easy for me. But, so was chemistry. Chemical equations just made sense. Had I not been chasing my father up the corporate ladder, I could have easily taken the path of the scientist and wound up doing research in some laboratory.

Instead, I became a Chemical Engineer. My father used to joke that this put me in the catbird seat because it gave me the ability to talk chemistry to engineers, and engineering to chemists. I went to work for DuPont at a Dacron® polyester manufacturing plant in Old Hickory, Tennessee. But, after six years on the "Dacron® farm," as one of my early colleagues described it, the company began to broaden my experience through stints in technical service, sales and marketing, strategic planning, and finally management. I was particularly good at analyzing market trends, predicting the future, and plotting strategic moves against our competitors in several different markets. In other words, I was good with numbers, and recognizing patterns.

DuPont was undergoing big changes back in the mid-1980s at the time I was a marketing and business strategist. Although I was interested in data-mapping and numerical analysis as a predictive tool, I was also interested in developing a deep understanding of how successful projects happen, and how successful change occurs. As a result, I developed a 10-step process that could be applied both to managing projects and creating organizational change. In essence, I was applying a basic understanding of numerology to the business world. And it worked!

As a recession hit in 1992, the golden age in DuPont came to a close. Many of the innovative management practices of the late 1980s disappeared as the company returned to an autocratic, command and control style of management. Unwilling to jump into the collective foxhole, keep my head down and wait for better times, I left DuPont at the end of that year. I started my own small executive coaching business in 1993. It was a watershed year.

At the close of 1995, another momentous event occurred. We met Joseph Rael, Beautiful Painted Arrow, a Native American mystic, medicine man, and visionary. He had "called" to my wife, Jeanne White Eagle, in a dream while we were doing conflict-resolution work in post-perestroika Russia.[1] Joseph taught us about the power of the vowel sounds as fundamental creative energies. He also taught us about the Native American Medicine Wheel. We began to do ceremonial vision-quest dances in which sound, movement and fasting combined to produce startlingly brilliant visions. Our lives turned 180-degrees topsy-turvy. We began living from inspiration, listening to our inner guidance, and stepping out in faith to follow our visions. It was huge. Life has never been the same.

During this period, while I was still making the transition out of the business world onto a more spiritual and grassroots-driven path, I remember having the first epiphany about a new system of numerology. It happened while I was flying to a business meeting. I realized that the vowel sounds (as pronounced in Spanish) – a, e, i, o, u, and y – should not get numbers assigned to them as is done in

---

[1] For the full story, read *Journey For The One,* by Monty Joynes, One Journey Publications, 2008.

traditional numerology. No. They represent the energies of the cardinal directions:

- A is the East
- E is the South
- I is the West
- O is the North
- U is the Center
- Y is the Above & Below

I also realized in the split-second of that epiphany, that the Native American Medicine Wheel is similar to the Tree of Life, the Kabbalah of Jewish Mysticism. The numbers represent the connecting paths between the vowel sounds and cardinal directions. And, wonder of wonders, just as there are 22 paths in the Kabbalah connecting the ten Sephirot, there are also 22 paths connecting the vowel sounds and cardinal directions on the Medicine Wheel!

"Wow!" I said to myself. "This is really cool! And, it is significant in a way that I *have* to investigate!" It was as if years of dabbling with traditional numerology, astrology and my long-held interest in applying the power of numbers to both life and business had come together in a scintillating vision of something new. I was in heaven.

In 1997, my wife went to spend a month in Guatemala with Don Alejandro Cirilo Perez Oxlaj, a K'iche Mayan priest and elder who is considered a prince among his people. He also came up to New Mexico and spent time teaching some of us about the Mayan Day Lords, and the Mayan Prophecies. I was like a sponge. I began keeping the count of the Mayan Days and studying their impact on my life. As I tracked the days in my personal journal, I also began to see the correspondences between the energies of the Day Lords from the Mayan spiritual calendar and the energies of the days calculated with my emerging system of numerology. Over time, this connection became stronger and is now a part of my system of Mystical Numerology.

The way this new system developed has been through flashes of insight – a sudden perception of the essential nature and meaning of an important part of the system, an intuitive grasp of how to proceed. When this happens, all the synapses in my brain seem to light up like a Christmas tree. Indeed, it is very much like Santa Claus has brought me a present in the form of a striking and illuminating discovery! But, these flashes of insight are also marching orders. When I receive them, the practical engineer part of me shifts into gear. I begin to enthusiastically investigate the new discovery. This is how Mystical Numerology has been developed.

Another one of these flashes of intuitive insight was that the Gregorian calendar was no longer suitable for this system of "numerology for the shift in ages." The Gregorian calendar starts and ends with no connection to any natural cycle. It is also a 12-month system that locks us into the inventive yet driven and volatile nature of this number. The new calendar was to begin close to the winter solstice (northern hemisphere), when the sun begins its return. And, it was to be a 13-month calendar! Hey, when it comes to the inner guidance I get, I just work here. My job is to keep saying yes.

As I began to work it out, what became clear is that fitting a 13-month calendar to a 365-day normal solar year means that all months except for one have 28 days, making for much more regular months. Finding the starting point for the calendar became a process of trial and error, and using the new calendar to calculate the Life Path of family, friends and famous people. When they fit, I knew I'd found the right day to begin the calendar – December 20.

This is how Mystical Numerology was developed. It was driven by *eureka* moments of mystical clarity, and then backed up by a lot of hard work to prove them out on a practical level. For instance, to validate the 13-month calendar that I created, I compiled hundreds of charts of friends, acquaintances, and famous people – analyzing their birth dates and entering the data into a searchable database to see if the resulting numbers fit what I or others knew about a person. I also created a searchable database of the numerology of important events throughout history to look for patterns in categories of events both natural (astrological events, earthquakes, volcanoes, storms, fires) and man-made (entertainment, economic, government & politics, religion, law, science & technology, wars & riots). This is an ongoing part of my research.

I also recognized that if NAMES can be analyzed through this "mystical science" of numbers, then so can WORDS. Following closely on the heels of this insight was another epiphany. Rather than just accepting the *traditional* meanings for the numbers, I realized that the *fundamental* meanings of each of the numbers can be derived by doing the numerology of individual words and phrases, and then looking for the concentration or central focus of meaning that emerges. This set me on a 6-year-long research project to confirm or modify the traditional number meanings that you find in typical books on numerology which, by the way, do not include meanings for the numbers 12 – 21. 11 and 22 are included in traditional numerology because they are considered "master numbers," but this also begs the question, "why" are they considered to be so. The answer to this question, and the meanings of the numbers emerged in the research that I did to compile a database of over 25,000 words and short descriptive phrases organized by the numbers 1 – 22, and categorized by things like positive and negative qualities, animal and plant associations, health and medical aspects, philosophy and religion, government and politics, business, culture, gemstones and colors, science and technology, work correspondences, places, and so on. What has emerged is fascinating and valuable. In fact, even though it sounds bold to say, it is not too big a stretch to say that my system of Mystical Numerology is one of the best researched systems of numerology on the market. Of course, it also offers a fresh look at an ancient science.

All of this has been a labor of love that I did for the sheer joy of satisfying that inner voice of discovery, the one that whispers in my ear, "How does the world *really* work? Are there deeper patterns that govern the actions of men and the forces of nature? If so, can these patterns be identified through their number vibrations? Can this study of numbers lead to self-discovery and a closer connection with the Divine Source?" These have been the questions that have moved this work forward. It was a personal journey, one that has paid many dividends to me, and to others with whom I've shared my new system – through workshops and personal readings. Now, that inner voice is telling me that it is time to share what I have learned more broadly.

Oh, yes, the last thing about Mystical Numerology is perhaps the most important: IT WORKS! And, it works magnificently well! I have done hundreds of Mystical Numerology readings and forecasts for people. I have never had anyone tell me that their reading didn't fit (although there have been one or two that were unhappy that it did). On the contrary, the great majority were amazed at the accuracy and depth of the information and insights that came out of just their full name and birth date. I have watched these people gain self-confidence and move forward in their lives with a greater sense of surefootedness in this often uncertain world. This, of course, has been the real pay-off for all of the work.

My fondest hope is that you will benefit from this new system of Mystical Numerology as much as I have, and that some of you will take the "research" that I have done even further – particularly extending it into different languages and alphabets.

More specifically, my research has focused primarily on English words and the Roman alphabet. Even so, when I do readings for clients in Israel, Norway, Germany or Croatia, as examples, people are frequently impressed with the accuracy and depth of the information – sometimes, even astounded. So, I suspect that what I have found out, and will teach you in this book, is true much more broadly than for just English speaking countries. But, I haven't yet done the fundamental research to prove it. It would be wonderful to explore the possibilities for collaboration with some of my readers to confirm my findings in other languages.

Chapter One:

Mystical Numerology – Getting Started

To become a true human, one must be conscious of listening and hearing the voice of the Great Mystery speaking through everything. ...The activity of sound is what made the people.

~Joseph Rael, Beautiful Painted Arrow~

Mystical Numerology is a system that is really based on sound and vibration. Everything in the universe is in a constant state of vibration. Everything from the smallest subatomic particle to the largest galaxy has a characteristic vibrational frequency, a characteristic sound. Sound has the power to create reality, and everything is vibrating-sounding-singing itself into existence.

The most fundamental energy in the universe may be consciousness, a fact that frontier science is beginning to confirm. Sound, directed by the energy of consciousness, has the power to create our reality. This is the reason that sacred chants are so powerful, why beautiful music or birdsongs can touch our soul, and why inspiring words can lift us up.

Energy directed by consciousness through sound and vibration creates the reality we experience. Mystical Numerology is the systematic study of the fundamental vibrations in words, names and dates that carry this power of creation. These vibrations are described by the vowel sounds, consonants, and the archetypal numbers 1 - 22. Mystical Numerology uses these fundamental sounds (energies) to "map" the patterns created by our names and the numbers of our birthdates so we can gain deeper understanding – of ourselves, of others, of relationships, of patterns that exist in nature and of events that happen in the world.

The Vowel Sounds

The vowel sounds represent the fundamental, formative energies of creation that carry the power of consciousness into manifestation as our reality. So, this is where our study must begin.

Each vowel sound represents a principal idea and has a specific place on the Medicine Wheel that is a metaphor for the universe, the circle of life, and the psyche. In Native American teachings, Great Beings stand as guardians in the gateways of each of the seven directions, very much like Archangels in Judeo-Christian or Islamic traditions. Such is the power of the vowel sounds. Each vowel sound stands for one of the seven directions, and carries the qualities associated with that direction as shown below:

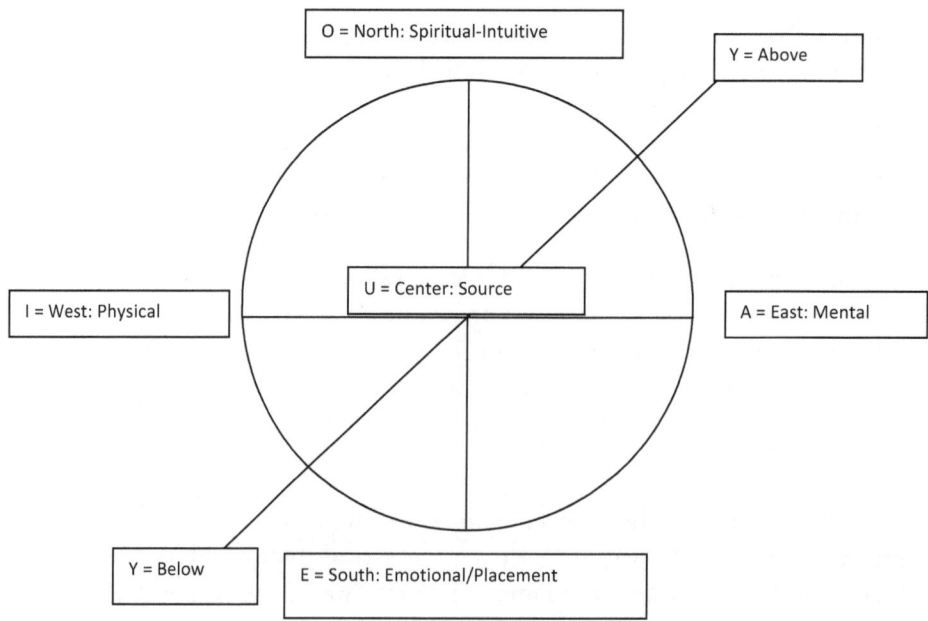

Medicine Wheel Directions & Meanings

In 1999, when my wife and I traveled to New Zealand, we took a canoe trip down the Wanganui River with members of the Owl Tribe of the Maori people. At an overnight stop at a Maori University, we gathered in a circle of some 50 people to say a prayer to bless the evening meal. We all joined hands in the circle. One of the female elders said, "Let us pray." Then, she began singing the vowel sounds, pronounced as they would be in Spanish: "ah, eh, iii, oh, and uu." It was the first time outside of the teachings of Beautiful Painted Arrow that we encountered another people who understood the power of these sounds, and had such reverence for their energies and their ability to connect us with the Divine. It was a teaching that I will never forget!

In October of 2000, we met a holy man in Israel. He was a Kabalist and rabbi, and he spoke to us about love in more ways than I have ever heard. We felt an immediate connection with David. A year later, he shared with us that there was a school for prophets 2000 years ago that used the vowel sounds in chants and songs as part of the training because they are such a direct connection to the Divine. Chanting the vowel sounds allowed these aspiring prophets to slip into the connected state of consciousness that allowed them to prophesy. The vowel sounds are very powerful energies, but somehow the knowledge of their power has been forgotten over the ages.

Hebrew uses the same vowel sounds as they are pronounced in Spanish: ah, eh, iii, oh and uu. It is an odd twist of fate that my wife, Jeanne White Eagle, and I would be introduced to their power by Joseph Rael, Beautiful Painted Arrow. I say it is odd because his ancient Spanish forebears were Sephardic Jews who settled in Spain during the Diaspora. The name "Rael" is actually a shortened form of "Israel." In the 1500s one of Joseph's paternal great great ... great grandfathers joined the military to escape the Spanish Inquisition and traveled to the New World with one of the explorers, perhaps Don Antonio Espejo who explored what is now New Mexico, or Juan de Zaldivar who came into Colorado and the San Luis Valley. This great great grandfather married a woman from the Southern Ute tribe. Joseph is part of this lineage that ties him back to Israel, and to the knowledge of the sacred power of the vowel sounds as fundamental creative energies. Perhaps the understanding that Joseph had of the vowel sounds originally came from Israel and the school for prophets. Joseph taught Jeanne and me this knowledge.

Then, in 2001, Jeanne and I wound up in Israel teaching about the power of the vowel sounds especially when used in spontaneous songs and chants. The teachings went full circle. I've always found this to be amazing!

Vowel Sound Meanings and Associations

Vowel	Direction	Meaning	Element, Color	Totems, Energies, Archangels
U	Center	The Source, God, Great Spirit, unity, the void; transformation, and the power of carrying.	The Void Purple	None
Y	Above & Below	The connection with other realities, dimensions & possibilities; Duality.	Wood Blue, Green	Unicorn, Vulture Zero-point Field
A	East	Mental realm, the place of new beginnings, sunrise, morning, childhood, purity, springtime.	Water Yellow	Wolf, Crow Raphael
E	South	Emotional realm, heart, inner child, youth, your place in the world, relationships, growth, noon, summer.	Fire White	Coyote, Spider Uriel
I	West	Physical realm, the body, health, reconciliation, adulthood, harvest, autumn, night.	Earth Black	Owl, Elephant Michael
O	North	Spiritual–intuitive realm, innocence & teachability, old age, ancestors, dreamtime, winter.	Wind/Air Red	Dragonfly, Bee Gabriel

Different traditions place different colors in the directions for the Medicine Wheel. The colors that I've shown come from a system taught by Joseph Rael, Beautiful Painted Arrow. The placements of the elements (wood, water, fire, earth and air) and the totem animals come out of my own research into the numbers of these entities and their best fit with the directions. The correspondence between the cardinal directions and the archangels is from their most common attributions.

A note about the vowel sounds before I describe their basic meanings. First, remember that A, E, I, O and U are pronounced as they would be in Spanish or Hebrew: ah, eh, iii, oh and uu. Second, the "Y" also has the *iii-sound*. The sound is the same as the sound for the "I," and yet the "Y" has a different energy than the "I." This is an important point. It is important to realize that individual letters and their different shapes carry different energies, and this affects their placement on the Medicine Wheel, and also their meaning. The "I" and the "Y" sound the same, but have different placements and different meanings due to their different shapes.

The fact that different letters carry different energies will also be important as we get into a discussion of consonants, names and words. I want to plant the seed now. Names or words that sound the same but are spelled differently (homophones) will have different energies. For example, my wife's name is *Jeanne*. She changed the spelling from her given name, *Jean,* when she was in her mid-30s. A little known but humorous fact is that the doctor who filled out her birth certificate actually misspelled her name as *Gene,* which is a man's name. The three names, Jeanne, Jean and Gene, all sound the same. But, they have quite different energies!

Enough said. Here are the basic meanings of the six vowel sounds:

Meaning of the "U" (pronounced "uu"): In the Medicine Wheel on page 20, the sacred center, represented by the "U," is the symbolic center of the universe, the unity of all things, the void or nothingness (no-thing-ness) from which reality emerges, and around which everything revolves. "U" is the Source that is beyond space and time. It is God, Great Spirit, Great Mystery, the Supreme Force – whatever you call the Higher Power. It is also represents the indestructible light body we call the Soul. As Jeanne White Eagle says, "In the soil of the soul lies the seed of all consciousness. From this seed, universes are born. From this seed, knowledge that you are Love is clear and unceasing." The "U" represents this place where the seed of consciousness resides.

The "U" represents the ineffable, the mystical and unknowable. It is the sacred beingness that is the ground beneath all things manifest, the "enfolded order" in our holographic universe from which everything unfolds. It is the energy of transformation, and the power of carrying. We cannot storm the gates to open the door to this sacred place. Rather, we must let go and allow ourselves to be carried by our Higher Power, our Spirit Guides and our Higher Self. In the numbering system of Mystical Numerology, the "U" and the zero are the same: U = 0.

Meaning of the "Y" (pronounced "iii"): The "Y" represents the spiritual axis that penetrates the center and connects the upper and lower worlds. It brings a connection with duality. Our three-dimensional world is woven upon the loom of polarities, and the "Y" represents the principal idea of polarity: "up above" and "down below," sky and earth, sound and silence, hot and cold, good and bad, white and black, love and hate, and so forth. It also connects us with alternate realities and alternative ways of seeing the world.

In the Native American mystical tradition, the "Y" is like the dance pole that stands in the center of the ceremonial dance arbor like a world axis. It brings guidance and inspiration from the upper realms, higher awareness, superconsciousness, and plants this new awareness deep in the earth, and in the fertile soil of the subconscious to become grounded where it will grow.

From a scientific standpoint, the "Y" represents the zero-point field that connects us with everything, everywhere at any instant across the infinity of space and time in the ever-present "NOW."

The A, E, I and O: To paraphrase Joseph Campbell, the dome of heaven rests on the earth and is supported by the energies of four cardinal directions, East (A), South (E), West (I) and North (O). The energies of the A, E, I and O are the "Four Winds," the Great Beings that stand guard in the four directions, exchanging energy with the center/navel and also between themselves. They are like the four archangels and the four seasons: "A" is East – Raphael, Spring. "E" is South – Uriel, Summer. "I" is West – Michael, Autumn. And "O" is North – Gabriel, Winter. My purpose for showing the correspondence between the directions and the energies of the four primary archangels is to emphasize that many religions have recognized the power of these cardinal points.

The energies of the directions are palpable, and those who are at all sensitive to energies can feel the different quality of each direction by turning to face it and becoming quiet. If you do this, you will notice a subtle difference associated with the energy of each direction. Another way to do this is to face the direction and chant or sing the vowel sound connected with it. Face East and chant "ah;" face South and chant "eh;" face West and chant "iii;" and face North and chant "oh." If you try this, you will feel the difference, and in doing so you will gain a new level of understanding about the energy of each of the vowel sounds.

Meaning of the "A" (pronounced "ah"): The "A" represents the mental realm, thinking and illumination. It is the East, place of new beginnings, sunrise and springtime. It has the quality of unity in diversity. Although systems differ, in the system that I was taught by Beautiful Painted Arrow, the "A" and East are connected with the color yellow, like the rising sun. It is the element of water, and the energy of purity, purifying and washing.

A predominance of "A" sounds in a name can bring a quick, analytical mind, and maybe even psychic ability. It can also mean that the person is good at starting things, creating new beginnings. But, the "A" can also bring a tendency to have a linear, analytical thinking style. Too much "A" energy can cause someone to be a bit judgmental, a purist who sees the world mostly in white and black, and misses the nuances in the shades of gray.

The totem animals are the wolf, crow and snake. It is also connected with the energy of the archangel Raphael.

Meaning of the "E" (pronounced "eh"): The "E" represents the emotional realm. It is the South, and the element of Fire. It is the place of the heart and emotions. It is the inner child, growth, and summertime. It is connected with the color white.

"E" is connected with *roots,* and deals with *placement* by which I mean knowing your place in the world, where and how you fit. The South is the place of relationships. We know who we are, and our place in the scheme of things through the relationships we have with people, places, things and events. When I say "people" I mean this in the expanded sense of not only humans but also as nature, representing what Beautiful Painted Arrow calls our "vast Self" – animal people, tree people, rock people, the winged ones, the ones that swim, and the no-leggeds and many-leggeds that crawl on the Earth.

An abundance of "E" sounds in a name helps a person to be expressive, and in touch with their emotions. People with strong "E" energy can be quite empathic and even clairsentient – knowing things through their feelings.

"E" is connected with the archangel Uriel. The totem animals are coyote, cheetah and spider.

Meaning of the "I" (pronounced "iii"): The "I" represents the physical realm, the manifested world. It is the West and the element of Earth. It is the body, physical awareness, and all things physical including health and fortune. It is the season of autumn and represents the harvest. It is the place of reconciliation.

An abundance of the "I" sound in a name can make a person strong, athletic and grounded. It also can give a person a powerful, kinesthetic "body-knowing."

The "I" is connected with the archangel Michael. The totem animals are owl, elephant.

Meaning of the "O" (pronounced "oh"): The "O" represents the spiritual-intuitive realm, the direction of the North. It is the wisdom of the ancestors, childlike innocence and teachability. It is winter, the time when the elders tell stories around the fire that communicate ancient wisdom.

An abundance of the "O" sound in a name can give a keen intuitive ability and a strong spiritual or mystical connection (not necessarily a religious one).

It is connected with the archangel Gabriel. The totem animals are the dragonfly, bee and badger.

Working with the Vowel Sounds

Example 1: The vowel sounds in a word describe its fundamental energies. For instance, "LOVE" has an "O" (spiritual) and an "E" (emotional). "LOVE" connects the spirit with the heart and emotions. The progression of vowel sounds can also be important and revealing. In the word "LOVE," the progression is "O" ⇒ "E." So, "LOVE" is a spiritual energy that gets experienced emotionally. See how this works?

Example 2: Take another example, "MONEY." The vowels provide the fundamental energies: "O" ⇒ "E" ⇒ "Y." Despite all the negative aspects of money, and its reputation for being the root of all evil, "MONEY" actually carries a spiritual energy that connects with us at a heart level, helps us define our "place" in the world (another aspect of the "E"), and connects us with other possibilities. This also teaches us that when our spirit and heart are in balance, and we are pursuing our dreams/possibilities, then we become magnetic to money.

Example 3: "WAR." In this word, the fundamental energy is "A," the mental realm, and the qualities of purity and new beginnings. War is caused by purists who see reality in terms of black and white, good and bad, "I'm right so you must be wrong." This energy lacks the ability to compromise, or see things as "both/and" instead of "either/or." The result of war is often to sweep away old systems and structures and create new beginnings, but it is never pleasant. There are better ways of changing things.

In each of these examples, you can gain additional insight into the word or name by chanting its vowel sounds. For "LOVE," chant "oh-eh." For "MONEY," chant "oh-eh-yy" (the "y" sound being pronounced like "iii"). For "WAR," chant "ah."

Looking at the vowel sounds and considering their meanings is also the place to start when looking at your name or analyzing the names of friends, family, and/or famous people. For instance, the fundamental energy in my name, "JOHN," is the spiritual energy of the north, the place of ancestors, storytelling and teachability. It is one of the reasons that I am attracted to the mystical and it gives me a passion for figuring out how things *really* work.

This is a small taste of the kind of insights that come from looking at the vowel sounds in names and in words. The next chapter will show you how to go deeper, and do vowel sound readings with names.

For now, it is important that we keep moving forward to keep the process interesting.

Chapter Two:

Working With Names: Vowel Sounds

What signifies knowing the Names, if you know not the Natures of Things?

~Benjamin Franklin, *Poor Richard's Almanac*, 1750~

Mystical Numerology allows us to see the true nature of things by looking at the names we give to them. My study of words and names in developing this new system of numerology has convinced me of two things. First, the names we choose to call people or things are not chosen by accident. There is a higher guidance at work behind the scenes. Second, the energy that vibrates in the sound of the names shapes the person or the thing. The name we were given at birth, or choose for ourselves at a later date, shapes our experience over time, and has a great deal to do with how we see the world and relate to it. Our name bestows upon us the characteristics and talents that we have, and magnetizes to us the people and resources in our lives and the types of events that we experience. It also draws us to the places where we feel most comfortable.

Mystical Numerology allows us to gain a deeper understanding of our lives, and the lives of our family, friends and colleagues. It can help us understand famous people and why they were/are famous or infamous – which is also sometimes a help to understanding ourselves at deeper levels. It can also help us understand relationships and why we fit with one person, or why sparks fly when we just can't seem to get along with another person we consider difficult or even intolerable. In short, the Mystical Numerology of names gives us a deep understanding into the nature of things.

Vowel sounds give information about the fundamental energies in a name, and how they flow. Looking at the vowel sounds is always the place to start when we analyze any name. This is a process that we started in Chapter 1 with the meaning of each of the vowel sounds. Now, we will take this understanding to a deeper level. You will see that a pretty good reading can be done simply by considering the vowel sounds in a person's name.

Vowel Sound Reading for a Name

The distribution of the vowel sounds in a name provides insight into the natural energies and inclinations of the person. To understand this, we will need to work with some examples. Then, you can try it with your own name.

The process is simple.

1. Count the number of each vowel sound and put them into the chart as shown below.

- Mental/East: **A**
- Physical/West: **I**
- Emotional/South: **E**
- Spiritual/North: **O**
- Source/Center: **U**
- Other Dimensions: **Y**

2. Take note of the <u>first</u> vowel because it has special significance.

3. Count up the total number of vowel sounds in the name.

4. Notice how many there are of each vowel sound: A, E, I, O, U and Y. If the name has lots of the same vowel, it tells you something important about how the person sees and interacts with the world.

5. If there are missing vowel sounds, note these in the chart. Missing vowel sounds are also important. Most people are missing some of the vowels.

6. Identify the order of the vowel sounds in the first name; this progression also is significant.

Example 1: ALBERT EINSTEIN

Albert Einstein was a German-born theoretical physicist who discovered the Theory of Relativity and is often regarded as the father of modern physics.

Vowel Distribution in the Name: Albert Einstein

- Mental/East: **A (1st Vowel)**
- Physical/West: **I, I**
- Emotional/South: **E, E, E**
- Spiritual/North: *missing*
- Source/Center: *missing*
- Other Dimensions: *missing*

In Einstein's name, we find six (6) vowel sounds: 1-A, 3-Es and 2-Is. "6" is the number of discovery and change (see Chapter 3 and the table of basic number meanings on pages 56-59). Many researchers have this number in their charts. The "A" is the first vowel and takes on special significance. The name *Albert Einstein* is missing the O, U, and Y. And, the order of progression for the vowel sounds in the first name is "A⇒E."

With this profile, we could expect that the lens through which Albert Einstein looked at the world would be a mental one, especially since the mental "A" is the first *letter* as well as first *vowel*. Yet, with 3-Es, he also had a strong feeling/emotional nature. And, since the number "3" is also connected with "idea," and "energy," it is very likely that Einstein's feeling nature was a fertile field for new ideas and discoveries.

Missing vowels in the full name indicate *areas of interest or development*. The missing O, U, and Y is the mystical/spiritual constellation, so we could have expected him to be a bit of a mystic and balance his science with intuition. Indeed, he once said, "intuition is more powerful than knowledge."

From the A⇒E vowel progression in his first name, "Albert," we can see that energy flows from the mind to the heart and emotions. Abstract ideas feed his feelings and emotional sense of the world. But, the "E" is also about delving deeply into the roots of things, and finding how things fit together. So, his research into the fundamental physics behind reality was also something that was deeply satisfying on an emotional level, and gave him a sense of place and order.

We will go deeper into the meaning of the first vowel and the missing vowels in the next section. For now, I am giving you just a taste of how the vowel sounds in a name can give you a first, but important glimpse into the nature of the individual.

Example 2: <u>HENRY DAVID THOREAU</u>

Henry David Thoreau had many talents. He was an American author, poet, naturalist, historian, philosopher, tax resister, surveyor and leading transcendentalist. He is best known for his book, *Walden,* and his essay, *Civil Disobedience,* an argument for individual resistance to civil government in moral opposition to an unjust state.[2]

Vowel Distribution in the Name: Henry David Thoreau

- Mental/East: **A, A**
- Emotional/South: **E, E (1ˢᵗ Vowel)**
- Source/Center: **U**

- Physical/West: **I**
- Spiritual/North: **O**
- Other Dimensions: **Y**

You will note that in his name, there are eight (8) vowel sounds, 2-As, 2-Es, and 1 each of the vowels I, O, U and Y. It is significant that there are no missing vowels. As names go, this is a fairly balanced distribution of energies, and would lead us to believe that Thoreau

---

[2] See Wikipedia.

would be a fairly well-rounded individual with a strong feeling nature and quick mind, good attributes for a writer. (It is interesting to note that he was actually baptized "David Henry Thoreau," but everyone called him Henry, and he later adopted "Henry David Thoreau" as his name.)

"E" as the first vowel will tend to make a person expressive, but also is about *placement,* or how things fit in the natural order or overall scheme of things. With 8 vowel sounds, "8" being the number of "power," we could expect Thoreau to have the power to push against the constraints and boundaries of society. And, the first-name vowel progression is E⇒Y which would indicate that emotional/feeling energy is connected with the ability to see the world in alternative and unconventional ways. Indeed, as a protégé of Ralph Waldo Emerson, Thoreau was part of the transcendentalist movement.

Example 3: MOHANDAS KARAMCHAND GANDHI

Let us look at a third example, this time of a famous ideological and political leader who was influenced by Henry David Thoreau's most famous essay: *Civil Disobedience.*

Vowel Distribution in the Name: Mohandas Karamchand Gandhi

- Mental/East: **A, A, A, A, A, A**
- Physical/West: **I**
- Emotional/South: *missing*
- Spiritual/North: **O (1ˢᵗ Vowel)**
- Source/Center: *missing*
- Other Dimensions: *missing*

What we find is that there are also eight (8) vowel sounds in the name, and "8," among other things, is the number of the leader (see pg. 57). The first vowel is an "O," giving Gandhi a spiritual focus. Six of the eight vowels are the "A" sound – the energy of the mind, and of new beginnings. So, his spiritual focus was projected through a strong mind, and desire for new beginnings. Six (6) is also the number of the people, so it is not surprising that his philosophy of mass nonviolent civil disobedience helped India gain independence (a new beginning), and inspired movements for civil rights and freedom across the world.

Interestingly, the K'iche Mayan correspondence for the number "8" is called "Tijax," and is the energy of cutting away what no longer serves. We will learn more about the Mayan correspondences later.

Gandhi is missing the E, Y and U in his name. Missing vowels define areas or dimensions of life that are in the shadow, in the Jungian sense of the term. A person is very often drawn toward these aspects as areas for development and exploration. In this case, the E, Y and U represent the emotions, alternate worldviews, and the power of the center or Source. In combination, it would draw an individual to develop the emotional aspects of himself (E), the connection with his Higher Power (U), while at the same time seeing the world anew (Y). Gandhi did this. He traveled all of India to connect with the people at a heart level, and saw the potential for an India without the British. He was the father of the modern India, but accomplished all that he did in a very centered way, remarking once, "I am a Hindu, a Muslim, a Jew and a Christian."

Example 4: WILLIAM BUTLER YEATS

Let us look at the Irish poet and dramatist, William Butler Yeats, who won the Nobel Prize for literature in 1923. Some feel that Yeats was the greatest poet of the twentieth century.

Vowel Distribution in the Name: William Butler Yeats

- Mental/East: **A, A**
- Physical/West: **I, I (1ˢᵗ Vowel)**
- Emotional/South: **E,E**
- Spiritual/North: *missing*
- Source/Center: **U**
- Other Dimensions: **Y**

Again, there are eight (8) vowel sounds. "8" is the number of power, and each of the last three examples (Thoreau, Gandhi and Yeats) have been men with 8 vowel sounds in their names. This imbues them with power, one of the qualities of the "8."

The first vowel is "I," meaning that Yeats tended to relate with the world around him first on a physical basis, especially with the first name vowel progression of I⇒I⇒A. People with "I" as first vowels tend to be *sensory thinkers*. In other words they see the world in terms of what

35

can be apprehended by the body through the senses of sight (visual), sound (auditory), taste (gustatory), touch (tactile), and smell (olfactory). Maybe this is partly responsible for his being such a great poet.

The distribution is fairly balanced except for the missing "O," the spiritual dimension. It is interesting to note that his father was an atheist. The combination of "I" as first vowel, and the missing "O," which defines the spiritual-intuitive realm as an area for development, may be the reason that Yeats was interested in magic and the occult in later years.

Example 5: <u>HELEN ADAMS KELLER</u>

Helen Keller is a woman who lost both her hearing and vision when she was 19 months old. But, she rose above these serious disabilities to become an author, political activist and lecturer. She was also the first deaf-blind woman to earn a Bachelor of Arts degree (Radcliffe, 1904).

Vowel Distribution in the Name: Helen Adams Keller

- Mental/East: **A, A**
- Emotional/South: **E, E, E, E**
  (1ˢᵗ Vowel)
- Source/Center: *missing*

- Physical/West: *missing*
- Spiritual/North: *missing*
- Other Dimensions: *missing*

There are six (6) vowel sounds in the name Helen Adams Keller. "6" is the number of polarities. It is also the number of people, and the awakener and influencer. Certainly, being born with her vision and hearing only to lose them at such a young age is the extreme in experiencing polarities. She also had to awaken her other faculties to be able to become all that she was. In doing so, she influenced many others, and awakened the potential for other deaf and blind people.

Her name is missing four of the six vowel sounds: the I (physical) as well as the O, U and Y (the spiritual constellation), almost as if her purpose was to develop physical capabilities that would provide a deep connection with her innate spiritual/intuitive abilities that would result in a unique worldview.

Her name has 4-Es and 2-As. "E" is also the first vowel. With E⇒E as the first name vowel progression, we can understand that Helen Keller's primary interaction with the world around her was on a feeling level. The 2-As in her name are both in her middle name, "Adams." The middle name acts as an "inner urge" that is present, important, but often unseen. In this case, since the "A" is also connected with visual sight, it might not be too much of a stretch to say that her sight was hidden, or an *inner* sight.

Example 6: LUCRETIA COFFIN MOTT

Finally, let us look at Lucretia Coffin Mott, a social reformer who was the initiator of women's political rights in the U.S. She is credited with being the first American "feminist" in the early 19th century.

Vowel Distribution in the Name: Lucretia Coffin Mott

- Mental/East: **A**
- Emotional/South: **E**
- Source/Center: **U (1st Vowel)**
- Physical/West: **I, I**
- Spiritual/North: **O, O**
- Other Dimensions: *missing*

Here we see the "U" as the first vowel, which is the power of carrying, like carrying a movement for women's political rights. She has "7" vowel sounds in her name, the number of the words "drive" and "crusade." Indeed, she was a crusader for women's rights.

The first name vowel progression is U⇒E⇒I⇒A. This could be read like this: A strong sense of her own center and ability to transform things (U) worked through her passion (E) to create change in the physical world (I) that led to new possibilities (A) for women in the United States.

Try this kind of analysis with your own name and see what initial insights you get. This will also provide a foundation for further exploration.

In this next section, we will look more deeply into the meaning of the first vowel, and the missing vowel sounds.

The First Vowel

When considering the vowel sounds in a name, the *first* vowel is important because it is like a lens through which a person sees and processes life. Of course, people are complex and we will certainly need to take into consideration more than just the first vowel for a complete understanding. Still, this is an important first step because looking at the first vowel will give important clues to how a person most naturally interacts with the world.

The basic meanings are shown below. You can use this as a guide to look at your own name, and those of your family, friends, coworkers, people in the news, historical figures, and so on.

You may find it helpful to refer to the Medicine Wheel Diagram below:

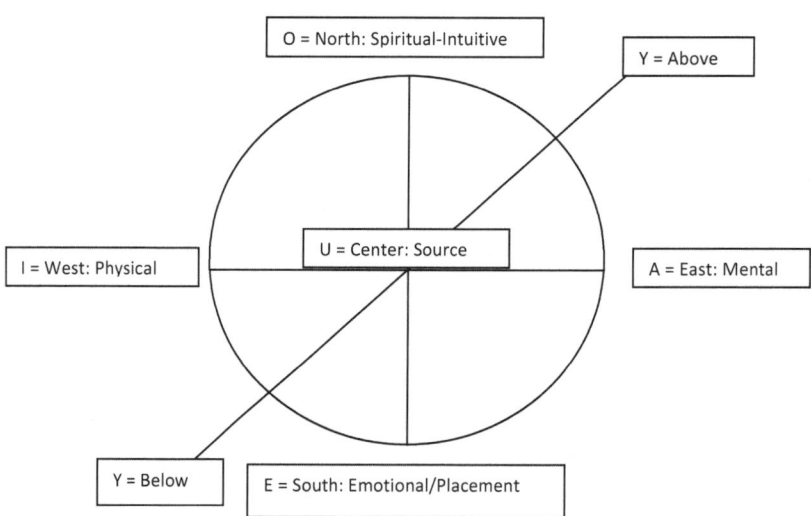

"A" as First Vowel: "A" sits in the East on the Medicine Wheel, and is a connection to the mental dimension of life. People whose names have an "A" for the first vowel are rational types, and are likely to have a quick mind. They tend to value objectivity, think about things before taking action, and make decisions through the use of logic and reason. When they process life experiences, it will generally be at the mental level first.

A quick mind is in many ways a blessing. It gives the ability to be fast in understanding and thinking. This mental agility can also mean seeing, understanding, or "getting" ideas and concepts before others do. Because of this, there is a need to develop patience with others who may be not be so quick to understand.

"A" is also about purity. So, with "A" as the first vowel, there can also be a modest tendency to be a purist and look at life in stark contrasts of right and wrong, good and bad, black and white. Coupled with an agile mind, these individuals need to guard against a tendency to make snap judgments and, in doing so, judge people, things and events a little too quickly.

The East is the direction where the sun rises. Its energy brings new beginnings. So, people with "A" as a first vowel, or with a predominance of this vowel in their name, make good starters. They are often adept at initiating new projects or stepping out in new directions in life – as long as they do not over-analyze things.

"A" is connected with vision and the visual sense, so people with "A" as a first vowel relate to things represented visually. For instance, Albert Einstein's "thought experiments" were visualizations such as what it would be like to ride a beam of light.

The "A" is also connected with an ability to see or receive visions, or receive information at a psychic, nonverbal level. As a first vowel, the "A" sometimes indicates an ability to be clairvoyant – as long as they are able to temporarily put rationality aside.

"E" as First Vowel: The "E" sits in the South on the Medicine Wheel. The south is concerned with issues of the heart, of relationship, growth and *placement* (e.g., what is my place in the world, where do I fit?).

The "E" as a first vowel suggests that his or her *first* interaction with the world is on an emotional, subjective, feeling level and through relationships. We know our place in the world because of how we relate to the people, places, events and things in the world around us.

The "E" as a first vowel tends to highlight the issues of relationship and finding one's "place."

These people tend to be expressive. This means that they are good at putting feelings into words. They may also *talk to think,* by which I mean that an individual with "E" as their first vowel might open her mouth to talk with no idea of what it is she is going to say. In fact, the act of putting an idea into words often helps her to clarify her own thoughts. This often makes these individuals good extemporaneous speakers. My wife, Jeanne, is like this.

Since the "E" is connected with emotions and feelings, people with an "E" as first vowel are most likely to receive information and insight on the emotional level through feelings first, and *then* process these feelings mentally at a cognitive level. These people will tend to make decisions on a subjective rather than an objective level.

People with "E" as a first vowel often have an empathic ability to feel what others are feeling around them. This is a wonderful talent, especially if developed intentionally. But, it can possibly lead to a problem of discriminating which feelings are theirs, and what feelings are being soaked up from others. This sensitivity can lead to boundary issues and the need to build a protective wall around themselves.

Sometimes the "E" as first vowel also indicates that a person is naturally "clairsentient." In other words, she may have an ability to receive precognitive information through feelings – such as knowing that something is awry with a loved one far away because her "gut" tells her so, or changing travel plans based on feelings and then finding out the flight she was supposed to be on crashed – that kind of thing.

People with an "E" as a first vowel are often concerned with what people think of them. They want people to "like" them, and will invest lots of energy to make this so – sometimes inappropriately giving too much of themselves to make it happen. If they perceive that somebody doesn't like them, it can even cause emotional pain and suffering.

"I" as First Vowel: The "I" sits in the West on the Medicine Wheel, the direction of the physical world. This includes physical awareness, physical energy and health, and physical abundance and prosperity.

"I" as first vowel suggests that a person's first interaction with the world around them is on a physical level. This means that people with the "I" as a first vowel, tend to be *sensory thinkers*. They gather information about the world around them through their senses of touch, sight, hearing, taste and smell. In other words, they tend to be kinesthetic. They can be quite brilliant, but it is their sensory experiences that feed their thinking process.

Because of this, a person with an "I" as first vowel may need to get into motion to think clearly. In other words, movement facilitates getting clarity about thoughts and feelings. My friend and mentor Beautiful Painted Arrow used to say that movement plows the field of consciousness to plant new seeds from the realm of ideas. It is good general advice to say: if you get stuck, move! But, this is especially true for these individuals.

People with an "I" as first vowel tend to be kinesthetic. In other words, they may sense in their bodies, or experience as part of their physical energy, things that happen around them. This can also be a powerful ability, but it takes practice. They may also be very instinctual.

These people are inclined to put their ideas into action and movement to create something practical in the world. They may be good finishers who like to see the tangible results of their accomplishments. They may express their love and affection in very tangible, practical ways.

"O" as First Vowel: The "O" sits in the North on the Medicine Wheel. The north is concerned with issues of teachability, storytelling, and guidance received from the ancestors, avatars and ancient masters (e.g., through a connection with the collective consciousness or field of knowing).

The "O" as a first vowel suggests that a person's *first* interaction with the world around them is on a non-rational, spiritual level. These individuals may be very active in the world, but they also tend to be "inner-directed."

Their thinking process is fed by intuition. Their motivation to take action is often sparked by a desire to discover how things work at a fundamental level. Having an "O" as a first vowel also provides

41

resources for the search because it helps these people to be more intuitive and open to following inner guidance.

Individuals who have an "O" as first vowel often know things without knowing how they know them. They can get flashes of insight, or fully formed concepts and ideas that get downloaded into their consciousness. This is great as a talent for discovery. The challenge sometimes becomes how to explain this in some logical, coherent way – especially to others. Or, how to translate these intuitive flashes and this inner-knowing into a practical plan of action.

First vowel (U): The "U" sits at the center of the Medicine Wheel. It gives a person a strong connection with the center of all things, the God-Source, Great Spirit, or Creator. These people have a natural ability to connect with the potential possibilities of All-That-Is.

With the "U" as first vowel, these people carry their "center" with them. This tends to make them expansive and, because of this, uncomfortable with boundaries and constraints.

They have the power of carrying and transformation. They are seed-carriers. This may possibly look like carrying ideas, visions, people and movements forward. Through their actions they can transform the world around them.

"Y" as First Vowel: The "Y" represents the spiritual axis that penetrates the center and connects the upper and lower worlds. It brings a connection with duality, the polarities that define our perceived reality in this three-dimensional world: "up above" and "down below," silence and sound, hot and cold, good and bad, white and black, sky and earth.

The "Y" as first vowel also connects individuals with alternate realities and alternative ways of seeing. It brings guidance and inspiration from the upper realms, higher awareness, superconsciousness, and plants this new awareness deep in the earth, in the subconscious, to become grounded where it will grow.

From a scientific standpoint, the "Y" represents the energy matrix that connects us with everything, everywhere at any instant across the infinity of space and time in the ever-present "NOW."

In the Native American ceremonial tradition, the "Y" is like the dance pole or tree that stands in the center of the sacred dance arbor, connecting the "up above" and the "down below." People with "Y" as a first vowel have a natural connection with other realities and dimensions, and an ability to see alternative ways of doing things. It also brings the power to actualize new ideas in the grounded, practical world.

As you digest the basic meanings of the First Vowel Sounds, I want to make a quick clarification. As I said previously, the first vowel is like a lens through which an individual tends to see and process life. It is a starting point, a home base, if you will. What this means is that a person who has an "A" as a first vowel, like my son Alan, has a natural inclination to see the world through a mental lens *first*. This doesn't mean that he doesn't also have deep feelings, or doesn't have intuitive insights. It just means that the place he naturally starts is by thinking about something. And, the same is true for the other vowel sounds. They define the natural home base or starting point.

First Name Vowel Sounds

In researching first names for my system of numerology, I collected over 7000 first names. It was casual but consistent research and certainly not exhaustive since there are websites that have more than 10,000 – 15,000 first names. The names that I collected came from famous people, friends and clients from around the world, and names found at random by, for instance, noting author names while walking through bookstores, or in the credits of a movie or TV series, or by collecting the first names of athletes from around the world while watching the 2012 London Olympics. While the names are predominantly American, English, or European, there are also African, Arabic, Israeli, East Indian, Latin American, Japanese, Russian, and (a few) Mongol and Chinese names.

All the time I was collecting these first names, I kept a running percentage for the distribution of first vowel sounds. What I noticed was that the percentages remained fairly consistent all the way from 1000 names to the present total of 7025. I am making an assumption that even if I had looked at 10,000 – 15,000 names, the overall percentages wouldn't be much different than those shown below.

By the way, when I began adding names from around the world, it did not result in a significant shift in the following percentages – something I found a little surprising. It would make an interesting study to go country by country and look at first name vowel sounds, but I will leave this for a future work.

That said, I believe that my research to date makes an interesting point about the *overall* consensus reality. Look at the rankings of names by their first vowels:

A = 38% (mental)	I = 15% (physical)	U = 7% (wisdom carrier)
E =22% (emotional)	O = 14% (spiritual-intuitive)	Y = 4% (alternate worldview)

Names that have either "A" or "E" as the first vowel sounds (60%) outnumber the next four vowel sounds put together (40%). *This means that the consensus reality is made up of thinkers and feelers* – with *thinkers* being in the overwhelming majority. If the first vowel in your name is I, O, U or Y, you might feel like you are wired a little differently – and, truthfully, you are!

Many people that I've met over the years automatically assume that we all see the world in the same way. But, this is not true. The world that I see when I look out of my eyes may be different than what you see. People *are* wired differently, and knowing this is very helpful. One way to begin to appreciate this is by looking at the first vowel in a name, because it tells something about how an individual perceives reality.

In hopes that you won't find it redundant, I will emphasize the meaning of the first vowel again, this time in the context of its place in the overall distribution shown above.

First Vowel (A): There are significantly more names (38%) that have "A" as their first vowel than any of the other vowel sounds. This means that roughly four out of every ten people are *thinkers* who interact with the world on a mental level first. They see their reality through a pair of glasses that are colored with what they *think* about the world. Generally speaking, abstract ideas will be as important and tangible to them as things that they can reach out and touch, or that can elicit an emotive or spiritual response. Generally speaking, they know things through a rational or an analytical process, may be fond of making lists and want to be organized, and will make a plan before doing something. They may also feel uncomfortable with being spontaneous or extemporaneous in new situations and surroundings. These people will most often say, "I *think* that _____." Or, "What do you *think* about ___." If you want to appeal to these people, it is a safe bet to be in a "head space" and interact on an rational, thinking level first.

First Vowel (E): The next highest number of names (22%) have "E" as the first vowel sound. This means that one out of five people are *feelers*. They interact with the world on an emotional, feeling level first. Relationships and social interactions are important. They tend to be expressive, may talk to think, and have little problem in talking spontaneously, off the cuff. In other words, they can stand up in a group of people not knowing what they're going to say, and just open their mouths and talk. They also find it helpful to *talk* about something in order to clarify what they *think* about it.

Even though they may need downtime to rejuvenate, these people are most often extroverted. They want to be listened to and have their feelings heard. Feeling "liked" is more important to these people than for the other groups. They will often "know" things because they just "feel" it. They will most often say, "I *feel* that _____." Or, "How do you *feel* about _____." If you want to appeal to these people, be a good listener, and interact on a feeling level. Share what is in your heart.

First Vowel (I): The next highest number of names (15%) have "I" as the first vowel. These people tend to interact with the world in a physical way and/or as sensory thinkers. They are generally kinesthetic.

They are often practical and pragmatic, focused on the here and now, and tend to be doers who get into action. Movement is important to these people. In fact, doing something active may actually help them get clear on what they think about something.

With these people, actions definitely speak louder than words. If you want to appeal to them, do something for them or with them.

First Vowel (O): An almost equal number of names (14%) have "O" as the first vowel sound. These people tend to see the world through spiritual-intuitive eyes, and are generally inner-directed. Their intuition and/or power to envision or imagine may be quite strong.

They get the world in very intuitive ways and often know things without knowing how they know. They may sometimes have a challenge in explaining what they see or discover in a logical, analytical or rational way. It is a growth area that takes time to develop.

These people like to see the big picture. While they can get down into the practical details, they generally enjoy the overview, and are often energized by future-oriented, theoretical ideas and concepts.

First Vowel (U): Only 7% of the names have "U" as the first vowel. These people are naturally connected to the God-Source even though they may not be aware of it.

They have the power of carrying in their names – carrying ideas, dreams, movements, and so on. They may be dreamers who have the power to create a following for their beliefs. Regardless of whether that is true, these people have the capacity to connect with perennial wisdom at deep soul levels. While they may do just fine carrying on a conversation with "small talk," you can best communicate with these people by going deep.

While these people can be dreamers, they also may have the capability to be quite disciplined and practical in order to carry these dreams forward – like Lucretia Coffin Mott who was the founder of the women's rights movement in the U.S.

First Vowel (Y): A mere 4% of the names had "Y" as the first vowel. These people see the world in creative ways and have a natural ability to think outside the box, the ability to see beyond what is considered normal or traditional. These people have the ability to push the envelope and help the rest of us see other, perhaps better ways of thinking about the world, or better ways of doing things.

Even if they seem very practical, they are probably ahead of their time in whatever is their passion. You can use these people as sounding boards for new ideas, or to stretch your boundaries.

By the way, these people need a relatively high degree of freedom. Forcing them into a traditional mold, or to adhere to a strict set of practices can be quite stressful for them, and over time it may be unhealthy. They do better in a flexible environment that has value for their novel ideas. For instance, they might never feel like they quite fit into a traditional business environment. They may hop jobs every couple of years to relieve the tension and need for more freedom. In harness to a constraining environment, their health may suffer.

Missing Vowels

The void left by missing vowels in a full name often acts like a vacuum to gently pull a person toward those areas of life.

At this stage of our process, we've tallied up the vowel sounds in your full name, or the full name of the person of interest whom you wish to analyze for insight. We've paid special attention to the first vowel in the first or given name. And, we've also noted which vowels are missing. The areas that are missing will also provide insight.

It is important to know that *missing* vowel sounds in your full name do not mean that you or the person you are studying is necessarily lacking or deficient in some way. Rather, the void left by missing vowels in a name often act like a magnet or vacuum to gently pull the individual toward those areas of life.

As noted previously, the missing vowels in a full name define areas or dimensions of life that are in the shadow, in the Jungian sense of the term. A person is very often drawn toward these very aspects as areas for development and exploration. They become areas of interest. We have seen cases in which debilities *are* reflected by the missing vowel

47

sounds, such as Helen Keller (pg. 36), but this is the exception rather than the rule.

A full detailed discussion of this topic is beyond the scope of this book – mostly because including it would make this introductory book too long. At this point, I wish to just make the point that insight can be gained by noting the missing vowels and the dimensions of life that are represented. For yourself, see if this doesn't give insight into areas of interest in your life. Also take a look at family, friends, and so on, to see if this doesn't provide interesting added information.

Here's a final example before we move on. Let's take a look at sixteenth century astronomer Galileo Galilei:

Vowel Distribution in the Name: Galileo Galilei – 8 vowels, 6 consonants

- Mental/East: **A, A (1ˢᵗ Vowel)**
- Emotional/South: **E, E**
- Source/Center: *missing*
- Physical/West: **I, I, I**
- Spiritual/North: **O**
- Other Dimensions: *missing*

Notice that the first vowel in Galileo's name is the "A," the mental dimension, the direction of the East where the sun rises. It is associated with new beginnings. The fact that Galileo was a brilliant man is not a surprise. In fact, he is considered one of the most brilliant men of any age.

The vowel sounds in a name represent fundamental energies. Galileo Galilei has 8 of them. The number "8" is about power … faith … being a leader or guide … engaging in pioneering activities, and pushing the boundaries. All of this fits what we know about Galileo. The telescope he invented allowed him to study the heavens. The result was that he knew the view of the universe taught by the Catholic Church was incorrect. And this got him in big trouble.

Missing U, Y: The name Galileo Galilei is missing the vowels, U and Y. Actually, I've chosen this example because the missing U-Y is the most common combination in all of the missing vowel categories. It is much more common, in fact, than missing any of the single vowels. In an interesting way, this missing combination defines t human condition. "U" is the connection to the God Source, Creator or whatever you choose to call your Higher Power. "Y" is the connection with knowledge and information from different dimensions of awareness and the power to anchor it into our grounded everyday reality. The combination of the two defines our sense of separation from our cosmic origin.

We are born into this 3-D reality and, for a brief time, we remember what our connection with All-That-Is is like. Then, we forget. We spend our entire lives attempting to make the connection again and find our way home. Feeling separation from our cosmic origins is part of the human condition. This is what the missing U-Y vowel combination is about: divine longing for wholeness. It is what drove Galileo to invent the first telescope and study the heavens. It is also an active force in many people, the following historical figures among them.

All of these historical figures are also missing the U-Y vowel combination:

Politics/Government: Adlai Ewing Stevenson, Adolf Hitler, Alexander Hamilton, Benjamin Harrison, Calvin Coolidge, David Lloyd George, Dwight David Eisenhower, Franklin Delano Roosevelt, George Washington, Hillary Rodham Clinton, James Madison, Levi Parsons Morton (USVP), Mikhail Gorbachev Sergeevich, Millard Fillmore, Ronald Wilson Reagan, Mohammed Elbaradei, Robert Michael Gates, Thomas Paine, William Jefferson Clinton.

Art: John Singer Sargent, Vincent Van Gogh.

Entertainment: Oprah Gail Winfrey.

Business/Finance: Aristotle Onassis, John David Rockefeller, John Pierpont Morgan.

Science: Alfred North Whitehead, Claude Levi-Strauss, Charles Robert Darwin, Galileo Galilei, Isaac Newton, Leonardo da Vinci.

Space: Valentina Tereshkova (first woman astronaut).

Educators: Doris Kearns Goodwin, George Washington Carver.

Medicine: Florence Nightingale.

Music: Andres Segovia, George Frederick Handel, Johann Sebastian Bach.

Writers: Beatrice Potter Webb, Catherine Drinker Bowen, Elizabeth Barrett Browning, Harriet Beecher Stowe, Jean Baptiste Moliere, Michele de Nostradame.

Chapter Three:

The Consonants & Number Paths

What we have called matter is energy, whose

vibration has been so lowered as to be

perceptible to the senses. There is no matter.

~Albert Einstein~

Vowel sounds in your name represent the fundamental energies of creation flowing into your life. The consonants provide a container for this energy and give it direction and purpose. Consider this visual metaphor: The vowel sounds are like the water flowing through a garden hose. The consonants are like the hose, itself, that points the energy of the flowing water in a specific direction so you can do something useful with it, like water your garden.

So it is with Mystical Numerology. When analyzing a word or a name, the vowel sounds give the principal energies – as we have already seen in Chapters 1 and 2. The consonants, and the number paths they represent, are channels through which these fundamental energies flow to create our reality and the different aspects of our lives. Each consonant has a number equivalent. This allows us to add up the consonant energies in a name and come out with a number total that represents the combined vibration so we can interpret the overall meaning.

Let us take a look at the Mystical Numerology number system, and the basic meanings of the numbers 1–22.

<u>Important Tip</u>: You may want to make a copy of the following chart by Xeroxing it, printing it out, or making a hand-written copy to use as your own easy reference chart as we proceed. You will find this quite useful until you commit the consonant/number correspondences to memory.

B	C	D	F	G	H	J	K	L	M	N	P	Q	R	S	T	V	W	X	Z
1	2	3	4	5	6	7	8	9	10	11	12	13	14	15	16	17	18	19	20

Note that the numbers 21 and 22 are not represented in the above chart. There are only 20 consonants in the alphabet, but there are 22 pathways connecting the archetypal energies on the Medicine Wheel. (See Appendix A for a more detailed description, including a Medicine Wheel "map" of the numbers).

For now, these are the important concepts to learn:

- The six vowels – A, E, I, O, U, and Y – are the principal energies and stand in the cardinal directions: east, south, west, north, center, above and below.

- The 22 numbers represent the 22 different pathways connecting the fundamental energies of the vowels/cardinal directions. They represent the 22 fundamental pathways for energy to flow in our lives.

The numbers 1 – 22 are archetypes similar to the Major Arcana of the Tarot deck. You can think of them as the directors in the 3-D movie that is our lives. They direct the six principal energies of the vowel sounds (A, E, I, O, U and Y) into physical manifestation in our perceptual reality.

Each name or word has a signature frequency that comes from the interaction of the consonants and their number values with the vowel sounds. It is this vibrational frequency that causes our reality to come into being. Our names and birth dates carry the vibrations that create our reality, give us our unique characteristics, and attract people and events into our lives.

More specifically, the number value of the consonants in people's names and the numbers in their birth dates give specific direction and shape to their lives. It is from the consonants in the name and the numbers in the birth date that we determine: Life Purpose, Life Path, Inner Urge, Legacy, Drive, Personality, Attainment Cycles, and Life Challenges. We will cover all of these as we proceed.

For now, let's start with the Life Purpose Number.

B	C	D	F	G	H	J	K	L	M	N	P	Q	R	S	T	V	W	X	Z
1	2	3	4	5	6	7	8	9	10	11	12	13	14	15	16	17	18	19	20

Using the above chart giving the consonant-number conversions, calculate the number value of the name you are currently using as your first name, the name by which you are called. This "first" name is the most frequently reinforced energy in your life. As such, it defines your "Life Purpose Number." This is the most important number of all. It tells you WHY you are here and WHAT you have come to do in this lifetime.

Remember:

• Only consonants are assigned number values; vowels sounds stand on their own and get analyzed separately as described in Chapters 1 and 2.

- Only double-digit numbers *greater* than 22 get reduced to a number between 1 – 22. For example, the number "58" reduces to a "13" (5 + 8 = 13). It is helpful to write the reduced number as "58/13" because there are other ways to arrive at a "13" (e.g., 49/13, 67/13, 85/13, and so on).

- When reducing numbers, stop when you get to a number that is between 1 – 22. For example, in reducing the number "58," *stop* when you get to the "13" since it is between 1 – 22. Do *not* reduce the 13 further to a 4 (1 + 3 = 4).

- Your *current* first name may be different from your *birth* name. The birth name is important and has a lingering effect, but the name you are currently using is most important. Look at the Life Purpose number from both names and see what the differences are – e.g., Kate vs. Katherine, Bill vs. William, Steve vs. Steven/Stephen, Chris vs. Christopher, Jeanne vs. Jean, Tim vs. Timothy, Tom vs. Thomas, Sue or Soozi vs. Susan, and so on.

- If you are using your middle name "Henry" (a 31/4) as your first name, instead of your given name "David" (a 23/5), then the middle name "Henry" determines your Life Purpose. In an example from the 2012 U.S. Presidential election contest, Willard Mitt Romney uses his middle name "Mitt" (42/6) so this determines his Life Purpose.

<u>Examples</u>

LEIGH = 9+5+6 = 20

JEANNE = 7+11+11 = 29 = 2+9 = 11

JOHN = 7+6+11 = 24 = 2+4 = 6

HILLARY = 6+9+9+14 = 38 = 3+8 = 11

LANCE = 9+11+2 = 22

BARACK = 1+14+2+8 = 25 = 2+5 = 7

JOSEPH = 7+15+12+6 = 40 = 4+0 = 4

FAIRUZ = 4+14+20 = 38 = 3+8 = 11

DVIR = 3+17+14 = 34 = 3+4 = 7

ANKE = 11+8 = 19

HAMID = 6+10+3 = 19

ANDREW = 11+3+14+18 = 46 = 4+6 = 10

HAGHIT = 6+5+6+16 = 33 = 3+3 = 6

Once you have calculated the number value for your first name, look at the table below to find the basic qualities of your Life Purpose.

Basic Number Meanings

The following chart is a primer on the number meanings, and will be your friend as you begin to work with the numbers to determine your Life Purpose, Life Path and other significant numbers. It is best to work with this simplified version of number meanings before going to a deeper level in Chapter 10. You may want to print it out, if you can.

Basic Meanings for the Numbers 0–22

NUMBER	BASIC MEANING
0	**The Unknowable** … God, Great Spirit, Great Mystery, Center, Unity; the Soul. The "enfolded order" from which everything emerges.
1	**Creator**, Creative Principle … Genesis, Mother, Birth, Potential … Breath, Superconsciousness … Clairvoyance, Knowing, Psychic … Self. Self-Interest … Innovate, Invent, Originality … Silence … Suddenness.
2	**Problem-Solver** … Masculine … Physical Reality, Perceptual … Equilibrium, Relationship, Reconcile … Concentration, Observe, Organizing Power … Count, Measurability … Acquire, Own … Security.
3	**Incubator** … Root, Origin, Idea … Energy, Speed … Activities, Agility, Do, Try … Carry, Convey, Mind-over-Matter … Objectify, Proof … Art, Science, Language … Candor … Urge for Relationship … Humor.
4	**Manager** … Manifested World … Reason, Order, Analyze … Work, Capability, Decision, Produce … Ego-Mind … Forgive … Seeing, Healing … Expanded Awareness, Ascend … Alliance, Freedom, Liberty, Justice … Song … Ascend.
5	**Bridge** … Medium … Goddess, Female … Fluidity, Balance, Harmony … Conceive, Create, Develop … Ask, Seek, Choose, Education, Learning … Words … Fertility, Nature … Friend, Family, Caring … Journey.

6	**Influencer** … awakener, intuitive, shaman … change, discover, research … trendsetter … teach, mentor, record … philosophy, governing principle … belonging, sharing, communicate … people, public, society.
7	**Idealist** … Mystic, Messenger … Vision, Visualize, Inspire … Drive, Personal Determination, Crusade, Achieve … Expert, Authority … Truth, Trust, Conscience … Linear, Logical, Precise … Study, Learn … Need to Give … Joy.
8	**Leader** … Love, Power … Faith, Expectancy, Miracle … Active, Pioneering … Ability, Competence, Purpose … Guide, Negotiator, Team … Willpower, Tenacious … Boundaries, Defender, Safety … Spontaneous, Optimistic.
9	**Foundation** … Earth, Light … Dream, Believe … Completeness, Drive for Wholeness, Mind-Body Connection … Executive, Fortune, Destiny … Caretaker, Giver, Diplomacy, Gratitude … Message, Music … Law.
10	**Seeker** … Ancestors, Awaken, Gate-Keeper … Seeker, Thinker … Understand, Wisdom, Mastery … Meaning, Objective Reality … Aim, Direction … Energizer, Organizer, Decisive … Outcome/Launch, Life Change.
11	**Connector** … Cultivator … Seer, Healer, Teacher, Shepherd … Change Agent, Futurist, Reformer … Strength, Action … Collective Outcome, Volunteerism, Equality … Musician, Sound … Manifestation, Prosperity.

12	**Achiever** ... visionary, pathfinder ... initiator, promoter, crusader, risk-taker ... creative forces, innovation, invention ... business, coordination, strategy ... service, therapy ... honesty, fair play ... woman/women.
13	**Builder** ... Life, Community, Grassroots ... Advisor, Authoritative, Expertise ... Goal-Oriented, Persistence ... Success, Wealth ... Giving Back, Selfless ... Choice Point, Personal Change, Paradigm Shift.
14	**Humanitarian** ... Peace ... Genetic Memory, Connectedness, Telepathy ... Harvest ... Affirmation, Belief ... Concreteness, Goal, Planning, Pragmatic ... Leadership, Individuality, Fame ... Mediator, Negotiation.
15	**Optimist** ... Extravert, Fun ... See, Heal, Psychic Abilities ... Support, Steadfast ... Functionality, Follow-Through, Tangible Result ... Turning Point ... Consensus Builder ... Businessman/woman, Judge, Plainspoken.
16	**Mastermind** ... Shape-Shifter, New Possibility, Fundamental Change ... Instinctive, Direct Knowing, Introspection ... Strategist, Synthesizer, Interpreter ... Logic, Pragmatist ... Hardworking ... Philanthropic.
17	**Transformer** ... Metamorphosis, Healing Process ... Miracle-Worker, Magic ... Being, Cause ... Beauty, Unconditional Love, Artistic Ability ... Enterprising, Doer ... Dialogue, Understanding, Public Relations ... Togetherness.

18	**Seed Planter** ... Hope, Ideas, Way-Shower ... Curiosity, Conceptualization, Acuity ... Act, Make, Accrue ... Persistent, Resourcefulness ... Stewardship, Sustainability ... Affable, Ally, Decency, Fair ... Administrator, Establishment.
19	**Guru** ... Augury, Lama, Deity ... Official, Power Issues, Decree ... Creed, Duty ... Male ... Agenda, Doing, Eager ... Urge, Nudge ... Web, E-mail, Data ... Voice, Candid ... Safe ... Agree ... Audit, Edit ... Egghead ... Body Image.
20	**Sage** ... Accuracy, Cogency ... Void, Fate ... Call, Hear, Debate ... Hero, Force, Fierce, Head-On ... Audacious, Avid ... Mobile ... Debut, Bloom ... Amiable, Abiding, Balm ... Joyful, Child ... Good Deal ... Barcode, Bank.
21	**Inner Guide** ... Guidance, Omen, Anima ... Educate, Focus ... Leap, Chance ... Grace ... Courage, Defend ... Coax, Enable, Engage ... Money, Play ... House, Name ... Beautify, Calm ... Aging ... Judicial, Jury, Plea.
22	**Guard**, Defuse ... Buddhahood ... Union, Ark, Equal ... Nuclei, Cohere, Meld ... Advice, Mold ... Noun, Fact, Oath, Map ... Reach, Climb, Voyage ... Succeed, Rich, Full, Enough ... Give, Offer, Beget ... Youth ... Joyous.

Once you've found your own Life Purpose number, calculate the Life Purpose numbers for your spouse or significant other. What insights do you get?

Now try calculating the Life Purpose numbers for family members, friends, coworkers, celebrities, people in the news, and historical figures. Play with it. Have fun. This can be a new world that is a doorway to deeper understanding.

The more you practice it, the quicker you will learn the consonant-number conversions. And, the quicker you learn these, the more fun it becomes to look at the Life Purpose numbers of people you know.

How I Derived the Number Meanings

I believe in the power of the sounds carried in words and names to create our reality. Because of this, I also believe that we can derive the meaning of each of the number archetypes through an analysis of the words and phrases we use. Over a period of years, I did just that. I analyzed over 25,000 words and short phrases, categorizing them by the numbers 1–22. (Remember, these are the archetypal numbers representing the 22 major pathways for energy to flow on the Medicine Wheel – see Appendix A). Then, I looked for the central focus of meaning that emerges. The meanings shown in the above Basic Meanings Chart came from this research. This is an aspect of what is new and fresh about my system of Mystical Numerology. I did not rely on the traditional meanings for the numbers. I *derived* them from the language.

Interestingly, many of the traditional meanings of the numbers 1-9, 11 and 22 are similar. But, there are also differences that emerge from this research, and nuances that generally get lost are uncovered – especially since the given meaning of a particular number is actually a cloud of meanings that coalesce around a focal point. While this additional information can complicate things, it also makes the numerology more accurate overall.

What is given above is a quick reference for each of the numbers, a primer, if you will. But, there is a lot more depth to each of the numbers. A more detailed description of the meaning of each number is presented in Chapter 10. This also includes an explanation of the shadow side or negative polarity of each number – something that most books on numerology don't show you. But, it is helpful to know both sides. If we know what is in our "shadow," we can better work with it and bring it into the light.

Chapter Four:

First Letter & Personality

Let us make distinctions, call things by the
right names.

~Henry David Thoreau, 1860~

The first letter of your first/given name is like the "rising sign" in astrology. It represents the public face that you show to the world, and gives insight to how people see you – your outer personality.

If the first letter is a vowel, it adds extra emphasis to the meaning of the "First Vowel" as described in chapter 2. For instance:

- A person with the first name of "Alan" will tend to have a sharp mind and be more intellectual or rational.

- A person whose first/given name is "Emily" will tend to have a personality that is expressive and relationship-oriented.

- The first name of "Ian" would tend to make a person sensory, and more connected with the physical world.

- The personality of "Owen" would be more intuitive and inner-directed.

And so on.

For names that start with consonants, personality traits and tendencies are described on the following pages. These descriptions are really a result of adapting the basic number definitions from pages 56-59 to the aspect of personality traits. Once you become familiar with the meaning of the numbers, you can do this for yourself. I've just done the work for you so you can use this section as a reference.

However, I am also introducing new information here. Each consonant is connected with the energy of a Mayan "Day Lord" (archetypal energy). There are 20 consonants in the English language alphabet and 20 Day Lords in the Mayan Spiritual Calendar[3]. These energies are linked. The correlations are given below:

B/1: Innovative, sees the potential in things; has a strong sense of individuality and may be strong-willed or, alternately, may struggle to find his/her sense of self.

K'iche Mayan Connection: "Batz" – the thread of life. These people have a sense of the past and future while staying in the "now" moment of the present.

C/2: Relationship-oriented; problem-solver and organizer; good powers of concentration and observation; may have a talent for acquiring things and establishing financial security; setting personal boundaries can be an issue – either something that they are good at, or struggle with.

K'iche Mayan Connection: "E" (pronounced Eh) – Destiny: These people are pulled forward along their path by the force of destiny.

D/3: Energetic doers, they like to get into action and "do" things; physical experience is important; may be good at socializing; they have the ability to carry and convey ideas.

---

[3] My thanks to both Don Alejandro Cirilo Perez Oxlaj, primary keeper of the teachings, visions and prophecies of the Mayan people, and to Cynthia Walker for teaching me this information.

K'iche Mayan Connection: "Aj" (the "j" is pronounced like a hard "h") – Power. These people have the kind of power that enables them to be an authority in their chosen field.

F/4: Productive worker; linear thought process, reason and order are important, has a tendency to be analytical; a capable decision-maker; personal liberty is important; may have a tough time backing down from strongly-held positions; forgiveness may be an issue.

K'iche Mayan Connection: "Ix" – the Earth, Jaguar. These people may have a strong connection with nature and her creative forces.

G/5: Creative and dynamic; a bridge between differing ideas or worldviews; outgoing and caring; strong connections with family and friends; seeks balance and harmony amidst chaos but can be impulsive and reckless.

K'iche Mayan Connection: "Tzikin" – the Birds. This energy is the intermediary between man and spirit.

H/6: Influencer, mentor; questions traditional ideas, seeks answers; may be a people person or connected with the public; a person of potentially strong polarities; a sense of place is important; may struggle with insecurity.

K'iche Mayan Connection: "Ajmaq" – Forgiveness and Reconciliation. It also represents ancient wisdom that comes from the brain in communication with the Spirit Guides.

J/7: Visionary and/or messenger; strong sense of knowing without knowing how he or she knows; knowledge and introspection are important; may have trust issues; also has earthy and linear sides, and the ability to be logical and detail-oriented.

K'iche Mayan Connection: "Noj" – Knowing. It is important to listen to and act on inner guidance.

K/8: Power, fortitude and directness; dynamic and action-oriented; inclined toward success; a leader/guide but also can be a team-player; romantic; can be a defender of others; may have control issues.

K'iche Mayan Connection: "Tijax" – Double-edged knife, cutting-away. These people need to learn to let go and allow a Higher Power to work through them.

L/9: Caretaker, diplomatic, altruistic, philanthropic – has the power to lift others up; often has connections with community groups, businesses, etc.; may have executive ability; attracts good fortune; can be a good storyteller.

K'iche Mayan Connection: "Kawoq" – home and hearth, the family. By extension, this energy also represents groups, the community, and society.

M/10: Seeker after wisdom and understanding; a thinker, scholar; energizer, organizer, can be decisive, good at setting a direction; has a strength in following through and producing collective outcomes; strong idealism.

K'iche Mayan Connection: "Ajpu" – Grandfather Sun, clarity, breath, hunter; bringer of spiritual and material certainty.

N/11: Connector, shepherd; may be a seer, healer or teacher; charismatic, has strong beliefs; may be a catalyst, change-agent or trailblazer; likes action; often service-oriented; may be a musician or work with sound.

K'iche Mayan Connection: "Imox" – Seer and Healer; this energy increases spiritual strength, opens the mind, and helps to manage change.

P/12: Achiever, planner, finder of new directions, crusader; innovator and risk-taker; strong value for service and honesty, can be a great therapist; dependable, faithful; good chief.

K'iche Mayan Connection: "Iq" – the Wind, the breath of the Creator. It is the principle of vitality that gives life and intuition.

Q/13: A "builder:" urge to build something practical and lasting; business savvy; goal-oriented; successful, reaps rewards for their actions; has a desire to give something back to the community.

K'iche Mayan Connection: "Aqabal" – Dawn and dusk; power of revelation, connection with beginnings and endings.

R/14: Networker, widely connected; ability to draw to themselves needed resources and people; pragmatic planner, grounded goal-setter; humanitarian, peacemaker; leadership ability.

K'iche Mayan Connection: "Kat" – The Net or Web – the energy matrix that connects all things ... and can create entanglements from which it is difficult to escape.

S/15: May have healing or psychic abilities; can be a unifying force and work selflessly for the common good; pragmatic and practical, good follow-through; tends to be optimistic and fun to be with; steadfast as a friend; may be plainspoken.

K'iche Mayan Connection: "Kan" – Serpent; an energy associated with the nervous system. It gives the power to continue to move forward even in the face of adversity. It is the energy of athletes, all kinds of games and high energy things. It gives a forceful personality. When angered, people with this energy can be suddenly fiery and ferocious.

T/16: Instinctive; hard-working, can be quite practical; synthesizer and interpreter, strategic thinker, logical; has the quality of direct-knowing; sees new possibilities, new frontiers; can be a shape-shifter, adaptable, culturally mobile.

K'iche Mayan Connection: "Kemé" – Death, harmony and rebirth; connection with the ancestors, particularly the Grandmothers. It gives personal magnetism, charisma and leadership qualities.

V/17: Enterprising, courageous, strong, intelligent, may exhibit deep understanding; may be a good advisor and/or work with the public; has the ability to transform things including self; artistic, likes beautiful things.

K'iche Mayan Connection: "Kej," the Deer, representing movement, the potential for things, and the power of new beginnings.

W/18: Way-shower, seed-planter, seeds new ideas; nurturing, bringer of hope; expands beyond existing limitations to help others feel free; loyal, affable, fair-minded; a good ally and friend; success comes from service.

K'iche Mayan Connection: Qanil – Rabbit, seed, semen; carries the codes for the creation of life; regeneration. These people are intelligent, sensitive, successful; a defender of the people.

X/19: Warm, high energy, magnetic to others; has the ability to attract followers, or work as an official of some kind; strong sense of duty, creed, and beliefs; can be quite grounded, strong affinity with the earth.

K'iche Mayan Connection: Toj – Payment, saying prayers of thanks for your blessings. These people are generally sensitive and energetic, strong and respectful.

Z/20: Audacious, stands his/her ground; can be an artist, sage, hero, or loner; has the ability to connect with the void from which all potential possibilities exist and from which all wisdom comes; amiable and joyful, has the talent to laugh at one's own foibles; may seem a bit spacey, at times.

K'iche Mayan Connection: Tzi – Dog, guardian of the home; the law and authority. These people are generally kind and cheerful. They believe in social justice, peace and spirituality.

Chapter Five:

Going Deeper With Names

Life must be lived on a higher platform, to which we are always invited to ascend; there, the whole aspect of things changes.

~Ralph Waldo Emerson~

Life Purpose, Inner Urge, Legacy & Drive

In Chapter 3, you learned the correspondence between the consonants and the number values shown again below. As you work more with converting the consonants in a name to numbers, you will soon find that you no longer need to refer to the chart. The key, of course, is practice.

B	C	D	F	G	H	J	K	L	M	N	P	Q	R	S	T	V	W	X	Z
1	2	3	4	5	6	7	8	9	10	11	12	13	14	15	16	17	18	19	20

I also introduced you to the basic meanings of the numbers 1–22 (see pages 56-59). And, you learned to calculate the Life Purpose number from the first name of a person. Now, it is time to take the exploration deeper.

Here's an important point that I would like you to keep in mind. Once you learn the techniques described in this book, a _lot_ of information about an individual can be found just from his/her name. You don't always know a person's birth date, but you always have their name. And, even if you only have a _first_ or _given_ name, you still can get an understanding of their Life Purpose, something about how the natural energy flows in their life (from the vowel sounds), and gain insight into their personality from the First Letter (Chapter 4). This is a very powerful tool to have in your toolbox.

On a personal level, I have used it to great advantage to understand myself better. It is a great tool for introspection. But it is also a powerful tool for understanding others in ways that can improve and strengthen relationships – with children, friends, family and others. It is a terrific and often quick way of gaining insight into people in business or at work, including potential clients. In short, with a little practice it can be one of the important arrows in your quiver.

In this chapter, I will show you how to determine your Life Purpose, Inner Urge, Legacy and Drive, the four aspects that come from your name.

Important note: Since Mystical Numerology deals with 22 archetypal numbers, all calculations that result in a number between 1 – 22 are not reduced further. For instance, a "15" does not get reduced to a "6" (1+5 = 6). It stands as a "15."

Life Purpose

This number tells WHY you are here in this lifetime and WHAT you are supposed to do. It is calculated by adding up the number values of the consonants of your first or given name, or that of the person you are analyzing. The Life Purpose is the most important number in the entire numerology chart.

It is important to use the _current name_ in cases where this is different from the birth name. When you change your name, or even use a nickname, it shifts your energy. The birth name has a lingering effect, like the sound of a bell ringing in the distance. After it has been struck, it continues ringing but gets softer as time goes by. So it is for names no longer used.

As an example, consider Katherine Anne "Katie" Couric, an American television journalist and author. She serves as special correspondent for ABC News, contributing to ABC World News, Nightline, 20/20, Good Morning America, and primetime news specials. "Katie" (24/6) is the name by which she is known, not "Katherine" (55/10), her given name. So, *Katie* is the name to use in calculating her Life Purpose number.

Some people use their middle names as their first name. I have no particular love for today's politicians, but as well-known individuals they sometimes make good examples. One such case is a 2012 U.S. Presidential candidate, Willard Mitt Romney. He uses "Mitt" as his first name. In effect, he has rearranged his name to be Mitt Willard Romney. So, you would calculate his Life Purpose number using Mitt (42/6). Willard (53/8) gets treated as his middle name, and would represent the Inner Urge described directly below.

Inner Urge(s)

This is an energy that is felt on an emotional level and is generally experienced as an inner, sometimes unconscious, motivation. As with the Life Purpose, the Inner Urge is calculated by working with only the consonants of the middle name, adding up their number values. People who have worked with traditional western numerology will find this different.[4]

When a married woman takes the surname of her husband as a last name, and shifts her own last name to a middle name, it becomes an Inner Urge.

Also, some people have more than one middle name. Consider former British Prime Minister Winston Churchill. His full name was Winston Leonard Spencer Churchill. In this case, both "Leonard" and "Spencer" represent separate inner urges.

On the other hand, when you look at names from the 1700s and before, it was not as common as it is today for people to have middle names. As examples, consider: Galileo Galilei, William Shakespeare, Christopher Marlowe, Thomas Jefferson, John Adams, Benjamin

---

[4] See Appendix B for a discussion of traditional systems of numerology.

Franklin, Thomas Paine, and so on. Of course, some people certainly did have middle names, such as: Johann Sebastian Bach, Wolfgang Amadeus Mozart, Giovanni Giacomo Casanova, and Samuel Langhorne Clemens. The point is this: *no middle name, no Inner Urge number.*

Legacy

This number represents the energy that carries forward beyond your lifetime, and often has an important connection with what you do in the world. It is calculated by summing up the number values of the consonants in your last name (surname).

For women, figuring out the "Legacy" number can be less than straightforward since it is still common for married women to take the surname of their husbands as their own last name. In this case, while the birth name will always have an influence, the current name is most important. The rule of thumb is: *when you change your name, you change your energy.*

Drive

This number is your *motivation,* the fuel that *drives* you along your "Path" to achieve your "Purpose." It is calculated from adding together the Life Purpose + the Inner Urge(s) + Legacy. This is equivalent to summing up all the number values for all of the consonants in your full name.

OK, now we have four numbers to look at when we are considering the Mystical Numerology of ourselves – which is great for introspection – and for looking at when we do the numbers of others. The same number chart (pages 56-59) is used in each case, but we must adapt the interpretation to the different aspects we are looking at: Life Purpose, Inner Urge, Legacy or Drive.

Let us consider an example from public life: HILLARY RODHAM CLINTON.

Hillary Rodham Clinton served as the U.S. Secretary of State from 2009–2012. In 2008, she competed against Barack Obama for the Democratic nomination to run for President and nearly won. Had she defeated Obama, it is very likely that she would have also beat Senator John McCain and become the first woman U.S. President.

Her birth name was actually Hillary Diane Rodham. When she married Bill Clinton, her family surname, Rodham, became a middle name. Using the consonant/number conversion chart, we can calculate the numbers of her name.

HILLARY RODHAM CLINTON			
38/11 +	33/6 +	49/13 =	120/3

Life Purpose from HILLARY = H/6 + L/9 + L/9 +R/14 = 38 = 3+8 = $\underline{11}$. Since the "11" is between 1 and 22, we do not reduce it further. What does this tell us about Hillary Clinton?

"11" is a Master number and represents a high-energy. From the number definitions on page 57, we read that "11" is the **Connector**. It is the number of the Change Agent and Reformer. It is Strength and Action. It is also the energy of the Seer, Healer, Teacher, Shepherd, and the number of Sound and Manifestation. All of these aspects tell us something about Hillary Clinton's Life Purpose, much of which she has already realized and some of which may still represent potential for the future.

Hillary Clinton is here in this lifetime to be a change agent and a connector. She was an important force behind Bill Clinton's successful bid for the U.S. Presidency in 1992 and his reelection in 1996. She is certainly strong and has demonstrated staying power in the high-adrenaline game of politics. And, as U.S. Secretary of State she traveled perhaps millions of miles meeting with heads of state and political leaders around the globe, connecting the dots in an expanding network of influence.

Inner Urge from RODHAM = R/14 + D/3 + H/6 + M/10 = 33 = 3+3 = $\underline{6}$. From the number meanings given on page 57, we see that the "6" is the **Influencer** and has to do with people, the public and society. It is also the Awakener, Trendsetter, and Mentor. These are, perhaps, fair descriptions of Hillary Clinton's inner motivations.

Legacy: from CLINTON = C/2 + L/9 + N/11 + T/16 + N/11 = 49 = 4+9 = 13. Since "13" is between 1-22 we do not reduce it further.

From the basic number definitions on page 58, we find that "13" is the **Builder**. It is about Life and the Community. It is the energy of Success and Wealth but also about selfless service and giving something back at the grassroots level for blessings received. It represents a person who is Authoritative, and has considerable Expertise. This is Hillary Clinton's "Legacy," what will live on after she has left political office and left her body. This is the part that the history books will write about her.

Drive from the sum of the number values of all the consonants in her full name, and also equal to the Life Purpose (38/11) + Inner Urge (33/6) + Legacy (49/13). This brings up an important point. When adding up numbers like this:

Always add the unreduced numbers and then reduce the final result.

DRIVE NUMBER = 38 + 33 + 49 = 120 = 1+2+0 = 3.

"3" is the **Incubator**. It is the number of energy in action that moves outward in all directions. It is the ability to delve into the origins and roots of things, and to carry and convey an idea. It gives Hillary Clinton the kind of energy she needs to compete at the highest levels in the political arena and move around the world.

See how this works?

Let's consider one more example before moving on. Let us look at the father of the atomic bomb:

JULIUS		ROBERT		OPPENHEIMER		
31/4	+	45/9	+	65/11	=	141/6
Purpose	+	Inner Urge	+	Legacy	=	Drive

Life Purpose from JULIUS = J/7 + L/9 + S/15 = <u>31/4</u>. From the table of basic meanings on page 56, we see that "4" is the **Manager**. Keywords include: Reason, Order, Analyze ... Work, Capability, Decision, Produce ... Alliance, Freedom, Liberty, Justice.

These are good descriptors for the man. He was a capable manager who managed a team of scientists in one of the biggest research projects of the day. He was a scientist whose stock in trade was reason and a lot of hard work. And, regardless of what you may think of nuclear weapons, he and his team felt they were working to maintain freedom and liberty.

Of course, eventually Oppenheimer would quote the Bhagavad Gita in speaking of the atomic bomb, "I am become death, the destroyer of worlds." It is also very interesting to me that if you look at the consonant values for "Atomic Bomb," you will find that it is a "40/4" energy, the same basic energy as Julius Oppenheimer's "4" Life Purpose.

Inner Urge from the middle name, ROBERT: R/14 + B/1 + R/14 + T/16 = <u>45/9</u>. The "9" is the **Foundation** (page 57). Keywords include: Executive, Fortune, Destiny ... Earth, Light ... Dream, Perceive, Believe ... Caretaker, Giver, Gratitude ... Law. Again, we get an indication of Oppenheimer's ability to manage people. The "9" is the executive, but it is also the caring executive. It is also the dreamer, and Oppenheimer was well-known to be a versatile scholar and quite philosophical.

Legacy: from the last name (surname): OPPENHEIMER = P/12 + P/12 + N/11 + H/6 + M/10 + R/14 = <u>65/11</u>. The "11" is the **Connector** (pg. 57). Keywords include: Change Agent, Reformer ... Strength, Action ... Seer, Shepherd ... Manifestation. Oppenheimer and his team of scientists, in developing the atomic bomb, altered the course of World War II and changed the world forever. His legacy is clearly one of "Change Agent."

Drive from the sum of the number values of all the consonants in his full name. This is also equal to the Life Purpose (31/4) + Inner Urge (45/9) + Legacy (65/11). Allow me to again emphasize this important

73

point: when adding up numbers like this, *always add the unreduced numbers and then reduce the final result:*

DRIVE NUMBER = 31 + 45 + 65 = 141 = 1+4+1 = 6.

"6" is the **Influencer** (pg. 57). Keywords include: Awakener … Trendsetter … Change, Discover, Research … Teach, Mentor, Record … People, Public, and Society. Oppenheimer's Drive or primary motivation was research and discovery. And, he certainly gave the world a wake-up call, made a tremendous change in world affairs that affected people and society everywhere. So, we can see that this Drive number fits him very well.

If you haven't yet determined these four numbers for your own name, I hope you will do so now to see how it fits. And, after you use the basic meanings on pages 56-59 to gain initial insight, go to Chapter 10 and find the more detailed description of the numbers. This will add even more insight.

As an introspective tool, Mystical Numerology will give you new insights and maybe even some inspiration for your future potential. It is also fun to look at the names of your family and friends. This is good practice, but also will result in new understanding. If you are anything like me, you will start to look at *lots* of names – family, friends, coworkers, acquaintances, celebrities, and also famous and infamous historical figures. The more you practice, the better you will get at adapting the interpretations of the numbers to the different aspects under consideration such as Life Purpose, Inner Urge, Legacy and Drive.

And, the quickest way to learn is to have fun – play with it like a new toy!

Chapter Six:

The 13-Month Mystical Numerology Calendar

> Time is an illusion. ... The only reason for
> time is so that everything doesn't happen at
> once.
>
> ~Albert Einstein~

There is a place or state of consciousness that is beyond time and space. It is the place of the infinite void, the cosmic womb, the place of unmanifest existence that is everywhere pregnant with infinite potential and possibilities. It is a state of being where past, present and future merge into the eternal NOW. It is from that place that we come, and from which this reality emerges.

Many of you have very likely experienced this state of awareness. It is available to us in meditation, in sacred ceremonies, in near-death experiences, and in traumatic moments when time seems to stop or proceed in freeze-frame.

I remember experiencing this for the first time when I was 13. It was so vivid that I even remember the date: Monday, March 4, 1963. I was late for school so my older brother, Russell, drove me in his beautiful, two-tone 1957 Ford. On the way, the hot ash of his unfiltered Lucky Strike cigarette fell on the seat between his legs. It diverted his attention, and while he was frantically trying to deal with the hot ash, the car drifted over to edge of the road, jumped the curb and smashed into a telephone pole. We were only going about 25 to 30-mph, but it was enough to total the car. Russ walked away with 60 stitches in his neck just under the chin. I went through the windshield and back. As I did, time stopped. I went to that place where time doesn't exist. Maybe I left my body for a brief few seconds. Whatever happened, the result was that I never felt my face hitting the windshield and going through it. I never felt the lacerations to my forehead, eyelids and nose that would require over 300 stitches to mend.

Joseph Rael, Beautiful Painted Arrow, who first taught my wife, Jeanne White Eagle and me about the power of the vowel sounds, would say to his students, "We really don't exist." It was and is still a mind-bender. What he meant is that we come out of nothingness, the pregnant void of all potential possibilities that is beyond space-time. We keep blinking on and off, appearing and disappearing as the inhalations and exhalations of the Great Mystery. Our minds are too slow to catch it except for once in a while in visions or ceremony or states of ecstasy when we can see that we are here and not here, here and not here – and so is all of reality.

The point is this. For all of our focus on time as a precise and unchangeable quantity, it is a very relative and arbitrary thing. Albert Einstein once explained it this way. "If you spend an hour with a girl that you love, it seems like only a second. But if you sit on a hot cinder for a second, it seems like an hour." His Theory of Relativity went on to explain that someone flying at just under the speed of sound in a jet aircraft at 38,000 feet will age slightly more slowly than a person on the ground.

All time is relative, and the way we divide it up is a choice, one that has certain consequences. We didn't always have 12 months in the year. In fact, in ancient times people lived by a 10-month calendar. It was Julius Caesar's astronomers in 45 BC that explained the need for 12 months in a year and the addition of a leap year to synchronize with the seasons. That was when the months

January and February were added to the calendar, and the original fifth and sixth months were renamed July and August in honor of Julius Caesar and his successor, Augustus – both of which were made 31 days long to emphasize their importance, another arbitrary choice. The modern "Gregorian" calendar that has become internationally accepted as the civil calendar was adopted by Pope Gregory in 1582.

The Julian and Gregorian calendars reconciled the solar year with the 12-sign zodiac but ignored any natural solstice cycle for a starting point. January 1 just starts where it starts. In some fundamental way, this doesn't make any sense. The shortest day in the northern hemisphere occurs at the winter solstice that usually occurs on December 21 or 22, after which the sun begins its return. In the southern hemisphere this is the summer solstice and longest day. But the same principle is true. The sun shifts on this date in relationship to the Earth. Why not begin a calendar on or near this date instead of ten or eleven days later?

Not to beat a dead horse, but the point is that our calendars are arbitrary choices. We have *chosen* to carve our years into periods of 12-months of varying lengths because Julius Caesar's astronomers saw the need to reconcile the solar year with the Earth's passage through the 12-signs of the zodiac. It is interesting to me that in 1995 Walter Berg and Mark Yazaki suggested that a 13-sign zodiac be adopted with the addition of the constellation Ophiuchus, the Serpent-bearer. This constellation has been known since at least the time of the great second-century astronomer, Ptolemy (90 AD–168 AD). Why is a 13-sign zodiac just now being suggested? Could it be a sign of our shifting consciousness?

Just for grins, consider that the reason that we divide our day into two 12-hour segments is also an arbitrary choice, not some immutable cosmic law inscribed in granite and brought down from the mountain top. Our 12-hour days and nights came from the Babylonians as long ago as

3500 BC. They were enamored with the number "12." That's also the reason we have only 12-signs in the zodiac, because the Babylonians, and the Egyptians after them, liked the number "12" and thought it would be great to divide the day and night into 12-hour segments. They also used a sexagesimal system (base 60) which is probably why the hours were divided into units of 60 seconds. It was a choice that came out of the consciousness of the day. It fit for them, but may not any longer be a good fit for the times in which we live.

We are in transformative times. People are waking up, spiritually. Individually and collectively, we are moving into higher states of awareness. Perhaps a 13-sign zodiac is a sign of the times. What I do know from my research into the numbers that form our reality is that the number "12" is an explosive number.

It has many wonderfully positive qualities. It is a visionary energy that acts as a gateway and allows us to be innovative and inventive. It can help us to be fearless and move in new directions. It is the number of religion and service and business. Yet, locking ourselves into 12-hour days, and 12-month years has a serious downside.

We would do well to also recognize that "12" is also the number of extremism and violence. It is the number of earthquakes and explosions, atrocities and holocaust. It supports rebelliousness and ruthless tyrants on one side, and defeatism, hopelessness and self-doubt on the other. We have seen enough of these negative energies both in modern times and through long centuries past. What we haven't considered is that our choice to divide up our year (and our days) into increments of 12 lock us into these patterns.

I developed *a new, 13-month calendar for my system of Mystical Numerology.* My initial inspiration came from the K'iche Maya spiritual calendar in which 20 Day Lords (archetypal energies) cycle through 13 different powers. I began to wonder what a 365-day solar year would look like if it were divided into 13 increments or powers. What I found was that it gives much more uniform months. In a non-leap year, all months except for one are 28-days in length – an even four seven-day weeks. And one month is 29 days. This seemed like a good thing, especially since "13" is considered a sacred number by the Mayans.

From my research into the meanings of numbers, I also found that "13" is a less explosive energy. It is the number of community and life and the power to build. It is the energy of the causal plane and unlimited potential. It fosters the paradigm shift and personal change that we need at this time in our history when we are about to emerge into a higher state of awareness. It is also the number of success and wealth, and bestows self-assurance, dynamism and expertise. As an added blessing, it is helps to promote goodness, selflessness, and a spirit of giving something back for what we receive. These are qualities that could shift old patterns and transform our world.

In Hebrew, the word for "one" is "Echad" (where the "ch" is pronounced as a hard "h" at the back of the throat). The gematria or numerology of "Echad" is 13 in the Hebrew system. So, there is also a mystical connection between the number "13" the concept of oneness.

The Mayan correspondence with the number "13" is the Day Lord called Aqabal (Aq'ab'al), the "dawn and the dusk." So, "13" also has a connection with beginnings and endings.

For all of those reasons, I believe that a 13-month calendar would be better to live by than the 12-month system we've had for the past 2000 years. That said, one of the best things about the 13-month calendar in the context of my Mystical Numerology system is this: It works!

While it took some time to determine just when to start the calendar, when the starting point (December 20) finally clicked into place, everything else worked. I began testing the 13-month calendar as the basis for interpreting birth dates in Mystical Numerology readings, analyzing hundreds and hundreds of famous people, friends and family. To my delight and surprise, the calendar gave accurate readings. I encourage you to try it, not only in Mystical Numerology readings for yourself and others, but as a calendar by which to live. Of course, as long as the accepted civil calendar is the 12-month Gregorian calendar, it is impossible to totally unhook from it. However, I have been using the 13-month calendar side-by-side with the Gregorian calendar now for years – and this I recommend doing!

The following chart shows the 13 months, the Gregorian Calendar dates for each month, the basic energies of each month, and the correspondence of each period with a Mayan Day Lord. The Mayan energies will be discussed more fully in Chapter 10 on the number meanings. I'd love to hear suggestions from my readers for the *names* of the months!

The 13-Months: Gregorian Calendar Dates & Energies

Month	Gregorian Dates	Energies of the Months	Mayan Energy
1	Dec 20 – Jan 16	**Genesis** ... Potential, Original Wisdom.	Batz
2	Jan 17 – Feb 13	**Relationship** ... Intention, Journeys, Our Path.	E
3	Feb 14 – Mar 13	**Activities** ... Energy, Ideas, Spiritual Power	Aj
4	Mar 14 – Apr 10	**Decision** ... Order, Reason, Expectation, Mother Earth.	Ix
5	Apr 11 – May 8	**Fluidity** ... Balance, Harmony & Chaos	Tzikin
6	May 9 – Jun 5	**Change** ... Discovery, People, Placement, Forgiveness.	Aqmaq
7	Jun 6 – Jul 4	**Trust** ... Vision, Knowledge, Judgment, Drive	Noj
8	Jul 5 – Aug 1	**Achievement** ... Imagination, Letting Go, Moving On	Tijax
9	Aug 2 – Aug 29	**Gratitude** ... Foundation, Family, Community, Destiny	Kawoq
10	Aug 30 – Sep 26	**Mastery** ... Outcomes, Clarity.	Ajpu
11	Sep 27 – Oct 24	**Manifestation** ... Knowing, Outreach, Change	Imox
12	Oct 24 – Nov 21	**Adaptability** ... Coordination, Compassion, Service, Vitality	Iq
13	Nov 22 – Dec 19	**Endings/Beginnings** ... Choice Points	Aqabal

On the following pages are two versions of the 13-month calendar. One is for a normal, non-leap year. The other is for leap years when an extra day must be added to the third month.

Up front, I offer apologies that the print is so small. The value of reproducing the calendar all on one page outweighed the confusion created by breaking the two tables in half to make the numbers bigger. Some of you might have to get your reading glasses or a magnifier to read it. But, if my own 63-year-old eyes are a fair test, the calendar conversion table should work for most people.

To read the calendar, you will see that the days, 1–29, are shown in the first column. The months, 1–13, are shown as columns M1–M13. In the monthly columns are the Gregorian dates. As an example, Day 1 of Month 1 (M1) is shown as Dec-20. Day 1 of Month 6 (M6) is May 9, and so on.

To convert a birth date to the 13-month calendar, locate the Gregorian calendar day, and see what day and month it is on the 13-month calendar. You will note that I use the Day–Month–Year format to work with dates. This is the convention that is common outside the U.S., and it will be important to adopt for working with dates in Mystical Numerology readings.

Example 1

My birth date is 21-February, 1950. It is a non-leap year, so look for the date in the first calendar. You will find it in the Month 3 (M3) column across from Day 8. So, on the 13-month calendar, my birth date is written as: 8–3–1950 (Day-Month-Year format).

Example 2

Barack Obama was born on 4-August-1961. You will find August 4 in the Month 9 column (M9) across from Day 3. So, in 13-month calendar format, Obama's birth date is 3–9–1961.

Example 3

OK. Here's a tricky one. For late December birth dates, you have to remember that the 13-month calendar starts on

December 20. So, *any birth date on the Gregorian calendar that falls between December 20 – December 31 rolls over into the next year* – that's the tricky part. My wife, Jeanne was born on 29-December-1943. On the calendar conversion chart for the common year, you will find December 29 in the Month 1 column (M1) across from Day 10. So, her birth date of 29-December-**1943** translates into 10–1–**1944** (D-M-Y) on the 13-month calendar.

Example 4

Dr. Suess, Theodore Suess Giesel, was born on 2–March–1904. 1904 was a leap year, so to convert his Gregorian calendar birth date to the 13-month calendar format, look at the leap year calendar. There, you will find his birth date in the Month 3 column (M3) across from Day 18. So, in the 13-month calendar format, the birth date for Dr. Suess is 18–3–1904.

How do you know which year is a leap year? They occur in 4-year intervals. This is because it takes 365 days, 5 hours, 48 minutes and 46 seconds for the Earth to make one revolution around the sun. That is 365.2425 days, very close to 365-¼ days. So, every four years, we add a day to the calendar to catch up. In any century, leap years are the years that end with the double digits shown in the following table:

Leap Years

00	20	40	60	80
04	24	44	64	84
08	28	48	68	88
12	32	52	72	92
16	36	56	76	96

For instance, the years 1900, 1904, 1908, 1912 and 1916 are leap years, and so on. Actually, any year with the last two digits that are divisible evenly by the number 4 is a leap year. Take any century and this is true. The years 1700, 1704, 1708, 1712 and 1716 are also leap years. So are 1852, 1876, and 1888. 2012 is also a leap year. When analyzing a birth date, make a quick check to see if it is in a common year or a leap year. Then, choose the 13-month conversion calendar chart that fits.

In the next section of the book, we will begin to use the basic tools to analyze names and put together a Mystical Numerology reading. That's the fun part!

The 13-Month Calendar Conversion – Common Year

(Note: Bolded letters in columns represent month beginnings: e.g., J = Jan, etc.)

Day	M1	M2	M3	M4	M5	M6	M7	M8	M9	M10	M11	M12	M13
1	**Dec** 20	**Jan** 17	**Feb** 14	**Mar** 14	**Apr** 11	**May** 9	**Jun** 6	**Jul** 5	**Aug** 2	**Aug** 30	**Sep** 27	**Oct** 25	**Nov** 22
2	21	18	15	15	12	10	7	6	3	31	28	26	23
3	22	19	16	16	13	11	8	7	4	**S-1**	29	27	24
4	23	20	17	17	14	12	9	8	5	2	30	28	25
5	24	21	18	18	15	13	10	9	6	3	**O-1**	29	26
6	25	22	19	19	16	14	11	10	7	4	2	30	27
7	26	23	20	20	17	15	12	11	8	5	3	31	28
8	27	24	21	21	18	16	13	12	9	6	4	**N-1**	29
9	28	25	22	22	19	17	14	13	10	7	5	2	30
10	29	26	23	23	20	18	15	14	11	8	6	3	**D-1**
11	30	27	24	24	21	19	16	15	12	9	7	4	2
12	31	28	25	25	22	20	17	16	13	10	8	5	3
13	**J-1**	29	26	26	23	21	18	17	14	11	9	6	4
14	2	30	27	27	24	22	19	18	15	12	10	7	5
15	3	31	28	28	25	23	20	19	16	13	11	8	6
16	4	**F-1**	**M-1**	29	26	24	21	20	17	14	12	9	7
17	5	2	2	30	27	25	22	21	18	15	13	10	8
18	6	3	3	31	28	26	23	22	19	16	14	11	9
19	7	4	4	**A-1**	29	27	24	23	20	17	15	12	10
20	8	5	5	2	30	28	25	24	21	18	16	13	11
21	9	6	6	3	**M-1**	29	26	25	22	19	17	14	12
22	10	7	7	4	2	30	27	26	23	20	18	15	13
23	11	8	8	5	3	31	28	27	24	21	19	16	14
24	12	9	9	6	4	**J-1**	29	28	25	22	20	17	15
25	13	10	10	7	5	2	30	29	26	23	21	18	16
26	14	11	11	8	6	3	**J-1**	30	27	24	22	19	17
27	15	12	12	9	7	4	2	31	28	25	23	20	18
28	16	13	13	10	8	5	3	**A-1**	29	26	24	21	19
29							4						

The 13-Month Mystical Numerology Calendar – Leap Year

(Note: Bolded letters in columns represent month beginnings: e.g., J = Jan, etc.)

Day	M1	M2	M3	M4	M5	M6	M7	M8	M9	M10	M11	M12	M13
1	**Dec** 20	**Jan** 17	**Feb** 14	**Mar** 14	**Apr** 11	**May** 9	**Jun** 6	**Jul** 5	**Aug** 2	**Aug** 30	**Sep** 27	**Oct** 25	**Nov** 22
2	21	18	15	15	12	10	7	6	3	31	28	26	23
3	22	19	16	16	13	11	8	7	4	**S-1**	29	27	24
4	23	20	17	17	14	12	9	8	5	2	30	28	25
5	24	21	18	18	15	13	10	9	6	3	**O-1**	29	26
6	25	22	19	19	16	14	11	10	7	4	2	30	27
7	26	23	20	20	17	15	12	11	8	5	3	31	28
8	27	24	21	21	18	16	13	12	9	6	4	**N-1**	29
9	28	25	22	22	19	17	14	13	10	7	5	2	30
10	29	26	23	23	20	18	15	14	11	8	6	3	**D-1**
11	30	27	24	24	21	19	16	15	12	9	7	4	2
12	31	28	25	25	22	20	17	16	13	10	8	5	3
13	**J-1**	29	26	26	23	21	18	17	14	11	9	6	4
14	2	30	27	27	24	22	19	18	15	12	10	7	5
15	3	31	28	28	25	23	20	19	16	13	11	8	6
16	4	**F-1**	29	29	26	24	21	20	17	14	12	9	7
17	5	2	**M-1**	30	27	25	22	21	18	15	13	10	8
18	6	3	2	31	28	26	23	22	19	16	14	11	9
19	7	4	3	**A-1**	29	27	24	23	20	17	15	12	10
20	8	5	4	2	30	28	25	24	21	18	16	13	11
21	9	6	5	3	**M-1**	29	26	25	22	19	17	14	12
22	10	7	6	4	2	30	27	26	23	20	18	15	13
23	11	8	7	5	3	31	28	27	24	21	19	16	14
24	12	9	8	6	4	**J-1**	29	28	25	22	20	17	15
25	13	10	9	7	5	2	30	29	26	23	21	18	16
26	14	11	10	8	6	3	**J-1**	30	27	24	22	19	17
27	15	12	11	9	7	4	2	31	28	25	23	20	18
28	16	13	12	10	8	5	3	**A-1**	29	26	24	21	19
29			13				4						

Chapter Seven:

Working with Dates

Do not go where the path may
lead, go instead where there is no
path and leave a trail.

~Ralph Waldo Emerson~

Now that we've learned how to convert the "normal" Gregorian calendar dates to dates on the 13-month Mystical Numerology calendar, we can begin to work with them. Aspects that are determined from dates include:

- Life Path
- Attainment cycles
- Personal year, month and day energies
- Universal year, month and day energies
- Life Challenges

The most important of these is the Life Path, and that is where we will start.

Life Path

Your Life Purpose (Chapter 5) is WHY you are here and WHAT you are to do. The Life Path is HOW you will get there. Another way to think of this is that the Life Purpose is your destination in life, and the Life Path is the road that takes you there. It is the best path to accomplish your Purpose.

Before showing some specific examples, there are a few general guidelines:

- It is important to use the *Day – Month – Year* (D-M-Y) format when writing birth dates.

- The reduced value for the year is used in calculating Life Path numbers, not the actual year. So the first step is to find the reduced value of the year by adding together the individual digits of the year:

  $2012 = 2+0+1+2 = \underline{5}$.

  $1972 = 1+9+7+2 = \underline{19}$

  $1995 = 1+9+9+5 = \underline{24}$.

- It is important to note that if the reduced value for the year is greater than 22, it is this number that is used to calculate the Life Path. The following examples will make this more clear.

- Also, if the day number is greater than 22, use the unreduced number in the calculation shown below.

- As an initial example, the Life Path for a birth date of 27 – 9 – 1999 (D-M-Y Format) on the 13-month calendar is calculated like this:

$1999 = 1+9+9+9 = 28$

Life Path = Day + Month + Reduced Year = $27 + 9 + 28 = \underline{64}$.

- If the resulting Life Path number is greater than 22, it is reduced to a number between $1 - 22$. So, the number 64 is reduced to a 10:

$6+4 = \underline{10}$.

Write the Life Path as: $\underline{64/10}$.

Note: It is good practice write both numbers – 64/10, as shown above. This is because there are other ways to get to an "10." We can have a simple "10," or we could have a 28/10, 37/10, 46/10, 55/10, 64/10, 73/10, and so on. Each carries the basic energy of the "10" while having different nuances of meaning, something that is good to be aware of even though a full discussion of this will be left for a future book.

SPECIFIC EXAMPLES

Once you have converted the Gregorian calendar birth date to a 13-month calendar birth date, the Life Path is easy to determine. Let's practice.

Example 1

Barack Obama, born on 4-August-1961. His converted birth date is 3–9–1961 (from the conversion calendar on page 85). *Remember, it is important to use the Day – Month – Year format.*

The Life Path is the sum: Day + Month + *Reduced* Year. If the result is greater than 22, we reduce it further. Here's how to make the calculation for Barack Obama:

Birth Year = 1961; *Reduced* Year = 1+9+6+1 = 17.

LIFE PATH = Day + Month + Reduced Year = 3 + 9 + 17 = 29.

Now, we must reduce the "29" to a number between 1-22:

LIFE PATH = 2 + 9 = 11.

So, Barack Obama has a Life Path of 29/11.

To interpret the basic meaning of Barack Obama's Life Path, we go back to the chart of basic meanings for the number "11" on page 57:

The 11 Life Path is the **"Connector."** Key words include: Healer, Teacher, Shepherd ... Change Agent, Reformer ... Strength, Action ... Manifestation.

This seems to fit what we know about Obama. To become the first black president of the United States, he certainly had to become the *connector*. He was, perhaps, the first candidate in history to make such extensive use of the Internet using Twitter and Facebook to connect with millions of young voters who turned out in droves to support him. Once in office, he has done what he could to be a change agent. But even if he had done nothing, the mere fact that he is the first black U.S. president is a huge change.

The role of change agent and reformer is a difficult one because it always activates and energizes the forces that resist the change. For instance, in taking on an overhaul of the healthcare system, especially in a very polarized period in American politics, Obama became a reformer but angered many powerful interest groups and stirred the already boiling political pot.

Also, given the wobbly economy that he inherited from his predecessor, a big part of his efforts were spent dealing with economic issues of manifestation: how to deal with the debt crisis and get the economy back on track. In fact, the economy has been perhaps the single largest focus of effort (and rhetoric) for his administration.

In Chapter 10, where we deal with the deeper meanings of the numbers, you will also note that "11" is connected with the Mayan archetypal energy called "Imox," the Seer and Healer. This energy also helps to manage the energies of change. So, this is also part of Obama's Life Path.

Example 2

René Descartes, born 31-March-1596.

Step 1: Convert the Gregorian Calendar birth date to the 13-month Mystical Numerology Calendar. 1596 is a leap year so we look at the calendar conversion chart on page 86. What we find is:

31–March–1596 = 18 – 4 – 1596 (Day-Month-Year format)

Step 2: Find the reduced value for the year:

1596 = 1+5+9+6 = 21.

Step 3: Add the Day + Month + *Reduced* Year to find the Life Path number:

18 + 4 + 21 = 43

Step 4: Since the result is greater than 22, reduce it further by adding the digits:

4+3 = 7

Step 5: Write the Life Path with both reduced and unreduced numbers:

43/7

Step 6: Find the basic number meaning on page 57 and then interpret.

The 7 Life Path is the **"Idealist."** Key words include: Visualize, Inspire … Drive, Achieve, Crusade … Truth … Linear, Logical, Precise … Study, Learn … Mystic, Oneness.

René Descartes (1596 – 1650) was a French philosopher who was very much an idealist, and very much concerned with truth. He is often credited with being the "Father of Modern Philosophy" due to his break with the traditional Scholastic-Aristotelian philosophy of his time because of its reliance on sensation as the source of knowledge. Descartes felt this method was prone to doubt and promoted the development of the new, mechanistic sciences as the basis for truth — certainly a more linear, logical and precise method!

It is interesting to note that from his first name, René, we can find that his Life Purpose is also a "7" (RENE = 14+11 = 25/7). So, his Life Purpose and Life Path numbers are both "7," a very *mental* number. The 7 connects the mind with the Source, East ⇒ Center (see map in Appendix A), making it no surprise that Descartes is the one who made the famous statement, "I *think* therefore I am." In important ways, this single statement shaped 400 years of Cartesian thinking.

I have to note that there is some irony that Descartes would promote logical precision since his given name, René, has 2-Es, the energy of emotions and the heart. Perhaps we could say that Descartes was *passionate* about promoting a logical search for truth!

<u>Example 3</u>

Tim Berners-Lee, born 8–June–1955.

Step 1: Convert the Gregorian Calendar birth date to the 13-month Mystical Numerology Calendar. 1955 is a normal, non-leap year, so look at the Calendar Conversion chart on page 85.

8–June–1955 = 3 – 7 – 1955

Step 2: Find the Reduced Year:

1955 = 1+9+5+5 = <u>20</u>

Step 3: Add the Day + Month + Reduced Year to find the Life Path number, and reduce it to a number between 1 – 22:

3 + 7 + 20 = 30 = 3+0 = <u>3</u>

Step 4: Write the Life Path with both reduced and unreduced numbers:

<u>30/3</u>

Step 5: Find the basic number meaning on page 56 and then interpret.

The "3" Life Path is the "Incubator." Key Words include: Root, Origin, Idea … Energy, Speed … Carry, Convey … Activities, Agility, Do, Try … Art, Science & Language … Humor.

Tim Berners-Lee is the inventor (incubator) of the World Wide Web that is a vehicle for carrying and conveying ideas of all kinds. The World Wide Web certainly has accelerated life all over the world, adding to a perception of the increasing speed of our lives. Indirectly, the web also supports art and science, and even language. What a perfect fit with his Life Path number!

By the way, his full name is: Timothy John Berners-Lee. But he goes by the name "Tim." If we were calculating his Life Purpose, we would use Tim and not Timothy.

Let's do one more example before moving on.

<u>Example 4</u>

Diana Frances Spencer, Princess Di, born 30–June–1961.

Step 1: Convert the Gregorian Calendar birth date to the 13-month Mystical Numerology Calendar. 1961 is a normal, non-leap year, so look at the Calendar Conversion chart on page 85.

30–June–1961 = 25 – 7 – 1961

Step 2: Find the reduced year:

1961 = 1+9+6+1 = 17

Step 3: Add the Day + Month + Reduced Year to find the Life Path number:

25 + 7 + 17 = 49 = 4+9 = 13

(Note that the "25" day is not reduced)

Step 4: Write the Life Path with both reduced and unreduced numbers:

49/13

Step 5: Find the basic number meaning on page 58 and then interpret.

The "13" Life Path is the "Builder." Key words include: Life, Community ... Advisor, Expertise, Authoritative ... Success, Wealth ... Giving Back, Selfless ... Grassroots.

Diana Frances Spencer was born into an aristocratic English family with royal ancestry. She became a public figure with the announcement of her engagement to Prince Charles whom she married on 29–July–1981 at St. Paul's Cathedral. The wedding was watched by a global television audience of 750 million people.

She became well known for her fund-raising work on behalf of international charities and for her support of the international campaign to ban landmines. Diana once said in an interview that she wanted to be "Queen of people's hearts." She was loved by millions, and it is safe to say that she achieved the status of an eminent celebrity.

Diana and Prince Charles were later divorced in August 1996. Just a year later, in August 1997, Diana was fatally injured in a car crash in the Pont de l'Alma road tunnel in Paris. Millions of people watched her funeral.

Her life embodied many of the qualities of her "13" Life Path such as: a heart-connection to a worldwide community; wealth and success; a selfless urge to give something back for all of her blessings; and a desire to build something lasting with her celebrity.

Note also that with the name "Diana" she has a "14" Life Purpose. One of the shadow aspects of the "14" is getting caught up in a web of relationship dramas from which it feels as though there is no escape. This also fits very well the events leading to her divorce and untimely death.

If you haven't already done it, calculate your own Life Path number and find the basic meaning for it on pages 56 – 59. Remember, the Life Path gives you insight on the best way to achieve your overall Life Purpose.

Now, calculate the Life Path numbers for your family members, friends, coworkers, famous people, and so on. The practice will help you get more comfortable converting Gregorian Calendar dates to 13-month Mystical Numerology calendar dates, as well as the basic meanings of the numbers. It will also give you additional insight into the Life Path of friends, family, and other people of interest.

Attainment Cycles

The Attainment Cycles are major life goals that represent something important that you are meant to achieve or learn and integrate into your life. You can think of them as important stops along your Path of Life where you gain important experience, knowledge and wisdom.

In other words, if you are headed from New York to San Francisco, it may be important to make stops: 1) in Washington, D.C. to study the three branches of the U.S. government; 2) at the Grand Canyon to take in its majesty and contemplate the power of nature; and 3) at Disneyland to learn about the creative and relaxing aspects of play. These three stops along the way are like the three Attainment Cycles.

Everyone has three Attainment Cycles. Each is active for a period of 29 years. This is the Mystical Numerology equivalent of the 29-year Saturn return cycles in astrology. In the hundreds of charts I've done on famous historical figures, and for friends and clients, I have confirmed that these are important stages in everybody's life.

The first lasts from birth (age 0) through age 28. The second lasts from ages 29 through 57, and is often referred to as the "Major Attainment" because these are generally the most productive years of a person's life. The third cycle lasts from 58 through 86. Starting at age 87, you come back to the beginning to the first Attainment to see if you've really learned what you need to learn.

Here's how they are calculated:

<u>Example 1</u>

Let us continue to use Barack Obama as an example. He was born 4–August–1961 (page 89), and his converted birth date is: $3 - 9 - 1961$ (Day–Month–Year format).

Step 1: Reduce the Year by adding each of its individual digits:

$1+9+6+1 = \underline{17}$

Step 2: Rewrite the Day–Month–Year using the reduced number for the year. The date now becomes: $3 - 9 - 17$.

Step 3: Add the <u>Day</u> and <u>Month</u> and reduce it to a number between 1–22, if needed: $3 + 9 = \underline{\textbf{12}}$. This is the *first* or Early Attainment (ages $0 - 28$).

Step 4: Add the <u>Day</u> and the <u>Year</u> and reduce it to a number between 1–22, if needed: $3 + 17 = \underline{\textbf{20}}$. This is the *second* or Major Attainment (ages $29 - 57$).

Step 5: Add the <u>Month</u> and <u>Year</u> and reduce it to a number between 1–22: $9 + 17 = \underline{\textbf{26/8}}$. This is the *third* or Sunset Attainment (ages 58–87).

Here is an easy way to picture it. Start by laying out the 13-month birth date in Day – Month – Year format, and then build a pyramid with the additions described in Steps 3, 4 and 5. Once you *get* the process, it is easy:

(Ages 29 – 57)

20

(Ages 0 – 29) **12**   **26/8** (Ages 58 – 86)

3 – 9 – 17

97

Step 6: Interpret the Attainment Cycles using the basic number definitions on pages 56–59.

Interpretation

President Barack Obama turned 52 in August 2012, so let's look at the Major Attainment Cycle for his middle years (ages 29 – 57), the one he is in now. It is the "20" Cycle. This is a cycle during which obstacles are often cleared away, and greater balance is available. It is a time when individuals may become clear about their passion or calling in life, as if fate is pulling them forward and opening doors. At this time, an individual can be audacious and act with greater force to achieve their desires. What could be more audacious than believing you could be the first black president of the United States?

It is also interesting that "20" is the number of *banks, loans and debts,* and look at what President Obama has had to deal with – the most serious meltdown of the banking system since the Great Depression!

The "20" is also the number of the "sage," and Barack Obama certainly comes across as sagacious and intellectual, a characteristic that is appealing for some, and not so much for others. Remember, 39% of the people have "A" as a first vowel in their name and tend to be thinkers (see page 45).

Example 2

Edna Saint Vincent Millay, poet: Born 22–February–1892. This is a leap year, so we determine the 13-month Mystical Numerology calendar birth date by looking at the conversion chart on page 86. We find that 22–Feb–1892 gives a converted birth date of: 9 – 3 – 1892 (Day–Month–Year format).

Step 1: Reduce the Year: $1+8+9+2 = \underline{20}$.

Step 2: Rewrite the Day–Month–Year using the reduced number for the year. The date now becomes: 9 – 3 – 20.

Step 3: Add the <u>Day</u> and <u>Month</u> and reduce it to a number between 1–22, if needed: 9 + 3 = **12**. This is the *first* or Early Attainment (ages 0 – 28).

Step 4: Add the <u>Day</u> and the <u>Year</u> and reduce it to a number between 1–22, if needed: 9 + 20 = **29/11**. This is the *second* or Major Attainment (ages 29 – 57).

Step 5: Add the <u>Month</u> and <u>Year</u> and reduce it to a number between 1–22: 3 + 20 = **23/5**. This is the *third* or Sunset Attainment (ages 57–86).

Here is the Attainment Cycle Pyramid for Edna St. Vincent Millay:

(Ages 29 – 57)

29/11

(Ages 0 – 29) **12**   **23/5** (Ages 58 – 86)

9 – 3 – 20

Step 6: Interpret the Attainment Cycles using the basic number definitions on pages 56–59.

<u>Interpretation</u>

Edna Saint Vincent Millay was certainly the best-known, best-selling female poet of her day. If we look at her Major Attainment, 29/11, we will see that it is a good fit.

Edna St. Vincent Millay inspired people and connected them through her poetry. And, she was certainly a change-agent and reformer who pushed back the boundaries for all women through her refusal to be hemmed in by the societal norms of the day. This showed her to be a woman of considerable strength. Interestingly, the word *famous* is also a "29/11" word. She won a Pulitzer Prize in 1923 for her poem *The Ballad of the Harp-Weaver*. She was, perhaps, the most famous and controversial American woman during the 1920s

Her Major Life Challenge was also an "11," which is the number of sudden and unexpected events. It is a tragedy that Edna St. Vincent Millay died early and suddenly at her home in Austerlitz, New York. Found at the bottom of her stairs, the coroner said she died of a heart attack due to a coronary occlusion or blockage. She was 58, and just entering her Sunset Attainment, a 23/5. The downside energies for the "5" include "energy blockage," "karma," and "chaos."

Example 3

George Gershwin, composer and pianist: Born 26–September–1898. This is a normal, non-leap year, so we determine the 13-month Mystical Numerology calendar birth date by looking at the conversion chart on page 85. We find that 26–September–1898 gives a converted birth date of: 28 – 10 – 1898   (Day–Month–Year format).

Step 1: Reduce the Year: 1+8+9+8 = <u>26</u>. Here, it is important to note that you do *not* reduce the "26" year further to a number between 1 – 22. The general rule is: don't reduce numbers until calculating the final result, in this case that would be the Attainment Cycle. Once we get to the final result, *then* reduce the number as shown below. This also applies to the day number.

Step 2: Rewrite the Day–Month–Year using the reduced number for the year. The date now becomes: 28 – 10 – 26. Note again that the Day and Year numbers are not reduced to a number between 1–22.

Step 3: Add the <u>Day</u> and <u>Month</u> and *then* reduce it to a number between 1–22: 28 + 10 = **38/11**. This is the *first* or Early Attainment (ages 0 – 28).

Step 4: Add the <u>Day</u> and the <u>Year</u> and reduce it to a number between 1–22: 28 + 26 = **54/9**. This is the *second* or Major Attainment (ages 29 – 57).

Step 5: Add the <u>Month</u> and <u>Year</u> and reduce it to a number between 1–22: 10 + 26 = **36/9**. This is the *third* or Sunset Attainment (ages 57–86).

Here is the Attainment Cycle Pyramid for George Gershwin:

(Ages 29 – 57)

54/9

(Ages 0 – 29) **38/11**   **36/9** (Ages 58 – 86)

28 – 10 – 26

Step 6: Interpret the Attainment Cycles using the basic number definitions on pages 56–59.

<u>Interpretation</u>

George Gershwin (Jacob Gershvin) was born in Brooklyn, NY to Jewish parents from Odessa in the Ukraine. The original family name was Gershowitz but his father, Moshe, changed the name to *Gershvin* sometime after immigrating to the United States from Russia in the early 1890s. George changed the spelling of his surname to *Gershwin* when he became a professional musician.

George Gershwin became interested in music at age 10. He published his first song in 1916, and scored his first big national hit in 1919 with his song *Swanee,* that Al Jolson heard Gershwin sing, and decided to sing in one of his shows. In 1924, Gershwin began collaborating with his brother Ira to write songs for Broadway musicals. In the same year, he wrote *Rhapsody in Blue* for orchestra and piano, his first major classical work.

His early Attainment cycle (ages 0–28) was an "38/11." Interestingly, "38" is the number of the "musician." It is also interesting to note that during his early years, before he changed the spelling of his last name, George Gershvin has a Drive Number of 92/11. The "11" is also the number of becoming "famous" (29/11).

His Broadway career was already underway by the time Gershwin turned 29 and entered into his second Attainment Cycle, a 54/9. "9" is the number of "music" and also "drama." In 1930, the musical comedy *Girl Crazy* was the first to win a Pulitzer Prize (for drama). In 1935, he wrote his most ambitious composition, the "folk opera" *Porgy and Bess*. It was initially a commercial failure, probably because it crossed barriers, but is now widely regarded as one of the most important American operas of the twentieth century. In 1936, Gershwin moved to Hollywood, commissioned by RKO to write the music for *Shall We Dance*. He died of a brain tumor just two months after its release in 1937, two and a half months shy of turning 39.

With the 38/11 energy of his early Attainment Cycle (musician) and the 54/9 Attainment Cycle (music) period in effect from age 29 until his early death, Gershwin was one of the most productive composers of his generation.

If you haven't already done so, calculate the three Life Attainment Cycles from your own birth date, making sure to first convert it into the 13-month Mystical Numerology calendar format using the calendar conversion charts on pages 85 and 86. Also make sure you write your birth date in the Day – Month – Year format before calculating the individual Attainments.

You can gain experience by also looking at family, friends, and other people of interest – something I still do!

There are descriptions of the Attainment Cycles in the next chapter (Chapter 8) that you can use as a reference.

Year, Month and Day Periods

When tracking time-related periods, we need to make a distinction between *Universal* years, months and days, and *Personal* years, months and days.

Universal years, months and days refer to the actual dates (converted to the 13-month calendar). They are "universal" because that same energy affects everyone, everywhere on the planet.

Personal years, months and days refer to how the energy of the universal dates affect you or the person you are studying on a personal level. This requires some extra, but fairly easy calculation.

Universal Years, Months, Days

Remember, Mystical Numerology uses a 13-month calendar, so *universal* dates refer to the converted dates using the calendar conversion tables on pages 85–86.

Example 1

Let's take the Gregorian calendar date of 4 – July – 1776, the day that the U.S. Declaration of Independence was approved. 1776 is a leap year, so we have to use the calendar conversion table on page 86. When we do, we find that the converted date becomes the twenty-ninth Day of the seventh month of 1776, or: 29 – 7 – 1776 (Day–Month–Year format).

Step 1: When calculating the Universal numbers, start with the year because we will use this in the other calculations.

Step 2: To find the Universal Year, all we do is to reduce 1776 to a number between 1–22 as follows:

1776 = 1+7+7+6 = <u>21</u>.

Step 3: To find the Universal Month, add the universal year, 21, to the converted calendar month, and reduce to a number between 1–22:

21 (Reduced Year) + 7 (Month) = 28

And: 2+8 = 10.

So, the Universal Month = 28/10.

Step 4: The Universal Day simply entails adding the day + month + year of the converted calendar date. Remember, we don't reduce the numbers until we get the final result:

29 (Day) + 7 (Month) + 21 (Year) = 57/12 Universal Day

Calculating the Universal Day for an event is identical to calculating the Life Path number using someone's birth date. The 4th of July, 1776 is the birth date for the Declaration of Independence. The Universal Day or Path number, 57/12, tells us something important about its energy and the principle that it embodies.

The next step would be to interpret what the number "12" means by referring to the basic number meanings on pages 56–59, or to the deeper meanings of cycles described in Chapter 8.

"12" is the Achiever. It is the number of visionaries, pathfinders, promoters, and risk-takers. It is the energy of innovation, invention and business. This is a fair description of the various facets of the American psyche. Also, 1776 = 21, and "21" is the energy of money – which, it seems, has become the "national project" of the USA.

Example 2

Let's take something more recent, like the first successful flight around the world with no refueling stops, a feat accomplished by the American adventurer, Steve Fosset. The starting date was 4–Mar–2005. Using the calendar conversion chart on page 85 we find that the date on the

13-month calendar is: 19 – 3 – 2005. This is the *birth date* for this event.

Step 1: Calculate the Universal Year by adding the digits of the year:

2005 = 2+0+0+5 = 7.

Step 2: To find the Universal Month, add the month and year:

3 (Month) + 7 (Year) = 10.

Step 3: The Universal Day is the sum of Day + Month + Year:

19 + 3 + 7 = 29/11.

Allow me to reiterate that calculating the Universal Day for an event is exactly the same as calculating the Life Path number for a birth date. Events have birth dates, too. The day that Steve Fosset began his around-the-world flight was the day this event was born. So the Universal Day is also the Path number for the event. It tells us something important about the energy of the day that this successful global flight began. And, being an "11" gives it an extra boost!

Again, you can interpret the numbers by referring to the basic number meanings on pages 56–59, or by reading about the energy of these periods using the descriptions given in Chapter 8, or to the deeper meaning of the numbers given in Chapter 10.

Interpreting Year Energies

When analyzing and interpreting the energy of any given year, it is helpful to look at two numbers: 1) the Universal Year (as described above), and 2) the energy given by the last two digits of the year.

Example 1: 2012

It is helpful to look at 2012 as also the 12th year of the 2000s.

As previously described, the Universal Year is simply the sum of all the numbers in the year, reduced to a number between 1 – 22:

2+0+1+2 = **5**.

The "double digit" year energy is denoted by the last two digits. If these digits are between 1 – 22, they are taken "as is." For the year 2012, the last two digits are 12. So 2012 also takes on the energy of the "12."

In interpreting the year energies for 2012, we would look at both the "5" and the "12."

Example 2: 1789

Let's look at the year 1789, the year that the French Revolution began with the storming of the Bastille. 1789 is also the 89th year of the 1700s.

The Universal Year is the sum of all the digits, reduced to a number between 1 – 22:

$1+7+8+9 = 25 = 2+5 = 7$

So, 1789 is a 25/7 Universal Year

Since the last two digits of 17<u>89</u> do not fall between 1 – 22, we take the sum to get the energy of the double digit year:

$8+9 = \underline{17}$

In interpreting the energies for 1789, we would look at both the "7" and the "17."

Personal Years, Months, Days

Finding your personal year, month or day requires blending the energy of your own Life Purpose number into the mix. If you are looking at the personal year, month or day for another person, it means integrating their Life Purpose number. It is simple but powerful. Once you know how to do this, you can track the energy cycles for yourself or others.

Example 1: Obama's Election Day

Let's return to Barack Obama one more time. And, let's take Election Day in 2008, the day he became the first black president of the United States. The date was: 4 – November – 2008.

Step 1: convert the Gregorian calendar date to a 13-month calendar date. 2008 was a leap year, so use the conversion calendar on page 86 to find that 4 – November – 2008 converts to 11 – 12 – 2008 (Day–Month–Year format).

Step 2: Calculate Obama's Life Purpose Number. For that, we use his first name, Barack and the consonant/number conversion chart on page 67. Remember to reduce the result to a number between 1–22.

BARACK = 1 + 14 + 2 + 8 = 25/7.

Step 3: To find the Personal Year for Barack Obama in 2008, add his Life Purpose Number to the Universal Year (UY). Remember to add unreduced numbers and then reduce the result to a number between 1–22:

2008/10 (UY) + 25 (Life Purpose) = 35/8 (Personal Year)

The year Barack Obama was elected was an "8" Personal Year for him. As you will see from the descriptions in the next chapter, an "8" year is a time of achievement and stepping into one's full power. "35" is also the energy of miracles.

Step 4: The Personal Month is calculated by adding the Personal Year (35/8) to the calendar month using the 13-month calendar (12):

35 (Personal Year) + 12 (Month) = 47/11

Note that "OBAMA" is also an "11."

Step 5: Obama's Personal Day on Election Day is calculated by adding the converted 13-month calendar month and day to his Personal Year:

11 (Day) + 12 (Month) + 35 (Personal Year) = 58/13.

"13" is the number of Endings and Beginnings, and favors those who are catalysts for change.

Example 2: Chuck Yeager & The Sound Barrier

Let's take the day that the sound barrier was first broken by Charles Elwood "Chuck" Yeager in the X-1 rocket plane on 14–October–1947.

Step 1: 1947 is a normal year, so using the calendar conversion chart on page 85, convert the Gregorian calendar date to a 13-month calendar date, remembering to put it in Day – Month – Year format:

14-October-1947 ⇒ 18 – 11 – 1947 (D–M–Y)

Step 2: Calculate the Life Purpose number for Charles/Chuck Yeager. Immediately, this causes a dilemma. Which name do we use? Charles is the given name, but Chuck is the name he was using at the time. My inclination is to always go with the name being used, but let's take a look at both for completeness.

CHARLES = 2+6+14+9+15 = 46/10.

CHUCK = 2+6+2+8 = 18.

Step 3: Add the Life Purpose number to the calendar year to find the Personal Year (PY) numbers:

For Charles: 46 + 1947/21 = 67/13 PY.

For Chuck: 18 + 1947/21 = 39/12 PY.

Step 4: To find the Personal Month (PM) numbers, add the calendar month using the 13-month calendar to the above results:

For Charles: 67/13 PY + 11 (month) = 78/15 PM.

For Chuck: 39/12 PY + 11 (month) = 50/5 PM.

Step 5: To find the Personal Day (PD) numbers, add the calendar day to Personal Month numbers above:

For Charles: 78/15 PM + 18 (day) = <u>96/15</u> PD.

For Chuck: 50/5 PM + 18 (day) = <u>68/14</u> PD.

"15" is the number of turning points and moving forward to overcome obstacles and achieve goals. It is a time for innovators and future possibilities.

"14" is the number of fame, and individual excellence but it is also carries the Mayan energy of "Kat" which is about escaping from the net – like breaking through the sound barrier! So, you can see the fit with Yeager's accomplishment – breaking the sound barrier – with the energies of his personal day.

<u>Example 3: United States</u>

You can do this same kind of analysis for other kinds of entities as well, such as businesses, countries, groups, and so on – as long as you can settle on the name to use.

For instance, if we were to look at the "personal" energies for the United States, what name should we use? There are four national name possibilities:

- United States
- United States of America
- America
- USA

If we take the day of the Declaration of Independence as the national birth date (4–Jul–1776 ⇒ 29 – 7 – 1776), we can look at the energies of the nation by calculating a "personal" year, month and day. Let's focus on the personal day.

Step 1: We already calculated the Universal Day or Path Number from the converted date (page 103–104):

29 + 7 + 1776/21 = <u>57/12</u> (UD or Path)

Step 2: Find the Purpose Number of the name you want to use. Remember that the Purpose Number comes from the *first name,* so even though there are four national names that we can choose from, two of them have "United" as the first name. Three possibilities arise for Purpose Numbers:

United States; **United** States of America = 30/3.

America = 26/8.

USA = 15.

Step 3: To find the "Personal" Day energy, add the Purpose Number to the Universal Day:

For United: 30 + 57 = 87/15 (Turning Points)

For America: 26 + 57 = 83/11 (Trailblazer, Manifestation)

For USA: 15 + 57 = 72/9 (Foundation)

Of these, the "11" might be the closest fit. This also indicates that "America" is the best name to use for any future analysis of the country.

See how it works?

Example 4: DuPont/Conoco Merger

Let's take a look at a Business. In this case, let's look at DuPont, and the day of its $7 billion merger with Conoco, the largest in history at the time. The date was 20–July–1981. Since I was a DuPont employee at the time, this is something that I know about at a personal level.

Step 1: Convert the Gregorian calendar date to a 13-month calendar date using the conversion calendar chart on page 85 (since 1981 is a normal, non-leap year):

20–July–1981 ⇒ 16 − 8 − 1981.

111

Step 2: Determine the Universal Day or Path Number for this date:

UD / Path = Day + Month + Year

$= 16 + 8 + 19 = \underline{43/7}$.

Step 3: Calculate the Purpose Number for the company, DuPont using the letter/number conversion chart on page 67:

DUPONT $= 3+12+11+16 = \underline{42/6}$.

Step 4: Calculate the "Personal" Day for DuPont on the date of the merger by adding the Universal Day or Path Number from Step 2 to DuPont's Purpose Number from Step 3:

PD = UD/Path + Purpose Number

$= 43/7 + 42/6 = 85/13$. (Endings & Beginnings)

Actually, this merger came about to avoid a hostile take-over attempt by Seagram Company Ltd., the largest distiller of alcoholic beverages at the time. The blocking move was successful, to a point.

When the dust settled, Seagram had three seats on the DuPont Board of Directors, and life in the company was forever changed. It was the end of the golden era and the beginning of a new era.

DuPont was known for the success of its *basic* research, the kind that invented new compounds like nylon and gave birth to whole new manufacturing industries. But, after the merger, the company began to put its research and development funds behind *applied* research which, basically, meant the end of new inventions and the attempt to wring as much value as possible from what already had been invented.

This kind of thinking also led to a round of corporate downsizing in 1987 when more than 11,000 employees were cut from the rolls worldwide.

To gain a facility or ease of performance in calculating the Universal and Personal numbers for yourself, other people, countries, companies, and so on, you've got to practice!

It is a wonderful introspective tool to get insight about yourself, but it will also give you a deeper understanding of others. So, pick people you are interested in, and events that you'd like to understand. Then, following the examples given above, have some fun!

Chapter Eight:

Attainment Cycles, Year–Month–Day Periods

Time is the meaning of life.

~Paul Claudel~

This next section is for use as a *reference*. It defines what each of the 22 archetypal numbers means as a temporary energy. Use these definitions for looking at all time-related periods or cycles, including tracking Personal or Universal Years, Months and Days, and also for insight into the meaning of Attainment Cycles.

Remember, Attainment Cycles represent major life goals to be attained over three separate 29-year periods, the period of a Saturn return cycle in astrology.

At the end of each of the number descriptions, I give examples of famous people who have a "major" Attainment Cycle (ages 29 – 57) that corresponds with that number. I have also shown the percentage of people who have this cycle[5] to give you an idea of how common or uncommon it is. You may find this to be a helpful reference for comparison with your own Attainment Cycle or those of other people.

---

[5] Percentage based on 850 people: famous individuals, clients and friends currently in my database at year-end 2012.

1

During a "1" period, there is an opportunity to give birth to something entirely new. "1" is originality and the power to innovate. It brings a natural ability to be a creator and give birth to new ideas. So it is a good time to begin a project, start a business venture, artistic endeavor, relationship or partnership. It is also a good time for a marriage or to renew commitments. In short, it is an auspicious time for planning, setting some goals, and beginning to act on your dreams. When a "1" period comes around, it is time to start your engine, put it in gear, and go for it! Anything that begins with enthusiasm and hope during a "1" period has a positive future.

This period also represents innocence, the self, selfhood and self-regard. So, whatever else you may create, you may also be creating a new you!

The "1" brings psychic energy, clairvoyance, and the ability to know things without knowing how you know. You may be quite practical in your outlook on life, but be aware that your inner abilities may be growing stronger during a "1" period.

Downside: Watch out not to get caught up in illusions that may not be real. You may also feel challenged by strong-willed individuals who play the role of petty tyrants whose purpose is to help you stand up for yourself.

The "1" can also represent the painful contractions of the collective birth process, and the suddenness of cataclysmic events which can totally reshape things in a twinkling of an eye.

Famous people with a "1" major Attainment Cycle

Although there are "1" day or month energies, *nobody* has a "1" Attainment Cycle just because in the calculation you add two numbers together to get a result. The lowest value possible is a "2."

2

In a "2" period, you may feel as if the unseen force of destiny is active in pulling you along. There is a connection with infinite possibilities and global consciousness operating behind the scenes. You can hone your intuitive skills to tap into this state of awareness. This can help you organize, make decisions, solve problems, define boundaries and set limits. In fact, you may find yourself in the role of "problem-solver" for others.

This is a period for gaining a deeper level of self-awareness, promoting communication and achieving collective consent. It is a good time to enter into new relationships, and/or reconcile with old friends or partners. It is also a good time to begin a business, start a negotiation, or to sign a contract. A "2" period is about equilibrium, so it is a good period to find balance in your life.

It can also be a good time to begin a trip.

Downside: This can be a time to confront fundamental problems in your life. While this often has a positive outcome, it may not feel very good as you are going through it. It may feel heavy, as if you are carrying a burden you cannot seem to put down. You may have a sense of loneliness or incompleteness. Alternately, this may be a period of friction with one or more people who act as adversaries. Or, there can be disruptive changes that act as a catalyst – perhaps by creating a sense of disenchantment, rootlessness or even alienation.

It will help you stay out of self-pity to recognize two things: 1) this time will pass; and 2) the deeper purpose of this time is to help you find a more sustainable balance in your life.

Famous people with a "2" major Attainment Cycle (0%)

You will find the "2" energy relevant mostly for day, month and even year energies (e.g., the year 2000 was a "2" year).

117

Although it is possible to have a "2" for an Attainment Cycle, it is very uncommon. Nobody in my current database of 850 people has one.

3

A "3" period is a time of movement, rebirth, expansion and growth. It brings an urge for relationships, so it can also be a time of greater joy, expression and sociability. It can be a period of creative awakening. It is a great time to expand your horizons, and a good time to motivate others. It is also a wonderful time to plan for some travel … or a return to your roots.

There is a connection with the collective unconscious that can bring new insights concerning your life or work, or a vision of something that is important for you to do. This period is when the seeds for new ideas or activities that have been incubating may begin to take root and grow. It is a good time to get into action to achieve short-term goals.

Downside: A challenge during this time is to not get stuck in the dramas of daily life. Don't take things too seriously. Watch out for anger issues and feelings of guilt, and do your best not to be passive-aggressive with those you love. Movement will be important for balance, and especially so in dealing with change. So, walk, dance, run or exercise. Get out and play – but within appropriate limits since the "3" energy can get a little wild. Greater clarity is available to you during this period.

Famous people with a "3" major Attainment Cycle (4.1%)

Boris Yeltsin, Elizabeth Blackwell, Fidel Castro, George Gordon (Lord) Byron, Henry Wadsworth Longfellow, Mohandas K. Gandhi, Phyllis Battelle, Steve Fosset, Tyrone Power, Wolfgang Amadeus Mozart, Ulysses S. Grant, Woodrow Wilson.

4

A "4" period is a time to get organized and make some decisions. It can be a very productive time, one of honing your capability to achieve needs and desires. It is a period of greater effort and perhaps even a time of overcoming some limitations. If this is the case for you, remember that your mind is very strong at this time, and you can use its power to bring dreams to fruition. Focus on what you most want to create, formulate a new strategy, make a plan, and go after it – even if you have to push up against conventional limits.

This is also a good time to build alliances, and to offer your time, energy and skills to help others. This is a way to stay in balance, open up emotionally, and turn away negative energy.

Downside: A "4" period builds inner strength. Sometimes this means that it can be a time of trouble. If this happens, consider that hurdles you may encounter may be there to put you onto a slightly different path, or to prompt you to let go of what no longer serves you. Issues may arise that require you to forgive yourself or others. These may include emotional issues such as jealousy, betrayal, possessiveness, shame, feeling unloved or even romantic rejection.

Alternately, you may be confronted by bossy people, people who want to pick a fight, or people who try to deceive you. Take care to not become fearful or paranoid, or take the bait and get into verbal battles or physical fights. Worse, perhaps, don't allow yourself to become emotionally detached and frozen. Rather, as much as you are able, practice forgiveness. Even if you must confront others and stand your ground, do it while seeing the word *love* in your mind's eye. Doing this shifts the energy and allows miracles to happen.

Famous people with a "4" major Attainment Cycle (6.4%)

Bridget Fonda, Charles Lindbergh, George S. Patton, James K. Polk, Jean Chretien, Josef Stalin, Lisa Marie Presley, Ludwig van Beethoven, Marion Davies, Maureen Reagan, Mikhail Gorbachev, Pat Benetar, Robert Burns, Robert Duvall, Rush Limbaugh, Sandra Oh, Thomas Paine, William Wordsworth.

5

The "5" period is usually fast-paced, upbeat and expansive. Its energy can feel like drinking water from a fire hose and, therefore, sometimes hard to handle. The "5" merges the infinite, spiritual dimension and the personal, emotional dimension of life. During a "5" period, you may receive insights and revelations from dreams and intuition, so pay attention.

The "5" energy wants freedom, change and spontaneity, and it doesn't like limitations or boundaries. Its influence can spark a feeling of divine longing. During this time, you may feel an urge to go on a quest or journey to explore new potentials and possibilities, or to develop a new idea. It can be a time of creativity, learning and personal growth. Pleasure, laughter and pain, chaos and harmony all of fall under the "5" energy.

During a "5" period, friends, family and community are in the spotlight. It is a time to strengthen family and social bonds. This is a time for working together with others – especially in a common cause, and/or for the common good. It is a good time to ask for a partner or a love relationship. It can bring greater success in business or in your job, as well as increased abundance.

The energy of this period is about the *flow* of abundance and prosperity into and through your life. It is an auspicious time to ask for personal or community abundance. The key is to ask for what you need, set your intention, and then get your ego-mind out of the way and allow events to flow. Something larger than you is in charge during this time!

Downside: This can be a time of chaos. You can feel more impulsive than normal, and have difficulty focusing on practical things. You can be overeager and too much in a hurry. This can result in hurry-worry and even recklessness. The "5" energy wants freedom and tends to scatter energies in too many directions at once. As a result, breaking commitments and being unfaithful to partners, beliefs or ideas is one of the downsides during this period. Consider that the energy of this time is helping you to learn to create a sense of dynamic but sustainable balance in your life. It is prompting you to work with a focused intention to create what most inspires you.

Another shadow side of the "5" energy is feeling blocked, stuck, and unable to free yourself from old habits. You can feel low on energy and be undemonstrative with friends and loved ones. Obsessiveness and addiction is a severe example. Sometimes, a fear of lack is what begins the downward spiral, causing you to withdraw into a suit of protective armor and become covetous of what others have, be it money, influence or power.

This can be a time of emotional pain and grief. If this happens, remember two things. First, this is a temporary situation. It is going to pass. Second, realize that to transform these heavy emotions, you must allow yourself to fully *feel* them (as opposed to going into denial). You don't have to feel them for very long, but you *do* have to feel them.

Experiencing emotional pain may just be an "AFGO" – Another Freaking Growth Opportunity. Yet, "5" is the number of karma. So, it may be that your karmic residue has walked out onto center stage to be recognized, dealt with and cleared away. Once you've processed the feelings, you no longer need to hang onto them. Give them the hook. Drag them off center stage and lovingly give them the boot!

Famous people with a "5" major Attainment Cycle (10.0%)

Alexander Hamilton, Andrew Jackson, Ayn Rand, Clare Booth Luce, Dolly Parton, Edgar Mitchell, Henry David Thoreau, James Dickey, Katie Couric, Lahiri Mahasaya (disciple of Mahavatar Babaji), Marian Wright Edelman, Michele de Nostredame, Oprah Winfrey, Theodore Seuss Geisel, Tim Berners-Lee, Valentina Tereshkova, Victor Hugo.

6

The "6" period brings a focus on relationships with people and things, for it is through relationship that we achieve a sense of belonging, and know our place in the world. This is a time to open your heart to receive ancient wisdom, and use this wisdom to bring balance in your relationships and activities. In the process, a clearing of obstacles may take place. It is a good time to make changes in your life, and find or renew love.

During a "6" period, clearing away obstacles often involves forgiveness. In fact, this is the *best* time to forgive yourself and others for past mistakes. It is an auspicious time to let go of resentments or guilt, and reconcile with friends, partners, coworkers or acquaintances. Forgiveness is often a key to emotional wellness and inner harmony. In turn, these are connected with physical healing. A "6" period is good for curing illnesses of all types, achieving harmony with the Earth Mother, and finding individual happiness.

During a "6" period, the life force or kundalini energy is activated. You may feel energized and more confident of standing in your own personal power. Your ability to connect with and influence others is strong at this time. There is an enhanced ability to communicate and share your talents. It is an opportune time to teach, counsel and mentor individuals and groups. It is also a good time to pursue personal justice, and defend or be an advocate for people who are less fortunate than yourself.

A "6" period can also be a time of mental stimulation, discovery, and breakthrough. You may feel more capable and more focused. Your intuition is strong and in sync with your instinctual drives. You may feel like each hair on your head is an individual antenna tuned to receiving intuitive insights. This can be a time of awakening during which you give birth to novel ideas and projects.

If you don't already keep a journal of your ideas and experiences, a "6" period is a good time to start one.

Downside: The highs of the "6" period can be stimulating and happy, but the lows can feel like a roller coaster. The shadow side of this period can be a volatile time of imbalance and polarities. Negative or codependent relationships surface to be dealt with. You can lose focus, feel insecure and indecisive, and start putting things off that really need to get accomplished. This can lead to feeling bad and even to chronic depression. An unfulfilled craving for connection may drive people with addictive personalities to become addicts at this time.

Alternately, you can become impatient and cynical, start taking shortcuts and breaking the rules. You can cut yourself off from others and become a lone wolf. Deep insecurities get covered up with a mask of aggressive and even abusive behavior. You can begin to think only of yourself. Self-aggrandizement and avarice are the next steps on a path to self-destruction and a self-created hell.

If you are headed down this path, the way out is through forgiveness of yourself and others ... and by practicing love and gratitude.

Famous people with a "6" major Attainment Cycle (9.3%)

Carl Friedrich Gauss, Diana Frances Spencer, Donna Reed, Doris Kearns Goodwin, Edward M. Kennedy, Ellen DeGeneres, Etty Hillesum, Fernando Botero, Gerald Ford, Gloria Naylor, Jane Bryant Quinn, Joe Frazier, John D. Rockefeller, Paul Cezanne, Robert De Niro, Ronald Reagan, Rosa Parks, Walt Whitman.

7

The "7" period is often a time of mental creativity, and it can manifest in two ways: receptive and active. It can be a time for marshalling your inner resources and energy in preparation for moving ahead in a more powerful and focused way. It is a favorable time for introspection, reflection and learning, a good time for nourishing the mind and improving the memory. During a "7" period, you can strengthen and hone your inner knowing by asking yourself questions and then listening to your inner guidance for the answers.

The "7" period can also be more active, and you will feel it. The "7" energy brings an inner knowing but can also bestow an ability to visualize the next steps along the path. It can be a good time to initiate new projects and ideas, and inspire others. You may feel energized with the personal determination and drive to achieve whatever goals you set for yourself. But, don't overdo it.

The "7" period is also one during which you will be guided to develop greater trust in yourself, in life, and in the Creator – sometimes through a period of inner struggle. It is important not to let yourself get too serious, or become overzealous in your work. There can be a tendency to overdo it, to put too much effort into whatever is your focus, and to hold on when you should let go. You will know when your level of trust is increasing when you allow yourself to experience joyfulness, and become more genial, playful and carefree. A good practice during this time is to start each day by filling yourself up with the feeling of joy!

Downside: During a "7" period, the energy often pulls inward and people become introspective. What is out of balance or karmic comes to the surface to be recognized. Whatever is out of balance in your relationships suddenly can be seen. In fact, it can give you a good smack. This can be a good time for harmonizing relationships but can also be a time of broken hearts.

During a "7" period, obstacles arise in your path; blockages appear and must be dealt with. This can cause you to feel inadequate or inferior, or forlorn. You can feel overcome with fatigue, and turned off and full of apathy. You can withdraw and become a loner. If this happens, know that it will pass.

Alternately, you can find yourself being foolish, absentminded or illogical. You may start to rush, and fall into hurry-worry. This can lead to psychic distress and irritability.

Guard against being directive, divisive or envious. Watch out for bigoted people who may cross your path during this time.

On a collective level, the "7" period can be a time when the karmic scales get balanced. It can bring radical change, social upheaval and rebellion.

Famous people with a "7" major Attainment Cycle (9.2%)

Aristotle Onassis, Bill Maher, Edith Wharton, Franklin D. Roosevelt, Giorgio Armani, Henry Kissinger, Humphrey Bogart, Jackson Pollack, Jennifer Love Hewitt, John Hancock, Karl Marx, Margaret Thatcher, Maureen Dowd, Mikhail Baryshnikov, Mordechai Richler, Naomi Judd, Otto von Bismarck, Rudolph Nureyev, Vera Marie Rosenberg, Vincent van Gogh, Walt Disney, William Tecumseh Sherman.

8

The "8" period is generally active and focused on achievement. It is a good time to get into action and concentrate on the practical, material aspects of life. Pursuing your goals at this time brings successful outcomes and good fortune, particularly when willpower is applied with a singular passion behind a singular purpose.

When an "8" period rolls around, you may feel more alive and energetic, and ready to step forward more fully into your power. It is a time that supports competence and ability in all its forms. The "8" energy supports leaders, guides, managers, negotiators, coaches and teams. It is also a good time for writers.

The "8" period supports beginnings. It is an opportune time to start new projects. In fact, it is a time that rewards independent thinking, a pioneering spirit, and leap-frog ideas that push the envelope. Be open to unexpected insights that feed your imagination. What you can imagine and infuse with the power of positive emotions, you can create. Miracles are possible during this time.

It is a good time for socializing, as well as strengthening community and family connections – especially so for close family ties. It brings the energy of happiness and optimism. It can also be quite a romantic time!

Moving ahead and stepping into your full power often requires letting go of what no longer serves you, including negative relationships and/or partnerships and alliances that no longer work. If you have resentments or grudges, this is the time to let them go, as well. Clearing our personal energy of what is weighing us down is often an important step to physical healing, and why an "8" period is a good time to pray for health and for healing serious illnesses.

Downside: The upside of the "8" period can feel really energizing and alive. The downside can feel just the opposite. It can be a time of break-ups, heartache and despair. You can feel weak, incapable and invisible. Personal identity issues and inner conflicts may arise. The inner turbulence may include worrying, self-judgment, and feelings of helplessness and worthlessness. It can be a heavy time of facing both inner and outer ordeals.

The more active side of an "8" period can be full of conflict and upheaval. There may be people on your path who are self-absorbed, inflexible, coercive, overbearing, insolent or full of vanity and bluster. It is a time that can try your very soul, and that is the point.

The way out of the downside is to practice the transforming power of love for yourself and others. It sounds trite, but it works.

Seeing through the eyes of love is powerful. By this I mean imagining the word "LOVE" in your mind's eye, and then filtering everything that you say through its energy. It also helps to practice breathing in the energy of love, and breathing out the energy of love. As you practice in this way, there will come a time when you are able to let go of the ego-mind's need to control, and can allow something larger to direct your actions. This will lead you back to the positive side.

Famous people with a "8" major Attainment Cycle (8.7%)

Albert Einstein, Arianna Huffington, D. H. Lawrence, Dietrich Bonhoeffer, Giovanni Giacomo Casanova, J. Robert Oppenheimer, J. R. R. Tolkien, Laura Ingalls Wilder, Lewis Carroll, Lucretia Coffin Mott, Lyndon Johnson, Martha Carey Thomas, Pierre Auguste Renoir, Richard M. Nixon, Samuel Langhorne Clemens (Mark Twain), Sandra Day O'Connor, Stephen Breyer, Tony Blair, William Lamb Melbourne.

9

The "9" period is generally a time of harvesting, so make sure you open to receive the fruits of your past efforts. It may also be a time where making connections with a community, or giving back in gratitude for what you receive becomes important. Giving back keeps the circle complete and continues the cycle of abundance.

The "9" energy is about foundations: either building new ones, or finding out where the cracks are in the current ones. A "9" period brings things back around to be processed (mentally, emotionally, physically, and/or spiritually) and then released. Old friends, old dreams, old memories, old actions that you've taken, all of these may come up like pop quizzes in school. If this is not always comfortable, it is often beneficial in establishing a firm foundation for the future.

A "9" period is also about the drive for wholeness and the need to connect with others. It is a good time for networking, and making connections between yourself and others in your sphere of influence. It is the best time to look to the common good and well-being of your family, group and community. It is an auspicious time to settle disputes in your immediate and extended family. On a collective level, the "9" period can have to do with the law, legal issues and decisions.

A "9" period also deals with abundance and prosperity. It tends to bring good fortune and optimism, and is a good time to ask/pray for greater affluence for yourself or success in your business. You can more easily focus on the bottom line, and settle problems of a financial nature during a "9" period.

A "9" period is a good time to make decisions, and to take actions to make your dreams and ideas concrete realities. The energy during this period also helps you finish what you have started. If you've been working on something and cannot seem to bring it to completion, the natural energy of this time will help you bring it to a close. This is true for all kinds of activities and projects, but also sometimes for relationships. A "9" period is a time to finish something. A "10" period is time to experience the outcome, integrate the lessons, and launch something new.

During a "9" period, you may feel as though you are being *pulled* forward by your destiny. It is a good practice to allow this to happen rather than letting your ego *push* you forward. Sometimes this is difficult, but it can be made easier by practicing gratitude for all of your blessings. Once you cultivate this attitude of gratitude, you will relax and begin to make decisions from the sense of being carried along by something that is larger than yourself toward a destination that is in your highest good.

Downside: The shadow side of the "9" period can bring all kinds of drama and personal travail that work against the innate drive for wholeness and connection with family, friends, community and society. These dramas can take a variety of guises including opportunism, divisiveness, power struggles and provocations. It can cause you to feel driven to achieve goals and finish projects. Don't take the bait. It is a path to being out of control. It will hook you and lead to a constellation of regrettable results, including some of the following: impracticality, tunnel vision, temptation, hubris, illicit activities, psychic tension and spiritual distress.

This time can also be a time of underachievement, feeling dispirited and uncertain about life. This can result in a sense of personal inadequacy, futility, disempowerment, and even abandonment.

Other people may attempt to manipulate you, or deceive you and take advantage of your good nature.

Coming back into balance requires clearing away whatever is blocking the desire for wholeness and connection. Loving family and friends are important, as is a supportive community. A healthy love for self and others is critical. Starting a discipline of gratitude for your blessings is a way to begin to shine a light that dispels the shadow. This is because once you realize how much you have going for you, you will be able to move forward with confidence and grace.

Famous people with a "9" major Attainment Cycle (10.1%)

A. E. Housman, Abraham Lincoln, Alice Paul, Beatrice Potter Webb, Charles Darwin, Christie Brinkley, Clark Gable, Douglas MacArthur, Dwight D. Eisenhower, Edward Teller, Eva Cassidy, Geena Davis, George Gershwin, J. Edgar Hoover, James Joyce, Jesse James, Josephine Hull, Milton Friedman, Nikita Krushchev, Paul Newman, Pierre-Joseph Proudhon, Stephen Hawking, Tommy Hilfiger.

10

A "10" period is a time of outcomes. "10" is the stage at which creation is complete and physical manifestation occurs. What you have been working on becomes an objective reality. So, during a "10" period, something is being completed and you are stepping up to a new level. It is beneficial to take some time to stop, to reflect, digest and integrate what has come before, and consider what is emerging.

A "10" period is often a time of new beginnings, a time of renewal. A new path may be stretching out before you that will take you in a slightly different direction, or a completely new one. It is a period of transition and transformation. It is a favorable time to launch new projects, ventures, or relationships. It is an auspicious time to make life changes.

A "10" period brings clarity and certainty. You can use it to sharpen the intellect and find the answers you seek. It is a good time to gain understanding, make decisions, put plans into action, and feel more secure about desired outcomes. It brings the power to overcome obstacles and move forward. It also supports a pioneering spirit and pushing up against boundaries to create something new.

This time also brings the ability to lead, or to transform things around you. It is a good time to step forward and take personal responsibility for a project or activity at work, in the community or at home. What you accomplish now can be growthful and purposive, and is in harmony with the energy of this period that supports being decisive and taking practical action.

At the same time, the "10" period is also a good time for socializing, making friends, starting relationships, and adding more romance to your life. Your ability to be empathic and connect at an emotional level with others is strengthened, and you may find yourself feeling more outgoing and friendly.

It is a time that favors artists: musicians, dancers, poets, singers, and also sculptors and carvers of wood. Any work done with the hands to beautify the earth is especially blessed during this period.

Downside: You can feel bogged-down, tangled up, and blocked energetically. A variety of emotions can create mental and emotional immobility, including worry, anguish, or even paranoia. Movement is important to stay in balance during a "10" period. So, if you are feeling stuck, move! Walk, exercise, dance, get up from your chair or couch and walk to the kitchen and back. Move!

You can make careless mistakes during this time, and this can cause you to feel naïve, stupid and even irrational. If this happens, break your routine. Stop. Find some quiet space to reflect and find the lessons being presented in what is happening. Let things settle before getting back into action.

This can also be a time of calamity, crisis and breakdown. It can be a time of personal darkness. Life may be asking you to transform in some way, to find completion in some aspect of your life before moving forward. Remember that even though you must go through the experience by yourself, you don't have to do it alone. Reach to your support network for help. Get help from your community.

The other downside of the "10" period can be encountering people on your path who are arrogant, egotistical, tactless and divisive. You might be the object of sarcasm and ridicule. If this is the case, do your best to not allow it take you out of your center by becoming defensive and angry. More than likely, a life change is occurring and a deep shift is taking place inside of you. Work on yourself and your own self-esteem. Remember, this is a temporary period. Things will change, and will get better in the end. As the saying goes in India, "If things are not yet better, then it is not yet the end."

Famous people with a "10" major Attainment Cycle (9.9%)

Anne Frank, August Strindberg, Berry Gordy, Christopher Marlowe, Eleanor Holmes Norton, Hank Aaron, Helen Keller, Horace Greeley, Jeanne Lane Pehrson (Jeanne White Eagle), John Quincy Adams, Joseph Rael (Beautiful Painted Arrow), Mae West, Oliver Wendell Holmes Jr., Simone Weil, Sophie Tucker, Susan Sontag, Vladimir Ilich Ulyanov Lenin, Virginia Woolf, William Butler Yeats.

11

The "11" period is a high-energy time during which you are likely to receive new insights, visions, and guidance, and have the opportunity to work with inspiration on a practical level.

This period provides an opportunity to receive a higher level of spiritual and psychic energy that comes in the form of information, guidance, visions and mystical experience. It is a time of increased receptivity, as if the hairs on your head are individual antennae connecting your intuitive consciousness to the realm of higher vision. Insights may come in a flash of intuitive knowing, or in dreams, or as a product of increased curiosity that motivates you to search for answers. You may receive innovative new ideas, gain a sudden new understanding about something, make a discovery, or have a creative breakthrough. Seers, visionaries and healers are favored during an "11" period.

This is an active period. Make no mistake about that. While it is a wonderful time for increasing your internal powers and strengthening your spirit, it is *not* a time to sit on top of the mountain and meditate.

When you get guidance during this time, it is a good bet that you are supposed to get into action and *do* something about it. This period may provide experiences that will prompt you to begin to share with others what you have to teach, or move you forward to become a trailblazer, change agent, or a reformer in some way. Your guidance may urge you to step onto a larger stage. You may build a foundation for something new. In doing so, you may become connected with a broad-based, even worldwide, cross-section of people – as happened to my wife, Jeanne White Eagle.[6]

Our friend, Joseph Rael, Beautiful Painted Arrow, described the "11" energy this way, "It is like being dragged by the feet, kicking and screaming over a cliff so you can learn that you can fly." What does that mean in practical terms? It means that you may be given guidance to do something that you are not sure *how* to do, or even if it is something that you *want* to do, but you feel compelled to go forward with anyway. An "11" period or cycle does not favor the faint of heart.

"11" is the energy of manifestation. So, it is also an auspicious time to focus your intention and attention to manifest your needs and desires, including creating an increased level of prosperity. "11" is also the number of *sound*. The Australian aborigines say we are singing ourselves and our world into existence. Whatever you want to manifest at this time will be aided by putting it into the spoken word through, for instance, affirmations. Just as powerful is to put your intention into a spontaneous song using the vowel sounds, *ah, eh, iii, oh* and *uu,* for they are the fundamental sounds of creation.

On an interpersonal level, this is a good time for cooperative ventures. You can connect with collective emotional knowledge and more easily pull a group together behind a vision or single purpose. It is a favorable time for volunteerism, charity and service-oriented activities. You can build social capital during this time, and bring projects, ventures and events to critical mass during an "11" day, month, year or cycle. Indeed, this can be a time when mass movements get started.

---

[6] Jeanne, who has a 29/11 Purpose, had a vision in 1996 on a 92/11 Personal Day that carried her (and me) to many countries around the world for the next 15 years! See *Journey For the One* by Monty Joynes, for details.

Downside: The challenge inherent in this period is that it can bring sudden changes and unexpected insights and events. It can also feel like being plugged into an electric socket, at first. Because of this, during an "11" period, you might *possibly* feel overwhelmed by intuitive insights, visions and guidance or an unexpected shift in the course of your life. A sense of psychic, cognitive and emotional overload can result. People may then seek to shut this new energy off through self-destructive and/or compulsive behaviors. This can lead to self-indulgence, self-pity or both. In severe cases, individuals shut down, become emotionally numb, passionless and neglectful or, alternately, belligerent and dominating.

A collective form of the shadow energy is materialism, power games, exploitation, ego-trips and the "we're-better-than-you" mentality. During this time you have to watch out for the crazies that may cross your path, especially the fanatic believers (religious, political or business), and their misguided ideas of righteous retribution toward others with different beliefs.

What is really at the core of these personal or collective behaviors is a fear of change, or an unwillingness to open to a more spiritual level that is seeking expression. A path back to personal balance is to put whatever fears you may have into a spontaneous song using the vowel sounds. This may sound crazy but it is effective. Sing the fear until it has no more energy. Then, with an open mind, listen for the guidance that comes through. … And follow it!

Famous people with a "11" major Attainment Cycle (10.1%)

Andres Segovia, Alexander Graham Bell, Bill Clinton, Edna Saint Vincent Millay, Elvis Presley, Ethel Merman, Gertrude Stein, Jane Goodall, Jean Baptiste Moliere, Johann Sebastian Bach, Kahlil Gibran, Michelangelo Buonarotti, Paramahansa Yogananda, Ralph Waldo Emerson, Richard Branson, Somerset Maugham, William Shakespeare, Walter Cronkite, Winston Churchill, Zora Neale Hurston.

12

The "12" period can be an exciting period of innovation, change and new directions. Its energy awakens intuition and brings increased vitality. During a "12" period, you may feel really alive and in touch with the deeper meaning of life as well as your own purpose for being here. It can be a productive period for moving forward to achieve your goals.

Use the energy of this time to make changes, find a new path, choose a new direction, make needed realignments, or learn something new. Things are malleable during a "12" period. It is a time for innovation and boldness. Your intuition is more active at this time, so don't be afraid to act on faith and take fearless yet purposeful risks based on your inner guidance. The secret to success at this time is to keep showing up, and keep saying "yes" to spirit. This, in itself, will set you apart from the crowd and move you closer to achieving your dreams.

The "12" period combines the energies of intuition and objectivity. Inspiration fuels idea-driven practicality and a desire to achieve goals. Anchor inner insights and visions with systematic investigation. Then move forward. This is a time to initiate new projects and endeavors and for creating forward momentum. It is a good time for planning strategies, coordination with others, and making acquisitions or additions. It can be a time of prosperity and plenty.

The "12" period favors honesty, fair play and service to others. It is a changeable time, and there can be many ups and downs. This can be stressful. It is important that you don't get out of balance, and so focused on being a crusader for your own causes and objectives that you trample on others in the process. Rather, seek to be the arbitrator and harmonizer whenever possible. When tensions are high, a talent for peacemaking is needed.

Pay attention to your physical body during this period. It is a good time for physical healing, especially since your body is likely to be feeling the higher vibration, and making shifts. You have to be adaptable during a "12" period. In the right setting and circumstance, this can be an appropriate time for playfulness, carefreeness and uninhibited actions, especially those that support your overall health and well-being. It can also be quite a romantic time for finding or deepening love relationships. Your sexual drive may be high.

During a "12" period, women and women's issues are in the spotlight.

"12" is the number of the global mind. On a collective level, it can be a period of *mass awakening.*[7] The "12" period fosters connectivity, group coherence, and shared meaning. It is the number of the social network and the energy of the larger whole. Issues of social justice take the spotlight as the rationale for the prevailing worldview is questioned. The result, especially during the longer periods (years and multi-year cycles), can be world-changing.

Downside: The "12" period can be an exciting time of change. But, remember the oft-quoted Chinese curse: May you live in exciting times. This can be a time of trial when your personal beliefs are tested. Adaptability is a virtue during this period. In surfing the waves of change, being adaptable will help you maintain your balance.

The downside, as with most numbers, can take a couple of different but related paths. Energies and events are shifting at this time. Things may seem to be out of control, and you may want to hang onto the status quo because it is a known entity. So, the "12" period can spark within you (or others) a need for control. It can cause you to fixate on goals, and put undue effort into your work. You can become a workaholic. You can get emotionally stuck, and take too narrow a view of your circumstances. It can be a time of self-doubt, when you feel inept. You may be tempted to see things as hopeless and adopt an attitude of defeatism.

The more active path of maintaining an illusion of control during this period is to become manipulative, egocentric, ornery and hypercritical. You may feel resentment and righteous indignation at those you feel are responsible for making your life difficult. It's "my way or the highway," you say, because *your* way and *your* beliefs are the

---

[7] The end of 2012, the twelfth year of the new century, has long been prophesied to be a time of mass awakening, sparking a shift in the collective consciousness.

right ones. Chances are, whoever your scapegoats are at this time, they are merely carrying your own inner projections.

"12" is the number of earthquakes, explosions, implosions, shockwaves and heat waves. During a "12 period, the creative forces inside and outside of us are very active. It can be a rebellious and iconoclastic time of pushing boundaries and buttons. It can be a time of emotional alienation, of highs and lows and bi-polar thinking. It can be a time when ignorant and vindictive people cross your path and test your beliefs. Tyrants take center stage to test the human spirit and urge us collectively toward social justice and solidarity with spiritual law.

It is important to remember that the "12" period offers us new directions, and the opportunity to make fundamental changes. Just when things seem to be falling apart, a chance for a new innovation presents itself. There is an opportunity to burst the cocoon and become a butterfly. Your intuition is strong during this period. The path to balance is to listen to your inner guidance, keep showing up, and keep saying yes to your better angels.

Famous people with a "12" major Attainment Cycle (4.4%)

Alan Greenspan, Alexis de Tocqueville, Anne Bronte, Frederick Douglass, James A. Garfield, James Monroe, Jann Wenner, John F. Kennedy, Konrad Adenauer, Liz Claiborne, Margaret Storm Jameson, Martin Luther King Jr., Nicolas Cage, Paulina Porizkova, René Descartes, Simone de Beauvoir.

[Note: U.S. Presidents Garfield and Kennedy, and Martin Luther King Jr. were all assassinated during this "12" Attainment Cycle, highlighting its sometimes explosive and unexpected energy.]

13

The "13" period or cycle is a time of endings and beginnings. Like the "12" it is a good time for change. But, the "13" is more volitional and less potentially explosive. It is about coming to a choice point. At this time, personal change is necessary and inner work is generally needed to make a fundamental realignment.

The focus of this time is on breaking free from an old habit or routine, cleaning up anything that is out of balance, and finding personal renewal in the process. Moving forward involves leaving something of the past behind so you can step more fully into your power. There is a strong connection with ancestral spirits and guardian angels. Don't hesitate to ask for help!

The "13" energy is about getting into action to do something practical. It is the urge to use your energy, talent and experience to build something, to procreate, to bring forth something into the world. What this looks like will depend entirely upon you, but the point is that this period is a great time to move a project forward.

The formula for success during a 13-period or cycle is this: well-defined goals combined with readiness, action, persistence, and an expectation of success. This brings accomplishment and produces prosperity. Try it out. Be bold and do whatever you do with self-assurance. The nice thing is that "13" is the energy of success and wealth. Whatever you do at this time may bring you added abundance!

This is a fortuitous time to find the middle ground that leads to joint solutions and social harmony. This time favors facilitators, catalysts for change, networking, volunteers, and grassroots efforts.

"13" is the power of caring and compassion for others that moves in a disciplined or practical way to serve the community. It is a time to give something of your energy, time and talent back to the people in return for the blessings you have received. Doing so at this time puts you in harmony with the energy of this period and satisfies a deep need to connect. It also helps to keep the fabric of society healthy, and brings many personal rewards – for it is in giving that we truly receive.

Downside: Feeling aimless like you don't have a clue about what direction to take, or feeling that your efforts are meaningless and likely to fail – these are both signs of being caught in the shadow energy of the "13" period or cycle. This darker side can create disorder, blind spots, and mistakes (at least perceived ones). You can feel miserable, moody, pessimistic and not at all sociable. In fact, you can withdraw and feel quite insular. Add in a touch of scarcity that often happens during this period to spice up your life – or the fear of it – and you've got the recipe for codependency, evasive behaviors, selfishness and even xenophobia – all of which are "13" shadow energies.

The more active shadow qualities include being over-dramatic, individualistic and willful, negative and ill-mannered. The negative side of the "13" period can also produce antagonistic, disobedient, confrontational, unjust or even treacherous behaviors. It is the energy of hatefulness, wrongdoing, human greed and fanaticism. Charlatans and corrupt people can cross your path. As a counterbalance, this is a good time to file lawsuits to seek justice!

Collectively, this is a time of sudden awakening that supports human morality, civil courage and the overthrow of tyrants and unjust systems. Yet, this almost never happens easily. As a result, the "13" period can be a time when social dilemmas take center stage. This can cause cultural upheaval, meltdowns and even revolutions.

All of the shadow aspects for the "13" have a common root: something is winding down and ending. The sun is setting on an old habit, routine, mindset, worldview or system. The sun is rising on something new. It is a new energy that is calling out for a shift or realignment or (re)awakening. The path back to the positive side is to stop holding on to the past so tightly and learn to let go more lightly; to wake up to the new possibilities and potentials.

One of the secrets to accelerating this inner shift is to gain some perspective by getting outside of your own problems or issues. Giving of your personal time, talent and effort to help your community in some way restores balance and can return you to the positive side of the "13" cycle or period.

Famous people with a "13" major Attainment Cycle (0.7%)

Emanuel Ofosu Yeboah, Emily Watson, Harry S. Truman, Kate Moss, Orlando Bloom, Susan Bromwell Anthony.

14

The "14" period is often a time of connections and relationships. "14" is the number of the *web* that connects us to all things in life. It is the power of connectedness, and not only to people and things, but also to ancient, ancestral wisdom that is part of the world mind and also carried as genetic memory in our cells. This connection can strengthen psychic experience and latent prophetic or telepathic abilities. It can also enhance the natural ability to influence things at a distance through the power of your thoughts and emotions.

This power of remote influence can bring you what you need and desire. During a "14" period or cycle, you can draw to you the people and resources needed to accomplish desired goals, and harvest rewards for past efforts.

It is a good time to make connections with others, and for networking to promote personal or business goals. The "14" period can be a vibrant, life-enhancing time during which you feel more articulate and have more confidence in your conversational abilities. This makes it a favorable time for negotiations, and also the mediation of disputes – especially since the "14" energy promotes fairness and peace. It is also a time for cooperativity, a time to be supportive, nurturing, and maybe a even a little protective of family, friends and coworkers. If you are drawn toward taking a moral stance and humanitarian pursuits, this is the time to step forward.

"14" is the number of objective judgment, structure, organization, and also the energy of setting goals and making plans. This is a great time to set some very practical, grounded, concrete goals – including ones for physical action such as starting a new construction project, renovation or remodeling, and so on.

The "14" period supports individuality, individual excellence and making personal gains. It is also the energy of leadership and fame. It may be the time for you to step forward, knowing that the "14" energy will bring to you the support you need, and will aid you in harvesting all that you intend, focus on, and work toward.

Downside: The "14" period can also get you tied up in the problems of life, and caught up in relationship dramas. The challenge during this period is to *not* get stuck.

The shadow side of the "14" energy of connectedness is the feeling of being trapped, ensnared in problems of your own making, and feeling as if there is no way out. This can include a constellation of issues such as: experiencing failures, confronting incompatibilities, going through marital discord and/or being in manipulative relationships.

Often what leads you into these deep shadows is judgmentalism, controlling behaviors and dogmatism. It can be a time of craziness, compulsion, drivenness and one-upmanship. If you have avoided becoming the aggressor, then you may be at the receiving end. At the very least, you are in a tight spot. At the extreme, it can be a period that is hazardous to your mental, emotional and/or physical well-being.

While the "14" energy can pull you into its trap, it is for the purpose of teaching you a necessary lesson. The good news is that once you understand the lesson, the key to your release will also be given. Generally, the dark side of the "14" energy activates when you forget your connection to the Source and slip into a mindset of separation and disconnection from others, and disconnection from your own power. Once you remember that the "14" is the web of energy that connects you with All-That-Is, and gives you the power to attract all that you need, you are free once again!

Famous people with a "14" major Attainment Cycle (0.4%)

Marcus Aurelius Antonius, Warren Buffet.

15

The "15" period is often a time to be pragmatic, and move forward to achieve practical, tangible results – even in the face of obstacles. The "15" energy is connected with the life-force, and this can increase physical energy. It can also energize your ability to focus on goals with a singular purpose, and bring the follow-through necessary to succeed. In short, you can set goals and make things happen during this time.

The "15" energy combines practicality and business savvy with a motivation to work on shared goals and cooperative efforts. It is a time when you may feel a stronger desire for social interaction, and you may be more extroverted and expressive, as well.

It is a good time for working with a group or community to make collective decisions – especially at the grassroots level. Speak your mind, but work to build consensus and have power *with* others instead of power *over* others. During this time, you may be challenged to subordinate your personal ego needs to the overall needs of others. And yet, even if this is the case, doing so will bring gratifying rewards and emotional fulfillment.

This can be a time for innovators. You can more easily see future possibilities. In fact, psychic abilities are naturally stronger at this time, and may be drawn upon to provide a pathway through creative doubt to new inspiration. You can take ideas and help them grow during this period. It is a time for visualizing what you want, and then taking the steps to bring it into materialization. It is a time of procreation, and a good time to be pregnant with new potentials. This is also true literally. It is a good time for hopeful mothers to get pregnant.

This is a time of turning points, a malleable space for second chances, and for reviewing old decisions and conclusions. Estranged loved ones may come back. Things that you have lost or forgotten may be returned. Friends who have gone by the wayside may come back around. Issues long dormant that you thought were put to bed for good may come up for review. This is a powerful time for reconciliation between friends, lovers, and marriage or business partners.

Being a time of turning points, reality is more malleable. This also makes this period an optimum time for healing. So, go see the healer of your choice. "15" is an energy that many healers and body-workers carry, so their work is more powerful and effective during this period.

The old saw is: "All work and no play makes Jack a dull boy." The energy of this period can create a singular passion to focus your power on achieving goals. This can make you boring. Remember to lighten up and have some fun. Laugh and tell a few jokes. Don't take yourself too seriously.

Downside: This can be a time of social pressure that can be a catalyst for you to feel apprehensive and angst-ridden. Unresolved issues can arise. A course of action that you have been pursuing may now become unsustainable. It can be exasperating. But, this is a time of turning points. Life is telling you to reconsider old decisions, and make new choices.

The self-defeating course of action is to feel displaced, withdraw emotionally, become socially isolated and resentful, and lock down into a bunker mentality. You can become spiritless and inattentive. Your mind can tell you lies like, "moving forward is an impossibility" or "taking action is pointless." This is not true. The "15" period activates the life-force energy, and gives you added strength to overcome obstacles. You only have to tap into this power, and decide you want to make a positive change.

The more active downside of this period is feeling antsy and high-strung, and acting out in rambunctious ways. Take care not to cross a line into unscrupulous behavior, or into corruption and/or vengefulness. Once you do, the pathway back to the light side is more difficult.

Famous people with a "15" major Attainment Cycle (1.0%)

Austin Dobson, Benjamin Franklin, Betty White, Don Zimmer, Franklin Pierce, James Earl Jones.

16

The "16" period can be a time of new possibilities, new frontiers and fundamental change. This can be exciting! But it can also be tough. During a "16" period, life sometimes puts you into a crucible and turns up the heat. But, even if a meltdown occurs, know that it is all part of the growth process, and you will likely emerge from it feeling stronger.

The "16" period gives access to great power. This is because the "16" is about matter in service to the higher mind. When a "16" period or cycle rolls around, you can get in touch with the forces of nature, connect more readily with your "inner genius," put new ideas into action, or launch a successful project. "16" is grounded intelligence that is linked to the physical world, so this time brings greater ability to achieve practical results, even with major projects. Natural aptitudes are strengthened. Adhering to a hard-working discipline during a "16" period is in harmony with the time and readily produces individual gains.

The "16" energy is a direct link with the collective mind and ancestral wisdom. It is a powerful time to connect with spirit guides, and open up to spiritual guidance and inner knowing. You may experience times of direct knowing – i.e. information being downloaded directly into your mind so you just know something without knowing how you know it! It is a time during which you can trust your instinctive actions.

Communication with higher beings and access to dimensional gateways is possible during the "16" period. It is a special time to cure serious illnesses, prevent accidents from occurring, and to ask for safe travels.

The well-being of society is in the spotlight during this time. People more readily understand how interdependent we all are, and how much we rely upon each other. There is a high degree of inequity aversion during a "16" period. In other words, it is a good time to take action to stop unfairness to other individuals or groups. Good intentions carry much more power than bad ones.

Downside: As described above, life can put you in a crucible and turn up the heat during a "16" period. A meltdown can occur. It can seem that you are caught in a stranglehold. The energy may feel constricted. Too many people see limitedness, as in the glass being half-empty instead of half-full. You become more aware of things like abuse, mismanagement and close-mindedness around you – and it is frustrating! Life's persistent questions can seem unanswerable and its problems seem irresolvable. What can you do?

This period can be a catalyst for pulling back from life, and becoming introverted and uncommunicative. It can also be a catalyst for bitterness. But, it need not be if you realize that during a "16" period something fundamental is shifting. *You* are changing in deep, but often unseen ways. The key to balance is to be kind and gentle with yourself and others. Take time for introspection. Know that this is a temporary period meant to bring new growth and new capacities. And, you are getting stronger – even if you cannot see it now.

Famous people with a "16" major Attainment Cycle (1.0%)

Anton Chekhov, Cary Grant, Danny Kaye, Douglas L. Wilder, Federico Fellini, Irving Beecher, Ken S. Keyes Jr.

17

The "17" period brings the energy of movement and the power of balance and sure-footedness. It is a time that favors *doers*. It is an excellent time to get into action, be enterprising, and move forward to achieve desired goals. This includes finding the job you desire.

The "17" energy gives a helpful boost to professionals in the material, cultural and spiritual worlds. It is a good time to explore new ideologies, put together a business plan, and do some empirical research or quantitative analysis. At certain times, this period can be used to peer into the future.[8]

This can be a time of change since the "17" energy represents metamorphosis – the power that turns the caterpillar into the butterfly. It is a time that emphasizes individual identity, personal autonomy and self-realization. So, it is a good time to make significant personal shifts, and confront whatever may be holding you back from being all you can be. You may also find that you can have a transforming influence on both people and events during this period.

A "17" period highlights the quest for understanding. This includes the search for the deepest truths that undergird our objective reality, but is also a time for promoting understanding between individuals and groups of people. "17" is the energy of togetherness, and also of dialogue. It is a good time to bring people together to explore ideas and/or forge a collective vision of the future. It is a period that favors group processes, public relations work, and healing processes.

The "17" period is an auspicious time to find greater balance in your life. The energy of the period helps to bring inner balance as well

---

[8] The great Mayan hierarchy of elders, wise ones and visionaries gather to analyze the future on "8 Kej," an energy connected with specific "17" periods.

as harmony with the natural world. Your ability to sense things on a kinesthetic, body level is likely to be stronger during this time, so pay attention to the messages your body gives you, i.e., through your belly brain or gut instincts. Indeed, one has access to the ground state of pure being during this period, and the psychokinetic abilities that can flow from it – something to experiment with, for sure. It can be a time for miracles and miracle workers!

Movement is often important to achieve balance during this time, so consider integrating exercise of some sort into your daily routine. Moving your body not only brings greater balance and helps with physical conditioning, it also opens a channel to higher wisdom, as well as heightened physical senses and sensual ecstasy. Kundalini meditation is especially effective during this time.

You may also find that any artistic abilities that you may have are enhanced – especially those that involve working with your hands or body in some way. Artistic endeavors can be another pathway to balance and harmony at this time.

Downside: The positive side of the "17" can bring power and focus. The negative or shadow side of the "17 brings negativity and a tendency toward shallowness and narrowness of thinking – but not necessarily *your* thinking. You might find yourself confronting (or being confronted by) fundamentalism in some form or fashion. You may feel misunderstood. You can feel subservient to forces beyond your control or, alternately, entangled in issues that cause feelings of possessiveness, and/or create separateness that can include estrangement in relationships or marital strife. Be sure that you don't overstep your boundaries and trample on others during this time.

The shadow of the "17" includes nervousness, temperamental or argumentative energies, and rebelliousness. It can be a catalyst for opportunistic behaviors and controversial actions. During a "17" period, you can be prompted to take a walk on the wild side and explore things considered taboo by society. Take care, as during this period people can binge on food, alcohol, or other sensory indulgences.

At a collective level, the "17" period can be a time of purification that brings dangerous times and the popular hysteria that often follows in its wake. It can be a dire time of mournfulness when people feel grief-stricken.

Famous people with a "17" major Attainment Cycle (1.5%)

Augustine Birrell, Edwin "Buzz" Aldrin, George Frederick Handel, Jacques Cousteau, James Madison, Jeffrey Katzenberg, Leonardo da Vinci, Michael Bloomberg, Muhammad Ali, Pierre Cardin.

18

An "18" period can be an active time when you are prompted to get into action to make something, or chart a new path, or explore new ideas. In fact, it is a time of good beginnings. Anything that begins during this period has a positive future. It is the best time to begin any sort of love relationship or business relationship and to win back something that was presumed to be lost – such as a lost love, or lost friendship.

The energy of this time brings blessings and hope. It is generally a time of greater abundance that brings the fruits of love and understanding.

"18" is recognized as the energy of creation by the Mayan people.[9] In their culture, the energy of this period is used to select and prepare the seed for cultivation during the next planting season. In a more general sense, the "18" energy applies to cultivating *anything* in the early phases of development such as children, animals, new relationships or partnerships, new businesses, jobs, projects or endeavors, as well as intangible qualities like ideas and visions, love and romance, understanding, respect, and so forth. In short, this is the time to plant the seeds for anything that you desire to manifest in the future. It is a time to ask Spirit for what you truly want.

During an "18" period, your emotional and mental well-being and the emotional and mental well-being of others step forward to demand

---

[9] See Chapter 10 for a description of the "18" energy that is called *Qanil* in the K'iche Mayan tradition.

your attention. And, since this time often brings blessings, this is generally a good thing. New possibilities open up. If you have been feeling lost, you can find your way again, or help others find their way. If your life is just fine, perhaps a new way or path reveals itself to expand your potential and broaden your horizons. You might find a new and better way to do something, or develop a new system as I did with Mystical Numerology.[10] You can be driven forward by a heightened sense of curiosity that is matched by the persistence and resourcefulness to make things happen in the "real world."

This is actually a good time for businesses and the governing administrators and boards to make collective decisions, and move forward with new projects. This is a time of social integration on a collective level, so it is also an auspicious time for business acquisitions in which two corporate cultures need to mesh in relative harmony. Only make sure that due diligence is given to basic, block-and-tackle issues, and that the focus is on being fair and honest.

Downside: The "18" period can be a time during which you are challenged to learn something new. At the time you want to get into action, you may have to deal with niggling details. On a larger scale, you may even find that you have to stand against the crowd for something you believe. Standing your ground is a positive aspect. Just make sure that it doesn't develop into a general attitude of stubbornness.

Guard against fear and superstition during this time. Fear can create a witch's brew of attitudes and behaviors including mistrust, self-justification, coercion, and territoriality. Alternately, it can also lead to a brooding sadness, a bleak outlook on the world, and an unhealthy meekness that inhibits positive thoughts and actions. You can fall prey to these shadow qualities during an "18" period, or find that others who carry these attitudes and behaviors cross your path.

During an "18" period, it is also prudent to be aware of others who attempt to take advantage of you and your good nature. Don't give in to hype, and don't let yourself be bluffed or cajoled into doing something that doesn't feel right.

---

[10] I created this new system of Mystical Numerology during an "18" Attainment Cycle.

Famous people with a "18" major Attainment Cycle (1.6%)

Alfred North Whitehead, Charles Evans Hughes, Florence Nightingale, Galileo Galilei, George Lyttleton, John Henry Newman, Richard Burton, Ruth Bader Ginsberg, Sylvia Plath, Thomas Jefferson.

19

When a "19" period (day, month, year or cycle) rolls around, life's events conspire to help you to remember who you really are, and where your power *really* comes from. The "19" period presents opportunities to be in service to the larger community versus serving yourself, and to choose wholeness versus separation. It is in this time that you begin giving something back in gratitude for what you have received so that your cycle of personal growth may continue. This period can bring greater physical energy in support of others as you step into your own power in a way that serves the people.

"19" is the number of the "guru." During this period, an emphasis is placed upon what you have to teach others. Alternately, it is a fortuitous time to find a spiritual teacher. It is also during this time that your life priorities come up for review, and it never hurts to have a little spiritual help to sort things out.

During "19" periods, it is really important say "thank you," to the Creator for all the blessings you have received ... and even ones that you *will* receive, or hope to receive. The teaching in this is that you can activate the positive aspects of this "19" energy by remembering that sincere gratitude and giving something back is important, and reaps qualities such as compassion, sensitivity, unity, and transcendence. It also keeps abundance flowing into and through your life. Keeping a list of people, things and events that you are grateful for is a good discipline at any time, but especially during this period.

The energy of a "19" period also makes this an optimum time to atone for any actions you have taken that may have been hurtful to others, or hurtful to Mother Earth. It is a time to release negativity and cut the cords that bind you to unhealthy patterns of behavior. It is the time to clear away financial and/or karmic debts so that good things will naturally flow into your life. The K'iche Maya use this energy as a time of payment. They offer their heartfelt thanks to the Creator, and make offerings to the ceremonial fire.

Downside: Power and control issues often come to the surface during this period. Watch out for arguments, accusations, libelous statements, and people who would bully you. The energy of this time can spiral out of control and turn from anger to rage. Guard against a desire to disregard rules and disobey authority. You can feel like going rogue at this time, or encounter scoundrels and disreputable people on your path.

It is natural to feel a little uncertain during this time. Do your best not to let this make you feel like an idiot, or stop you from moving forward. If you have any phobias – exaggerated, illogical fears – they will likely surface. This is a good time to confront them.

During a "19" period, people can be more inclined than normal to corruption, vice and actions that cross the line into moral depravity. Be aware that engaging in seedy or disreputable behaviors may have unfortunate and lasting effects.

Famous people with a "19" major Attainment Cycle (1.5%)

David Livingstone, David Lloyd George, Francis Bacon, Helen Gurley Brown, Isaac Newton, Jim Carrey, Konstantin Stanislavsky, Richard J. Daley, Robert E. Lee, Thomas Riley Marshall.

20

During a "20" period, you may find obstacles and doubts being cleared away resulting in greater balance. The obstacles may be inner stuff that surfaces to be processed and released. So, it may not be all fun and games. But, this is the time to request divine intervention to help confront any kind of issue or solve any type of problem. If you are dealing with any kind of legal issues, this is the best time to take action and ask that justice be done.

This is a time of greater power, almost as if an unseen hand is guiding your actions. You may become more centered in the realization of who you are and where your true power comes from. Your body may feel stronger, and you may feel more drawn to the spiritual dimension of life. Pay attention to your dreams, as well as the synchronicities that happen to give you practical inspiration during this period.

This is a good time to pursue a regular course of exercise or a fitness regimen of some kind. Keeping your body fit will also help you bring in the spiritual energy you may require to meet life head-on.

This period is the time of the hero's journey or quest, something that you must experience alone even if you have the support of friends and family. The key is to have the audacity to take the leap of faith, to go on the quest even if it scares you. Significant growth lies at the end of the journey.

Actually, this can also be a joyful time when you can trot out your inner child and have some fun! Don't forget to laugh! It will keep everything else in perspective. Indeed, being with amiable, like-minded people, letting your hair down and having a good laugh will help you stay in balance during this time.

Downside: This can be a period of doubt when you must confront your inner fears, including a fear of being alone. The life experiences you may go through during this time are varied – health problems, relationship issues, problems with your job, legal issues, and so on – but the common thread is feeling like you are on a lone path walking through a dense jungle. Your progress may feel blocked and you can have trouble finding your way. You can feel like you are lost and in limbo waiting to be delivered back into the fullness of life. If you see the people and events during this period as part of the archetypal hero's journey, it may help you to move through it. Be audacious. It is not a time for sissies.

There can be a natural tendency to avoid problems and issues that you need to confront head-on. You can become ego-bound and adopt unhealthy behaviors that include a fierce defiance of authority, as well as deriding or blaming others for problems that are really your own outward projections. Conversely, you may find others blaming, deriding or even mocking you at this time.

This is a time for the judicious use of force in overcoming obstacles, breaking free of the bondage of overly constraining roles or identities, and for shifting off of dead-end paths. But, don't go overboard and adopt stubborn or obdurate behaviors.

Be on the lookout for loony people and buffoons who can stand in your way during this time. Don't allow them to befuddle your mind and push you off-center.

Famous people with a "20" major Attainment Cycle (2.9%)

Barack Obama, Daniel Webster, Donald Rumsfeld, Eartha Kitt, Harriet Beecher Stowe, Howard Hughes, James Watt, Janis Joplin, Karl Wallenda, Nicolaus Copernicus, Tenzin Gyatso (H. H. The Dalai Lama), Sai Baba, Thomas Johnathan (Stonewall) Jackson.

21

A "21" period opens you up for guidance and higher insights. You may, therefore, be more open than normal during this time. This means that you will also be affected by both inner and outer events more than is normal. This makes it a good time for personal renewal. As a part of this, it is a great time to review old structures and patterns in your life to see what fits and what doesn't. It's a period to integrate inner polarities and strive for wholeness.

This can also be a time of expansion and sometimes sudden changes. The "21" period puts you in touch with your soul's purpose, and presents you with an opportunity to make a course correction. A "21" period is a time to ratchet up your courage and make that leap of faith that will bring your inner and outer life into balance.

This period is also connected with money and your ability to attract more of it. Here is the key. To have more money you must first let go of any fear of lack that you have – e.g., focusing on what you *don't* have, including being afraid you don't have enough. It is helpful to release an attachment to money in any kind of needy way because this simply reinforces the same fear.

Next, realize that *money is linked to the energy of play* in the sense of letting go of worry, adopting a childlike innocence, and losing yourself in the moment. If you can find a sense of play in your vocation, then you've got a leg up on creating more money. The openness to play also opens the gateway to inner guidance. Childlike innocence allows you to follow the guidance. When you do, you make yourself magnetic to the money needed for you to achieve your soul's purpose.

Following inner guidance means showing up and saying "yes" to that voice inside of you, or to the gut-level sense of knowing that you are supposed to do something – even when you don't really want to do it. This also takes some courage and a little bit of audacity. There is a reason why the "cougar" is one of the totem animals for this number, because the "21" energy, while expansive, is not for the faint of heart. "Yeshua" is also a "21," and you can imagine how he felt when the priests of the temple traditions attacked him because his ideas were revolutionary for the times. Truthfully, they still are. The courage to follow inner guidance is part of the "21" energy.

This is a good period to seek an accord with others. It is a good time to educate yourself and others, and create understanding for your position, beliefs or worldview. It is a time to inspire trust and confidence in others. The energy of the period helps people make good choices and cut through extraneous information to focus on the most important goals.

This can be a time that brings a sense of calm. It is a good time to beautify your house and your surroundings. It is a time to feel good about what you have accomplished, have a little fun and enjoy the good life. In doing so, you will also help others to do so, as well.

Downside: You will know if you are in the shadow energy of the "21" period if you feel like you are blocked and unable to accomplish your goals, or that you are seriously constrained and feel as if you have no choices available to you. Life can also feel dull and lacking in freshness and originality.

Alternately, it can be a very exciting time but not in a good way. You may be confronted by those you consider enemies. People may speak or act with malice, be mean to you, or even gang up on you. You can feel under siege. The natural reaction is to be afraid. It may take great courage to stand your ground and defend your ideas and beliefs, or even your physical person.

Deceit and fraud are both "21" energies, so guard against those who would take advantage of you at this time. Be on the lookout for bogus deals, or ploys to take your money, or people who attempt to coax you into doing something you don't feel good about. This can be a challenge since the energy of this time can make you feel a little shy, baffled or even flakey. Stay focused, if you can!

Part of the "21" downside is mania. If you have a tendency toward hyperactivity or overstimulation, it can become activated during this period. Be careful of mood swings, particularly the excessively elevated ones. Take note, this is an especially bad time to use alcohol, marijuana or drugs as a way to compensate for feeling hyper. It will only add to a tendency for disorganized behavior. In addition, the vortex of energy during a "21" period can pull you onto a path of decadence and deterioration. It can be difficult to pull yourself back out.

A "21" period can bring up aging issues. If you are relatively young, this aspect of a "21" period won't have much effect. But, if you are getting older it might. Aches and pains you never would have given a second thought when younger, now can cause you wonder if they represent the new normal. As a retired university professor friend wrote to me, aging presents "the dilemma of a polarity of a yes or no: either you accept as a cosmological flow the falling change [in health], or don't accept it because we may yet have some determining input in the aging process." The "21" period can bring this dilemma into the spotlight.

Famous people with a "21" major Attainment Cycle (2.8%)

Chester A. Arthur, Edgar Allan Poe, Eduard Manet, Esther Williams, James Earl Carter, Jean-Marie Roland, Lawrence Edward Grace Oates, Rutherford B. Hayes, Samuel Foote, Sri Yukteswar Giri, Steve Earl, Sylvia Pankhurst, Vidal Sassoon, William Jennings Bryan.

<u>22</u>

During the "22" period, divine energy flows into the earth and gets anchored into its core. It is a period of expanded possibilities and potential, and can be an extended period of balance – especially as month, year or multi-year cycles. There is the potential to experience a grounded connection with the earth and a simultaneous openness to new inspiration.

This period is about love in service to higher goals, and service to others – family, work group, people in your sphere of influence, the larger community, the nation and the world. There are energies afoot in our increasingly polarized world that seek to separate and divide us – religious conflicts and politics being the two most prominent examples. The energy of the "22" period is about what holds everything together. It helps to bring people together to create union and equality. Any actions that you take at this time to defuse arguments and tense situations, and create connectedness and understanding will be augmented and increased in effectiveness.

The truth is that we are all energetically interconnected in ways that frontier science is proving to be true but most people do not yet realize. In addition, we are all equally special. The energy of the "22" period is about that equal specialness and interconnectedness. Those that work selflessly for the good of the whole should be honored, especially at this time.

This is a grounded, pragmatic time that is about creating something tangible from ideas, dreams, visions, insight and inspiration. Your ideas can have more than normal practical impact during this time, and you can work with greater effectiveness to achieve practical goals. The energy of the period will help you mold and shape your ideas and projects, or those of other people. It is also a good time to offer advice and counsel. The "22" energy will pull you toward success and fill up your coffers, and make sure you have enough. In essence, this can be a very productive period, if you apply yourself. So, don't be afraid to reach for the stars as you pursue your dreams!

This can be a period when life is full and times are good. It is a favorable time to take a trip or voyage – especially to the sacred power spots on the planet. It is a time to honor the Earth Mother and the guardian spirits that inhabit sacred places. The energy of this period supports those who are amicable, joyful and kind in their relationships, and who bring cheer to lighten and brighten the day of others.

Downside: The natural energy of this period acts to pull things together and fill things up. It brings success to actions on behalf of the common good. Yet, there is a shadow that comes with this period, and it is deep for those who act to cause divisiveness and separation. The shadow-side energy can create myopia, highlight deficiencies, and aggravate maladies.

The balanced "22" energy brings a grounded connection with divine energy. The shadow-side of this same energy is a catalyst for ungrounded, spacey individuals to act out with inane, silly or imbecilic behaviors and actions bordering on lunacy.

As the "22" energy breeds success and prosperity, one of the shadow-side aspects can spin out of excess. There is a natural tendency toward being a playboy or party girl during this time. Bawdy behavior and illicit affairs can result.

Perhaps the deepest shadow of the "22" is that it can generate greed. Whether this comes from a fear of lack, or from having great success and wanting more, the basic issue is feeling that you don't have enough. This is a good time to take stock of all your blessings, and recognize that the energy of the time will bring you all that you need. Still, some people will feel that they have to deceive others to get what they want. Be on the lookout for them.

Just as the natural positive energy of the "22" seeks union and is about what pulls things together to cause them to cohere, there is an opposite force acting to pull things apart. The way this manifests is to spawn bigots and hate groups. It is regrettable but true. The key is this: the positive energy that holds things together is *always* more powerful than the negative force attempting to pull things apart. Always! And, *that* is a thought to live by.

Famous people with a "22" major Attainment Cycle (2.1%)

Benny Hill, Eudora Welty, Garrison Keillor, George W. Bush, George Washington, (Captain) James Cook, Jane Horrocks, Kevin Costner, Lou Diamond Phillips, Marcus Tulius Cicero, Nelson A. Rockefeller, Oliver Hardy, Patricia Neal.

Chapter Nine:

Life Challenges

It is not because things are difficult that we do not dare; it is because we do not dare that things are difficult.

~Seneca~

Everyone has three Life Challenges that last for a period of 29 years. The first goes from birth (age 0) through 28. The second lasts from 29 through 57, and is often referred to as the "Major Challenge." The third lasts from 58 through 86. Starting at age 87, you start back around the cycle again with the first challenge.

Here's how they are calculated:

<u>Example 1: Barack Obama</u>

Let us use Barack Obama one last time. Actually, using Obama for the different calculations gives you an overview of the different techniques as you look back at previous examples. So, there's a method to the madness.

Obama's converted birth date is: 3 – 9 – 1961 (see page 82, example 2). Remember, this is Day–Month–Year format.

Step 1: Reduce the Year by taking the sum of the digits:

$1+9+6+1 = \underline{17}$.

Step 2: Rewrite the Day–Month–Year using the reduced number for the year. The date now becomes:

$3 - 9 - 17$.

Step 3: To find the first or Early Challenge (ages 0 – 28), calculate the difference between the Month and Day:

$9 - 3 = \underline{\mathbf{6}}$.

Step 4: Next, calculate the difference between the Year and Month to find the third or Sunset Challenge (ages 58 – 87) – when you see the graphic below, doing it in this order will make sense:

$17 - 9 = \underline{\mathbf{8}}$.

Step 5: Finally, calculate the difference between the Early Challenge and Sunset Challenge (the results of the two previous calculations) to determing the second or "Major Challenge" (ages 29 – 57):

$8 - 6 = \underline{\mathbf{2}}$.

This is Obama's current challenge.

Step 6: Here's the easy way to write it out when you are doing a chart. It helps to see it:

3 – 9 – 17

(Ages 0 – 28) **6**   **8** (Ages 58 – 86)

2

(Ages 29 – 57)

Step 7: Look up the meaning of the "2" challenge from the definitions given in this chapter under "Life Challenges," and see how it fits for President Obama.

<u>Interpretation</u>

At this current writing in 2012, President Obama is being challenged to find and maintain balance. He started in 2008 with his own Democratic Party in control of both houses of the U.S. Congress. But, Republicans won control of the House of Representatives in the 2010 midterm elections. Since then, Obama hasn't really found the balance between assertiveness, establishing boundaries and extending olive branches to make deals that work for both sides. It is quite likely that he has felt a strong sense of alienation from Congress.

<u>Note</u>: We can now show the completed birth date pyramid showing both the 3 Attainments and 3 Life Challenges. Here's what it looks like when we put these together for Barack Obama:

(Ages 29 – 57)

20

(Ages 0 – 28) **12**   **26/8** (Ages 58 – 86)

3 – **9** – **17**

(Ages 0 – 28) **6**   **8** (Ages 58 – 86)

2

(Ages 29 – 57)

Example 2: Princess Diana

Let's take another look at Princess Diana. From page 94, we see that her converted birth date is: 25 – 7 – 1961 (Day – Month – Year).

> Step 1: By reducing the birth year to a 17, we get: 25 – 7 – 17. Note that we *do not reduce the day to a number between 1 – 22*. This is important. For the purpose of calculating Challenge Numbers and Attainment Cycles, we do <u>not</u> reduce numbers in the birth date. If we do, it will change the result. If necessary, we reduce only the resulting Challenge number.

> Step 2: Lay the birth date out in Day–Month–Year format. In this format, the difference calculations as described in example 1 above become fairly self-evident. The result is another triangle chart:

25 – 7 – 17

(Ages 0 – 28) **18   10** (Ages 58 – 86)

8

(Ages 29 – 57)

> Step 3: Interpret Princess Diana's "Major Challenge" (ages 29-57)

Interpretation

Even Princess Diana couldn't escape the turmoil that sometimes comes with the "8" challenge that can include: despair, heartache, conflict and upheaval. It can be destructive. It is so sad that it was personally destructive in a way that led to her sudden, tragic death.

Example 3: Albert Einstein

Let us consider the famous scientist, Albert Einstein. He was born on 14-March-1879.

Step 1: 1879 is a non-leap year so we use the chart on page 85 to convert it to a 13-month calendar date:

14-March-1879 ⇒ 1 − 4 − 1879.

Step 2: 1879 is a 25/7 year, but remember: for the purpose of calculating Life Challenges, do <u>not</u> reduce this number to a number between 1 − 22.

Write out the 13-month calendar birth date in Day − Month − Year format, and make the difference calculations to find the 3 Life Challenges, as follows:

1 − 4 − 25

(Ages 0 − 28) 3   21 (Ages 58 − 86)

18

(Ages 29 − 57)

<u>Interpretation</u>

Einstein actually did his most important work in his early years. In 1905 he published 4 papers that laid the foundation for modern-day quantum physics. He was just 26 at the time. In his early years, Einstein was a bit of a rebel, and had a dislike for authority. This is actually quite in keeping with the Early Challenge of the "3" which is about focusing the energy of the inner genius and not scattering energies in too many directions at once.

In his middle life, ages 29 − 57, Einstein's Major Challenge was the "18." This is about cultivating and nurturing the seeds of the new ideas he planted, and sometimes standing against the mainstream worldview in order to show others the new way. He published his General Theory of Relativity in 1911 when he was 32. This made him world famous, and he once quipped, "To punish me for my contempt for authority, fate made me an authority myself.[11]" But, he was continually passed over for the Nobel Prize in physics until 1921.

Einstein's Sunset Challenge, ages 58 – 86, was the "21." This is about having the courage to stay open to his intuitive guidance, and keep showing up and saying "yes." He was looking for a unified field theory that would unify all the branches of physics. He never found it, but kept working toward it. In some ways, he was hobbled by his own success which limited his ability to consider novel approaches. He also was uncomfortable with all of the implications of the quantum physics for which his theories had laid the foundation. He kept defending his own ideas that had become out of step with the times. This is also part of the "21" Challenge.

Last word on calculating Challenge numbers

1. Writing the converted birth date out in Day – Month – Year format makes the three *difference* calculations for the three challenge numbers pretty obvious.

2. Don't reduce the *Day* number or *Reduced Year* number even if it is above 22.

3. Do reduce any resulting "challenge" number that is above 22.

Life Challenge Descriptions

A description of each of the 22 Life Challenges is given below. Following each of the descriptions, I have provided a list of famous people who have that particular challenge as a "major challenge" (ages 29–57). I have also included a percentage representing the frequency with which this challenge occurs based on 850 people in my combined databases of famous historical figures, plus those clients, friends and family for whom I have done charts and kept records.

---

[11] See Einstein: His Life and Universe by Walter Isaacson, Simon & Shuster, 2007.

It is interesting to note that the most frequently occurring major challenge is the "2" – *Balance, Boundaries and Burdens* (almost 1 in 10 people). The next most frequently occurring challenge is, not unexpectedly, the "4" – *Order, Limitations and Work*. Tied for third place, this is followed by the "1" – *Individuation and Originality,* and the "5" – *Sustainable Freedom*. A very close fourth place goes to the challenge of the "6" – *Relationships, People and Placement*. The least frequent of the challenges are "18" through "22," with "22" being the most rare.

0: Staying Centered

The zero-point is the center, the God Source or Higher Power. As a *challenge* number, it represents the need to stay centered, and the importance of connecting with one's Higher Power.

Famous people with a zero major challenge (4.2%)

Adolf Hitler, Booker T. Washington, Charles Darwin, Dwight D. Eisenhower, Larry Flynt, Laura Ingalls Wilder, Lord Byron, Margaret Thatcher, Mark Twain and Vincent Van Gogh.

1: Individuation & Originality

The challenge of the "1" is about individuation, self-actualization, independence and standing on one's own two feet, and learning how to focus on goals. It also is the challenge of originality and the ability to seed new ideas into the world.

Famous people with a "1" major challenge (8.1%)

Doris Kearns Goodwin, Hilary Clinton, Jimmy Carter, John Adams, Lahiri Mahasaya, Oscar de la Renta, Robert De Niro, Simone Weil, Theodore Roosevelt, Victor Hugo, Walt Disney, and William Randolph Hurst.

2: Balance, Boundaries & Burdens

The challenge of the "2" is about finding balance and setting appropriate boundaries. Sometimes, this is about balancing a need to be assertive and speak one's mind with saying what needs to be said in a diplomatic way. Quite often, achieving balance that is sustainable longer term also requires setting appropriate boundaries.

Appropriate boundaries are like the structural supports and walls of a house. They define a moral code by which to live. And, just as people who want to enter the house have to come in through the door, appropriate boundaries limit access so that others don't drain a person's energy, or take advantage of his or her talents and time.

The "2" is the number of perceptual reality and often requires that a person develop the skills of observation, concentration, and the ability to focus her efforts. Sometimes, the "2" challenge requires one to deal with a sense of burden, disenchantment, alienation, and/or a sense of rootlessness. Particularly in younger life, there can be a tendency toward rambunctiousness and negotiable virtue.

Famous people with a "2" major challenge (9.3%)

Alexander Graham Bell, Barack Obama, Bill Clinton, Elvis Presley, Gertrude Stein, Harriet Beecher Stowe, Helen Keller, Henry Wadsworth Longfellow, Immanuel Kant, J. Robert Oppenheimer, Jackson Pollack, James Joyce, John Henry (Doc) Holliday, and Kahlil Gibran.

3: Movement, Focus & Creative Achievement

The "3" is the number of energy, ideas, movement, expansion, and sociability. The challenge of the "3" makes a person susceptible to getting stuck – mentally or emotionally. When the energy gets stuck, it can get buried as repressed desires and/or manifest as anger somewhere down the road. The "3" is usually about remembering not to take things too seriously, and remembering that movement and play will often help a person to make breakthroughs and open up to his or her "inner genius."

Alternately, the "3" can also be about absentmindedness, or a tendency toward wild living. In this case, the challenge is about learning to put down roots, focus, and not to scatter and dissipate one's energy in too many directions and activities at once.

The "3" also represents the challenge of creative achievement. It is about carrying and conveying ideas through the vehicles of language, art or science.

At a macroscopic level, it is the challenge of transformation that comes from giving roots to new ideas that then have a ripple effect through the joint consciousness that connects us all.

Famous people with a "3" major challenge (8.1%)

Alan Greenspan, Clare Booth Luce, David Bowie, Dietrich Bonhoeffer, Esther Williams, John F. Kennedy, John Galliano, John Kerry, Josef Stalin, Mikhail Gorbachev, Mordechai Richler, Simone de Beauvoir, William Shakespeare, and Winston Churchill.

4: Order, Control & Work

The challenge of the "4" is about learning to focus energy in a practical way to create something tangible. It is learning to create order in one's life, sometimes out of chaos.

This challenge often involves overcoming limitations, especially in the earlier years of life. There is a strong connection with feeling unloved early in life that can lead to issues such as jealousy and possessiveness. The "4" challenge sometimes has an important connection with the "father" in early years.

These early life factors can lead to a need to be in control. While control can manifest in positive ways such as independence and a strong work ethic, it can also show up as aggressive and bossy behaviors. The challenge of the "4" is to overcome these hurdles in a good way.

The "4" challenge is also about learning that "work is worship." In other words, where you put your efforts is important. Work is a way of serving. Work and service to others takes us higher. It is a way to ascend to a higher level of consciousness.

5: Divine Longing & Sustainable Freedom

The mystical meaning of the "5" is the merging of the infinite spiritual-intuitive realms with the personal emotional sphere of life. On a practical level, it brings "divine longing," a desire for freedom, and discomfort with boundaries and rules. Achieving a constructive and sustainable sense of freedom is the overall challenge. This requires adaptability, creativity, education, and making appropriate choices (e.g., choosing balance or imbalance).

The challenge of the "5" requires one to develop focus, and the ability to deal with the chaos that often comes with a highly creative nature. There is often a tendency to scatter personal energy in too many directions at once, including romantically.

The person with a "5" challenge must also confront ego issues and develop humility.

6: Relationships, Placement & Ancient Wisdom

"6" is the number of people, placement and polarities. The challenge of the "6" is about finding balance in relationships and responsibility, and finding one's place in the world. It is about stepping into a sense of personal power and confidence in one's own abilities.

The "6" challenge deals with polarities – the highest highs and lowest lows. Being off-balance with a "6" challenge can look like impatience, belligerence and volatility, indecision and being tongue-tied, having negative and/or codependent relationships, and a tendency toward duplicity. Most of these are covers for lacking confidence in one's own capabilities.

"6" is the number of people, public and society. People with a "6" challenge may have an empathic connection with others that can sometimes feel overwhelming and scary. The challenge is learning how to open one's heart to connect and work with people while still maintaining one's own center and sense of self. The "6" challenge also often deals with issues of forgiveness and reconciliation.

The "6" is the awakener, influencer and mentor. And, there is also a challenge of opening up to ancient wisdom that flows from the spiritual dimension into the heart – and then *using* it in some practical way on behalf of the whole.

Famous people with a "6" major challenge (8.0%)

Artur Rubenstein, Betty Friedan, Edward M. Kennedy, Elizabeth Barrett Browning, Fidel Castro, George W. Bush, Horace Greeley, Martin Luther King Jr., Mel Gibson, Michel de Nostredame, Mitt Romney, Oprah Winfrey, Sylvia Plath, and Warren Buffet.

7: Trust, Knowledge & Joy

The "7" challenge deals with being overly serious, idealistic and driven to become successful by worldly standards. It brings a tendency to be a little too linear, logical and precise. Balancing these tendencies is the major challenge of the "7."

There is a need to lighten up and allow joy into one's life. There is also the need to learn to trust – trust in oneself, trust in others, and trust in life. Ultimately, this kind of trust must come from developing a reverence for life, cultivating the innocence of "beginners mind," and the "teachability" that results. This leads to greater tolerance and respect for others and, ultimately, a more egalitarian worldview.

There is also another dimension to the "7" challenge that lies in the quest for knowledge. The "7" challenge brings a desire to explore the world and learn how things work at a fundamental level (sometimes

167

this becomes a need to know more than others). The challenge is not only the exploration and acquisition of knowledge – that's the fun part. The deeper challenge is to become a teacher and share with others the life experience and wisdom that is gained.

Lao Tsu could have been talking about the challenge of the "7" when he said, "Seek first to be the master of yourself, then Lord over all you see."

Famous people with a "7" major challenge (6.5%)

Aristotle Onassis, Calvin Coolidge, Charles A. Lindbergh, David Livingstone, Douglas MacArthur, Eduoard Manet, Francis Bacon, Isaac Newton, Leonardo da Vinci, John D. Rockefeller, Karl Marx, Paul Newman, Richard Nixon, Stephen Breyer, and Susan B. Anthony.

8: Love, Power & Letting Go

The challenge of the "8" energy can bring despair, heartache, weakness, feelings of helplessness, and the tendency to be fatalistic about life – especially in the earlier years of one's life. At its worst, its energy is like a tornado. It can bring conflict and upheaval, and be destructive.

This challenge often requires that a person let go of what no longer serves her so she can step into her full power. Conflict, upheaval, heartache and other life shocks are often the spur to forward movement, and the catalyst for healing and harmonizing the mental, emotional, physical and spiritual energies.

In traditional numerology, the challenge of the "8" is most often connected with "material mastery." I have also found this to be true, but in way that is different than normally thought. The world teaches that success in getting what you need comes from having the power to influence or control the people, resources and events necessary to achieve one's goals. At a fundamental level, this is not the essential truth. Abundance and prosperity really come from the Creator, the Source of all things. The deepest lesson of the "8" is that we are being carried by something that is much larger than us.

The "8" challenge is in learning that true generative power comes from love. Learning this requires a radical surrender to one's Higher Power by which I mean the conscious merging of the self with the larger Universal Will. From this connected state of consciousness, a person can act with confidence and spontaneity knowing that he or she is *always* supported and carried.

This doesn't mean becoming airy-fairy and ungrounded. On the contrary, it means shifting out of ego-mind to act on inspiration in a practical way while pulling up above the daily dramas to know that everyone is carried by a loving power that always acts in one's best interests and for one's highest good. Yet, this is difficult work. It is no small, easy feat to get the ego and ego-based fears out of the way – especially when the world teaches us that this is craziness.

Famous people with a "8" major challenge (5.8%)

Jeanne Lane Pehrson (Jeanne White Eagle), Joseph Stalin, Lyndon B. Johnson, Marcus Tulius Cicero, Mohandas K. Gandhi, Robert Motherwell, Nicolaus Copernicus, Tenzin Gyatso (H. H. the Dalai Lama), Thomas Jefferson, William James, and Wolfgang Amadeus Mozart.

9: Caretaker, Gratitude, Drive for Wholeness

The "9" challenge is to remember that personal power will ultimately come from working for the benefit of others. The "9" is the challenge to be a compassionate executive, caretaker and/or diplomat who has everyone's best interests at heart while not losing oneself in the process. There needs to be a balance between giving and receiving. There is a danger of defining oneself in terms of taking care of other people's needs, including the needs of a group, or even the needs of the nation. This can happen for purely altruistic reasons, but can also stem from neediness born of a desire to be liked and respected.

Another aspect of the "9" challenge is learning to meet life's challenges with an awareness of one's blessings and an attitude of thankfulness and gratitude. The "9" challenge often brings things back around to be processed – mentally, emotionally, physically and spiritually – and then released. Old friends may come back into your life, and old dreams, old memories, or old actions taken may come up for review. If this is not always comfortable, the learning this prompts is often beneficial for establishing a new foundation for the future.

Intrinsic to the "9" challenge is also the importance of a loving and supportive family and community. The Mayan correspondence with the "9" is called Kawoq, and is about home, hearth and family. The influence we have in the world begins with the family and ripples outward to the community, society, the nation and beyond.

Famous people with a "9" major challenge (5.3%)

Abraham Lincoln, Charles Darwin, D. H. Lawrence, Edward Teller, Edwin (Buzz) Aldrin, Marian Wright Edelman, Max Plank, Oliver Wendell Holmes Jr., Ronald Reagan, William Jennings Bryan, Yukteswar Giri (guru of Yogananda), and Yves Saint Laurent.

10: Mastery, Pioneer, Gatekeeper

The "10" as a challenge is about mastery and wisdom. It is the challenge of the seeker of meaning and the need to understand. It challenges a person to push the boundaries and be a pioneer in his or her chosen field. It requires developing a strong sense of self-confidence – and even idealism – to be able to step fully into one's power. It also requires taking personal responsibility and learning to finish what one starts. The path to mastery often entails a period of personal struggle and self-doubt. It seems to be the way of things.

In walking the path of mastery, people with a "10" challenge develop the ability to set the direction for others. They make good counselors, can be decisive and practical, and have an ability to manifest abundance in their lives. They can be energizers and organizers – people you might call movers and shakers.

These people are gatekeepers between the manifest world we perceive as objective reality and the unseen unity of the spirit world. Their challenge on a spiritual level is to become aware of this, and integrate it into their understanding and actions. This is not an easy task since it means swimming upstream against the current of the prevailing worldview. However, if and when people with the "10" challenge learn to bridge the practical and spiritual realms, they can become ceremonial leaders, and step into the role of cultural leadership.

The darker side of the "10" challenge has to do with arrogance, egotism and the abuse of power. The people experiencing this side of the challenge exhibit one-sidedness in their thinking, and tend to polarize people in their sphere of influence. They can be crisis-mongers who feed off the energy of worry, anguish and struggle.

Famous people with a "10" major challenge (4.8%)

A. E. Houseman, Donald Rumsfeld, Howard Hughes, J. Edgar Hoover, James Dean, Joseph Rael (Beautiful Painted Arrow), Karl Wallenda, Rush Limbaugh, Ruth Bader Ginsberg, Thomas Johnathan (Stonewall) Jackson, Tony Blair, and Virginia Woolf.

11: Intuition, Change Agent, the Unexpected

The "11" brings a two-pronged challenge. First, it requires opening to receive a higher level of spiritual and psychic energy. Second, it requires one to develop the ability to handle the energy and insights without being overwhelmed.

This energy comes through in the form of intuitive information, guidance, poetic imagination, dreams, visions and brilliant flashes of sudden understanding. It can prompt one to become a cultivator of innovative new ideas, an entrepreneur, a reformer or agent for change, a healer, emancipator, musician, or a teacher. People with this challenge can be involved in creating a critical mass for change.

This high-energy challenge comes with a price. First, it is the number of shifts and changes. One who has this challenge must become adaptable, stay flexible and learn to expect the unexpected.

Second, it can *possibly* lead to being overwhelmed by intuitive insights, visions and guidance. A sense of psychic, cognitive and emotional overload can result. The challenge is to not become unfocused, disorganized, changeable and indecisive, or adopt self-destructive, compulsive or belligerent behaviors in order to shut off the flow of insights and visions.

Famous people with a "11" major challenge (5.3%)

Benjamin Franklin, Betty White, Claude Levi-Strauss, Edna St. Vincent Millay, Ernesto "Che" Guevara, Harry S. Truman, Herbert Hoover, John Hancock, John L. Lewis, Michael Bloomberg, Mikhail Baryshnikov, Somerset Maugham, and Vera Maria Rosenberg.

12: Creative Forces, Innovation, Service

The "12" is Divine power that opens a gateway to spiritual intelligence and the creative forces of the universe. It is the high and sometimes explosive energy behind mass awakening, world-changing ideas, and issues dealing with the social order and the larger whole such as social justice.

It is a visionary energy, and as a personal challenge number it can light a person up like a Christmas tree. So, the first inherent challenge is learning to harness the amount of energy that it brings. This often requires a person to get clear on his or her life's purpose, not always an easy task in itself – especially during the formative years.

The "12" challenge is to channel this energy to move in new directions, become an initiator of new ideas and innovations, be a passionate crusader for causes, and one who drives energetically forward to achieve success in one's chosen field. People with a "12" challenge are generally not shrinking violets. They have the power and strength to be a leader, and can be uninhibited and fearless risk-takers.

The "12" also challenges a person to be concerned with uplifting the human spirit, and involved in service to others. People with this challenge may make good strategists, business people, arbitrators, therapists and body-workers, and can be involved in peacemaking activities.

The "12" energy can be intense and sometimes explosive. So, people with a "12" challenge need to allow themselves to be carefree and playful once in a while. They need to guard against extremism, rebelliousness, or being moralistic and self-righteous. This challenge can also cause a person to deal with a need for control, and confront issues of self-importance, excessive individuation and a tendency to be manipulative.

Famous people with a "12" major challenge (5.4%)

Anton Chekhov, Carl Sandburg, Eleanor Holmes Norton, Giulio Andreotti, J. Pierpont Morgan, Joe Frazer, Johann Sebastian Bach, Paulina Porizkova, Sarah Palin, Walt Whitman, William Butler Yeats, William Tecumseh Sherman, and Woodrow Wilson.

13: The Present, Choice Points, Community

"13" is the *now moment*. It is the energy of life experienced in the pure present. The "13" challenges us to stay present in the here-and-now. This is where the magic is. It is the nexus point for all of the energy and information that flows into the world, and thus brings intuitive insights and revelations, and the ability to move beyond constraints to think outside the box. The here-and-now is also the launching pad for concrete action, the place of readiness to move in any direction, and the place of personal change.

The "13" challenge urges one forward to do something practical, to build something tangible and lasting in the *real* world. People with a "13" challenge often become goal-oriented, independent, develop persistence, and become authorities in their chosen field.

The present moment is like a pivot around which life turns. So, it is the place of change points, of endings and beginnings. The "13" challenge is also to recognize when one door is closing and another is opening, and then doing the work to release the old and embrace the new. Morrie Swartz summed this challenge up nicely when he said: "Don't hold on too long, but don't let go too soon. Find a balance."

Note that "13" is also the trickster. So, inherent in the "13" challenge is maintaining a sense of humor when it appears that life is throwing a few curve balls.

"13" represents the community, the fabric of society. It is the will to connect. It is also the need to agree, and finding the middle ground that leads to joint solutions. The challenge is to reach out, be a volunteer, be active in the community and help promote social harmony. People with a "13" challenge may also play the role of catalyst for others going through personal change.

Those with a "13" challenge need to guard against being directionless and pessimistic. There is a danger of becoming codependent, an underachiever, and adopting an attitude that life is meaningless.

Famous people with a "13" major challenge (2.7%)

Dr. Albert Schweitzer, Andres Segovia, Boris Berezovsky, Howard Stern, James A. Garfield, James Monroe, Jean-Marie Roland, Jeffrey Katzenberg, Lawrence Oates, Muhammad Ali, Robert Burns, and Robert E. Lee.

14: Connectedness, Harvesting, Dramas

The "14" is the energy of connectedness and cooperativity. It also represents the genetic memory carried in our cells. It is fertility and growth, but also the harvest. It brings the power to connect with people, and to draw to yourself whatever you desire – including abundance and fame. Therefore, the challenge is to be open fully to receive the fruits of your efforts. This is not as easy as it might sound since we are taught that goods and services are scarce, and we live in a survival-of-the-fittest world.

"14" represents possibilities and propagation, but also objectivity, and organization. It brings a challenge to take pragmatic action to achieve individual excellence, and make the world a better place. Indeed, "14" is the energy of the humanitarian and of peace – perhaps because it is the ability to deal with apparent opposites – e.g., dealing with potential possibilities while using objective judgment and taking pragmatic action.

The "14" challenges a person to accept responsibility for these abilities and step up to the plate as a humanitarian, peacemaker and translator of ideas. It also is the challenge to maintain a higher perspective and not get caught up in the web of everyday dramas such as relationships, marital strife, family bickering, money issues, politics in the work place, and on and on ad nauseum.

People with a "14" challenge need to guard against pessimism, judgmentalism and dogmatism. This challenge can bring heartbreak, separation and social isolation. One may also have to confront issues of incompatibility, marital discord and manipulative relationships. This challenge may also make one inclined toward drivenness, controlling behaviors, and a little craziness – as in marching to a different drummer.

Famous people with a 14 major challenge (1.8%)

Alfred North Whitehead, Lord George Lyttelton, Grover Cleveland, James Watt, Janis Joplin, Kirstie Alley, Lou Diamond Phillips, Mack Sennett, Nelson A. Rockefeller, Patricia Neal, and Sophie Tucker.

15: Practicality, Follow-Through, Centeredness

"15" is the number of functionality, practical utility and tangible results. It brings a challenge to develop the fixity of purpose and follow-though to get things done. It is the challenge of overcoming creative doubt, inattentiveness or an inclination toward wishy-washiness to become steadfast in one's beliefs, work, relationships, and the support given to others – even against social pressure, tradition or fears about reputation. These are characteristics that can make one a good businessman, businesswoman, or judge. Truthfully, learning to work with unbending intent is very beneficial to most professions, including for writers and musicians.

"15" is the number of social interaction and the sense of belonging. For the person with the "15" challenge, the need for social connection is present, but the ability to be an extravert, optimist and consensus builder may need to be cultivated over time.

People with the "15" challenge can be too direct, and may have a tendency to run people over. They may need to learn to balance being plainspoken enough to say what is on their mind with the politeness that allows them to be heard. As these lessons are learned and integrated, people with a "15" challenge can be fun, and good with jokes and comedy.

"15" brings psychic abilities and the ability to heal. The challenge is centeredness. The person with the "15" challenge must learn not to allow psychic sensitivity to nonphysical information pull him or her off-balance. Rather, they need to learn to utilize this sensitivity for the benefit of others.

175

People with a "15" challenge are prone to inattentiveness, fragmentation, and creative blocks. They need to guard against becoming overly-analytical, cynical, resentful and socially isolated.

There is also a danger of feeling a chronic sense of apprehension that can lead to a mindset that life is pointless.

Famous people with a "15" major challenge (2.0%)

Andrew Jackson, Booker T. Washington, Colin Powell, David Lloyd George, Edgar Allan Poe, George Frederick Handel, Georges Bernanos, Jeffrey Immelt, Jim Carey, Konstantin Stanislavski, Naomi Judd, and Viktor Shauberger.

16: Collective Mind, Instincts, Fundamental Change

The "16" energy is tied to the collective mind and brings a heightened sensitivity to collective energetic shifts. It is a pipeline to ancestral wisdom – particularly from the grandmothers. It brings a strong mind coupled with instinctive knowing, natural aptitude and ability. The challenge is how to use this energy.

The positive side of the "16" challenge inclines a person toward discipline and hard work, a grounded wisdom, and an underlying trust in life. It is a coherent, propulsive energy that has the power to manifest one's intentions, or make significant shifts in the physical world. It challenges a person to cultivate positive thought patterns, good intentions, and the awareness that what he holds in his mind is what will be created.

People with a "16" challenge must learn to be adaptable. They carry the energy to be a shapeshifter, which is to say the energy to be culturally mobile and adaptable to one's environment and life situation. The "16" challenge can urge one forward to discover new possibilities, seek out new growth, and promote fundamental change.

This is not an easy challenge to carry. It can even blow the ego apart. Thus, in traditional Tarot decks, it is called the "Blasted Tower." The challenge is to live up to the potential of this power without being drawn into the shadow side, which may come from the unknowing sensitivity to chaotic and unsettling shifts in the mass consciousness.

It can make a person feel constricted and uncommunicative or, alternately, moody and prone to acting out. It can show up as surliness, testiness, and thoughtless, unsympathetic or biting remarks – even dirty tricks. These behaviors are an attempt to anesthetize the feelings that can include emptiness and a fear of being useless.

The person with a "16" challenge would do well to avoid alcohol because drunkenness is also one of the shadow aspects.

Famous people with a "16" major challenge (2.3%)

August Strindberg, Babe Ruth, Daniel Webster, Eartha Kitt, Eudora Alice Welty, Jacob Bronowski, Jack London, James Madison, Jean Baptiste Moliere, Max Eastman, Paul Keating, Robinson Jeffers, Rob Lowe, and Savielly Tartakower.

17: Transformer, Understanding, Entanglements

"17" is the number of the zero-point field, the energy matrix that fuels your DNA, your heart, and all of life. It represents the titanic power of unconditional love that is available to everyone. Illumined adepts know how to use this power to fuel psychokinetic abilities and magic. This same power is behind the striking process of metamorphosis that turns a caterpillar into a butterfly.

On a practical level, the "17" challenge is to be a transformer – in both senses of the word. A transformer transfers electrical energy from one circuit to another, generally to step down the energy for practical household use. Just so, the person with this challenge takes the energy of unconditional love and makes it available to others on a practical level through their work and daily actions.

In the other sense of the word, the "17" brings a challenge to transform the world and change it for the better – a process that necessarily begins with oneself. "17" is the energy of pure being, and it forces one to see beyond appearances to the essence of things. Thus people with a "17" challenge often acquire deep self-knowledge and can help others do the same.

The "17" challenges a person to take positive action and do something enterprising – especially in ways that create understanding and foster self-realization. This can include working through artistic ability, dialogue and group processes, empirical research, business planning, various healing modalities, public relations, social activism, and so on. The "17" challenges a person to get involved and engage with people in pursuit of the deepest truths. It dares one to see beauty in the world – and then to act from that place.

The person with a "17" challenge needs to guard against entanglements, and getting caught in a narrowness of thinking that is, basically, an avoidance strategy.

Not addressing misunderstandings when they arise, putting on airs, becoming ostentatious and addicted to the game of acquiring more and more *things* are other ways of pushing away the deeper exploration into self and the world.

Famous people with a "17" major challenge (2.0%)

Alice Paul, Bill Maher, Sir Compton Mackenzie, Dolly Parton, Galileo Galilei, Geena Davis, Julian Barnes, Malcolm McLaren, Nikita Krushchev, Rudolf Nureyev, Steve Earl, Sylvia Pankhurst, and Vidal Sassoon, and (Hedwig) Vicki Baum.

18: Planting Seeds, Hope, Nurturing Growth

The "18" is the elemental power of the creative world that is encoded in the DNA and carried in an embryo or seed out of which grows the mature flower, fruit, animal or person. To paraphrase William Blake[12], "18" is the archetypal energy of the world in the seed, and eternity in the hour.

The challenge of the "18" is to plant seeds, and to cultivate and nurture things in their early phases of growth – ideas, projects, businesses, children, relationships, plants, animals, and so on. It is also a challenge to create hope through one's actions or one's work, and to help others find their way by expanding and illuminating the path forward. This is not a common challenge. Only one in a hundred carry it.

---

[12] See the poem *Auguries of Innocence* by William Blake; written in 1803 but not published until 1863 (which is, interestingly, an "18" year!).

This challenge generally comes with persistence, resourcefulness, mental acuity and, sometimes, an insatiable curiosity. People who carry it are generally affable, have a highly developed sense of fairness, and are often concerned with mental and emotional well-being of others (and sometimes of themselves). They often work within the establishment while pushing against its boundaries. Indeed, there is an innate ability to stand firm against the current of the mainstream worldview in order to show others the way.

People with an "18" challenge need to guard against fear and mistrustfulness. This can lead to behaviors that include stubbornness, moral absolutism and an intransigent attitude that can be abrasive, coercive, fiery and damaging to both self and others. At the other end of the spectrum, there is a challenge of not being too meek. There needs to be a balance.

Famous people with a "18" major challenge (1.0%)

Albert Einstein, Jane Horrocks, Jennifer Love Hewitt, Kevin Costner, Oliver Hardy, Paul Cezanne, and William Lamb Melbourne.

19: Authority, Duty, Vices

"19" is about power issues, and the challenge is to choose whom you serve: yourself, or a Higher Power or authority. Closely connected to this is the challenge of duty, which is to say faithfully performing one's moral or legal obligations, tasks, or services, particularly those arising from one's position in life.

This challenge includes finding the appropriate balance between duty and personal freedom, and between respect for authority and one's individual self-interest. It is neither desirable nor healthy to have a rigid sense of duty that continually forces one's nose to the grindstone, or to have an overly-strict adherence to authority or creed. As Albert Einstein once said, "Blind belief in authority is the greatest enemy of truth." Of course, neither is it healthy to be too much the rebel or iconoclast.

People with the "19" challenge have the ability to become a guru, an authority or official of some sort. And, ironically, this sometimes occurs as a result of success in their chosen field, and despite whatever previous contempt they may have had for authority on the way to their success.

The "19" challenge includes discriminating between urges that are beneficial and uplifting and those that lead to vices, and negative or addictive behaviors. Other challenges include being over-eager or over-candid. There can be a tendency to argue and even to be a bit of a bully. The person with a "19" challenge also needs to guard against phobias and exaggerated fears.

Famous people with a "19" major challenge (0.7%)

Carl Laemmle, Dave Attell, Frank Hague, and Mick (Michael Kevin) Taylor.

20: Void, Hero's Journey, Laughter

"20" is the energy of the void that is pregnant with potential possibilities. Within this no-place is a great treasure, but entering the void to claim it can be a scary thing. This is the hero's journey. People with a "20" challenge are called to take it at some point in their lives, and meet their fate head-on. This often requires developing the qualities of audacity and fierceness, and an understanding of how to use their inner force to achieve external goals. They may have an inclination for defiance against authority, but this is not always a bad thing.

The challenge of the "20" includes sometimes feeling blocked, in doubt, alone and in limbo. These people can be a target for blame and derision, but also need to guard against blaming others for their life's problems. They need a good emotional support structure because they are, at the extreme, candidates for suicide. This is one of the reasons they need to develop a fierce determination to meet life head-on.

People with this challenge can be over-analytical and linear. They need to learn to lighten up and laugh, be joyful and amiable, and remember their inner child.

Famous people with a "20" major challenge (0.5%)

Andy Kaufman, George Burns, Humphrey Bogart, (Arthur Annesley) Ronald Firbank.

21: Guidance, Courage, Money, Grace

This number represents guidance, courage, grace and money. The challenge of the "21" is to have the courage to show up and keep following inner guidance, keep saying "yes." It is the challenge to stay open, and allow oneself to play – a very creative state. Staying open also means allowing the energy of grace to carry you, something magical that can happen when invited.

"21" is connected with aging, staying engaged in the world, and continuing to educate yourself and others. The "21" can also be about having the courage to defend your ideas.

There may also be a challenge acquiring or dealing with money – including gambling and a tendency toward decadence. *Play* and *money* are both connected to the "21" energy, so there is a need to find the appropriate balance between the two.

Judicial proceedings, going to court, can also be part of the "21" challenge.

Famous people with a "21" major challenge (0.4%)

Alexander Humphreys Woollcott, Susanna Hoffs, and Ronald Arbuthnott Knox.

22: Union, Succeed, Giving Back

Only one person in a thousand carries this challenge, making it the rarest. "22" is the energy that draws things to the center and holds them together. It is union, the ability to cohere but also to mold or give shape to things. It is the energy to reach and succeed. It has a natural ability to give advice, and guard what is important.

The challenge becomes how to step into this role of one who creates union, helps to shape and give context to things. It is also the challenge to open up to the success and riches that life brings, and then give something back.

The other side of this challenge is defined by the flip side of those qualities described above. The person with the "22" challenge needs to guard against being greedy and inclined to deceive others, and falling victim to hate and bigotry. Alternately, one may face the challenge of shutting down and becoming emotionally numb.

People with a "22" challenge can offend others, sometimes unintentionally because of a playful earthiness. Indeed, there can be a tendency to be a bit of an imbecile and pursue inane follies on a lark. This challenge can also lead one to be bawdy by which I mean being a playboy or party girl and having multiple affairs (especially when young).

Famous people with a "22" major challenge (0.1%)

Baron Charles de Montesquieu.

Chapter Ten:

Number Meanings: Going Deeper

All is numbers.

~Pythagoras~

The basic number meanings given in the charts on pages 56–59 are a good start. They give the *essence* of each number. As such, they are relatively simple and a wonderful aid to learning and working with the power of the numbers. As we have seen, these basic interpretations can be adapted to provide insight on Life Purpose, Life Path, Attainments, Challenges, and more.

However, each number is really more complex, and there are multiple dimensions that are not covered in the simple distillation on pages 56–59. In this chapter, I will take you on a journey of exploration to show you the deeper layers of meaning for each number. It is meant to be a reference for you to refer to over and over. Actually, I know of no other book on traditional numerology that delves as deeply into the multiple meanings of the numbers – including the negative or shadow qualities normally not given.

The discussion for each number begins by showing its place on the Native American Medicine Wheel map (see Appendix A). Each number is the connection between two of the seven cardinal directions – East, South, West, North, Above, Below and Center – and the vowel sounds that represent those directions. These vowel sounds can be chanted or sung[13] to get more information about the number in question, something especially good to do if you are seeking additional clarity about your Life Purpose or Life Path number.

To make sure this is clear, the *sound* for each individual number comes from its place on the Medicine Wheel map (Appendix A), and not the actual vowel sounds in the word we use for that number. For example, consider the number "1." "1" is the number that connects the God-Source/Center (U) with the spiritual-intuitive realm of the North (O). Using the sound of the U and O as pronounced in Spanish (or Hebrew), the chant for the number "1" is "uu-oh." Its place on the Medicine Wheel remains the same whether we call this number *one* (English), *uno* (Spanish), *ein* (German), *echadh* (Hebrew), or *odin* (Russian).

Science has recognized that the electron that whizzes around the nucleus of an atom really exists as a cloud of probabilities. Our reality is built from many atoms coming together with their individual cloud of probabilities, so it should not be a surprise that there is also a cloud of possible meanings for each number across the spectrum from mystical to mundane, from light to shadow, and positive to negative. I've shown this cloud of meaning for each number as a grouping of Keywords, each of which comes out of my research to redefine the number meanings.[14]

For each number, I have included an expanded list of Keywords that are grouped into four different categories: Mystical, Collective, Positive and Negative/Shadow keyword associations. Each of the keywords comes from my research into the number value of words where I calculated the Purpose number of over 25,000 words and short meaningful phrases (e.g., *need to connect, logical mind, organizing power*, etc.) and sorted them by the numbers 1 – 22. The keywords shown for each number are the result of that research.

---

[13] Creating a spontaneous melody or song using the vowel sounds that represent the number is a wonderful way to gain added insight and clarity. Try it!

[14] Each Keyword has the numerical value of the number that it helps to define. For instance, all the words shown for the number six have "6" as their reduced value (e.g., 6, 24/6, 33/6, 42/6, 51/6, 60/6, and so on).

To be more specific, each of the keywords shown for the number 9 has a reduced value of "9" for its Purpose number (the sum of the consonant values). This is similarly true for all the other numbers with the exception of the 1 and 2. Because there are so few numbers that have an actual reduced Purpose number of 1 or 2, I have reduced some "10" words to a "1" (1+0 = 1) where they fit the meaning of the "1" – words like *mother, creator, genesis,* and *psychic.* In a similar way, I have reduced some "11" words to a "2" (1+1 = 2) where they helped to define the meaning of the "2" – such as *equilibrium, measurability, observation, physical reality* and *relationship.*

You will also note that when you get to the numbers 18 – 22, there are less Keyword associations and, especially noticeable, there is a scarcity of keywords around totem animals, powers, colors, gemstones, science-related fields and work areas/associations. This is not because these numbers are in any way more limited and less important. It is simply because there are less English words that add to those numbers.

The *negative qualities* of the numbers are not generally talked about in books on numerology. I believe this is short-sighted. Our perceived reality is strung on the loom of polarities: positive/negative, up/down, hot/cold, good/bad, white/black, light/dark – you get the point. Each number also has both positive and negative poles: an upside or light side, and a downside or shadow side. You may notice that the dark or negative qualities of the numbers are often the flip-side or opposites of the positive ones. This is in no way something that was planned in advance. It just came out that way in the research. In addition, you might find that the numbers that shine the brightest often have the darkest shadow.

Our personal numbers, such as our Life Purpose and Path, have the potential for good or ill depending upon our worldview, our approach to life and the actions that we choose to take in response to the events in our life. So, although the majority of books on traditional numerology do not cover the shadow aspects of the numbers, I believe it is important to know what is lurking in our shadow in order to bring it into the light. This is part of what makes our free will so powerful. An understanding of both sides is important. It helps us not only be fully informed, but also helps to maintain balance in life.

For each number, the Keywords are followed by an in-depth discussion of the number meaning in several different contexts:

- As a Personal Number: Purpose, Path, Drive, Legacy, and so on;

- An expanded description of the Mayan archetypal energies that are associated with each number;

- An exercise that explains how chanting the vowel sounds that represent each number can be helpful.

- Each number's connection with totem animals, recognized deities and powers, colors, gemstones, science aspects, and the work-related areas and associations[15] that are in harmony with each number.

- Famous historical figures that have each individual number for their Purpose, Path, Legacy or Drive Number and the frequency of its occurrence.

In short, you will find a lot of valuable information given in this section that is supported by fundamental research, and that you cannot find in any other book on numerology. When you are working with the Mystical Numerology of names and dates, you will find it to be a rich treasure trove of information that will provide many deep insights about yourself and about friends, family members, coworkers, acquaintances, celebrities and other famous people. Enjoy!

---

[15] Remember, in addition to the Purpose and Path numbers, the last name (Legacy Number) often has an important connection with the work or career that a person chooses.

Expanded Number Meanings & Associations

1 (B): **Creator, Potential, Selfhood**   <u>Chant</u>: uu – oh

Medicine Wheel Path: Center/God-Source ⇒ North/Spiritual Dimension.

Mystical Keywords: Creator, I AM, Cosmogenesis, Archetypal World, Inter-Dimensional   …   Absoluteness,   Undifferentiated   … Superconscious   …   Inner   Awareness,   Clairvoyance,   Psychic, Channeling … Out-of-Body Experience (OBE), Supernatural.

Positive Keywords: Potential, Creative Principle, Spiritual Drive … Breath … Birth, Genesis, Mother, Egg, Planting … Sentience … Gnosis, Knowing … Be, Silence, Inward, Meditative State … Instinctual Unconscious … Innocence, Childlike, Newborn, Wonder … Self, Selfhood … Self-Interest, Self-Regard, Self-Reliance … Moral Sensibility … Innovate, Invent, Originality … Suddenness.

Negative/Shadow   Keywords: Maya,   Dark   Energy   … Incomprehensible, Phantom, Undifferentiated, Vacant … Ignoramus … Wretchedness, Prostitution … Strong-Willed, Obey … Self-Interest, Self-Flagellation, Self-Inflicted … Squeamishness, Suppressive … Cataclysmic Event.

As a Personal Number: "1" is the impulse from the God-Source that connects with the spiritual-intuitive dimension of life. It is the archetypal world that arises out of this connection and exists beyond both space and time. "1" is the Creator, the "I AM," absoluteness, the incomprehensible, zero-point energy, the undifferentiated pre-space out of which the material world and our reality is born. Having the "1" as a personal number is linked to having a strong spiritual drive.

As a personal number, the "1" gives a natural connection to the supernatural   world,   out-of-body   experiences,   psychic   energy, clairvoyance, channeling, or what is called *second sight* in the vernacular. With the "1" energy, insights may come with suddenness like a flash of lightning out of the blue, giving the ability to know without knowing how you know.

"1" is the Mother principle, the egg or ovum, the processes of genesis, planting, and birth. It is the creative principle, the quality of originality, and the power to innovate and invent. So, people with "1" as a personal vibration tend to be innovative and original. Other "1" qualities include childlike innocence and a capacity to see the wonder in life.

"1" is the number of birth, the newborn and the sunrise. People with "1" as a personal number will often be involved in the beginning phase of things: new ideas, nurturing newborn children, cultivating plants in their seed phase, or the initial startup phase of new projects or ventures.

"1" also represents the "self," selfhood and those qualities linked to the self and the individuation process such as developing self-reliance and self-regard. In addition to a positive self-interest, these are the qualities that enable a person to stand on his/her own two feet and make his or her way in the world.

Downside: The shadow side of the "1" energy is "maya:" the sense-world phenomena that conceals the unity of absolute being, separating us from the divine – in other words, illusion. It also could be described as those things that are incomprehensible or un-figure-outable.

As a personal number, the shadow side of the "1" can be a vibration that separates by bringing an unhealthy focus on self-interest, a "me first" attitude. It can create a strong-willed nature that seeks to suppress the free will and originality of other people. Alternately, it can cause an internalization and drawing within that results in self-flagellation and self-inflicted misery.

Note

Having a "1" for a personal number is rare but there are examples. For instance, Abraham Lincoln was commonly known as Abe. "Abe" is a "1," and his life exemplified some of its characteristics. For instance, he was involved in the birth of the Republican Party, and became its first president in 1860. He was known as "Honest Abe," had a strong sense of moral sensibility, and had an unpretentious persona of trusting innocence. Lincoln was swept along by the cataclysmic events that led to the American Civil War, was known to have precognitive dreams, and was also a victim of the suddenness of his own death by assassination. All of these are aspects of the "1."

The other way a person may have the "1" as a personal number is as a Drive Number (sum of all the consonant values in one's name). My name, John Brady Pehrson, is an example. The consonants sum to 100/1. Over the years, I have been involved in many different start-ups. I am often better at starting things than finishing them. Of course, giving birth to this new system of Mystical Numerology is also an example of the "1" energy.

Mayan Connection

The "1" is connected to "Batz," the "Thread" that connects past, present and future. Batz is the Creator and start of life. It represents infinite time and unity, and it presides over the future. This sign symbolizes cosmic phenomena and original wisdom.

Exercise

Chant or sing[16] *uu – oh,* the sounds for the "1," as a meditation to open yourself up for insight on a psychic level, and become a channel for new ideas and creations.

Famous "1" People

Purpose (0.1%): Abe Lincoln.

Drive (1.3%): Alberto Gonzales, Benjamin Harrison, Ernestine Ulmer, Floyd Patterson, Harry S. Truman, Yevgeny Zemyatin.

Totem Animals: Bee, dragonfly.

Deities: Jesus.

Powers: Breath, Bringers of Light, Sunrise.

Colors: alabaster, colorless ... silver ... mushroom, tortoiseshell.

---

[16] Sing the vowel sounds while making up a spontaneous melody. You can also chant or sing *silently* by hearing the sounds in your mind. Try it!

Gemstone: aragonite.

Science-related: cosmogenesis, quantum physics, mystical science ... baryonic dark matter, subatomic matter ... information field, zero-point ... electrical circuitry, electric current, geomagnetic activity ... perpetual motion.

Work-related Areas/Associations: mind reader, psychic, trance channel ... writing craft ... apprenticeship, drag queen, exterminator, fire department, free enterprise, Internet education, neuroscientist, research chemist, seamstress, social philosopher, traditionalist.

2 (C): Problem Solver, Organizing Power, Relationship

Chant: uu – iii.

Medicine Wheel Path: Center/God-Source ⇒ West/Physical Dimension.

Mystical Keywords: All Possibilities, Infinite Possibility ... Astral Travel, Ancient Mysteries, Mystical Experience ... Perfect Knowing, Perfect Communication ... Perceptual Reality, Physical Universe, Womb, Living Matrix ... Global Consciousness, Master Program.

Collective Keywords: Relationship ... Cooperative Social Glue, Collective Consent, Equality ... Ecological Sustainability; (-) Social Stress ... Mob, Psychological Warfare ... Religious Fanaticism.

Positive Keywords: ... Now, Pivotal Moment ... Forward-Thinking ... Conscious Intention, Mental Trial Run ... Observe, Observation, Concentration, Conscious Intent, Quiet Determination ... Self-Awareness ... Fathering, Masculine, Problem-Solver ... Organizing Power, Well-Established ... Reconcile, Equilibrium, Unselfishness, Need to Take Turns ... Sponsorship, Steadfastness ... Count, Possession, Acquire, Own ... Boundary, Security, Personal Justice.

Negative/Shadow Keywords: Alienation, Rootlessness, Paralysis, Captive ... Disruptive Change, Irrational Impulse, Rambunctiousness ... Burden, Dense, Fundamental Problem ... Alienation, Disguise, Disenchantment, Incompleteness, Lonely, Self-Pity, Vacuum ...

Friction, Adversary, Ill-Treatment, Invasiveness ... Misogynistic ... Bottomless Pit, Pestilence ... Forfeit, Exit Strategy.

As a Personal Number: "2" is the impulse from the God-Source into the physical dimension. It is the master program that defines perceptual reality, the womb and living matrix for all potential possibilities. It is the pivotal "now" moment around which both past and future revolve. It is in this "now" moment that the "self" enters into the physical nature of perceptual reality and becomes self-aware. At this stage, the self still has access to perfect knowing, and thus the "2" represents the ancient mysteries, mystical experience and connection with global consciousness.

The organizing power and problem-solving ability of the "2" nature flows from this powerful connection with all potential possibilities. People with a "2" as a personal number carry these abilities, often with quiet determination. They generally have well-developed powers of observation and concentration.

As the "2" is the impulse to enter into the physical world, it is also connected with the need to acquire and own things, and have possessions. This, in turn, is connected with the need to set boundaries, have security, and the desire for personal justice and equality. People who have "2" as a personal number are often adept at setting appropriate boundaries and defining systems.

The "2" defines the realm of human relationships because once there are two we have the possibility for relationship. "2" as a personal number brings a need to share with others, and a desire to create equilibrium. The "2" person often has a generous, unselfish nature and the quality of steadfastness in relationships. "2" is the number of sponsorship, collective consent, and is the cooperative social glue that holds things together. People with "2" as a personal number may be good workshop or process facilitators.

You will note that the keywords for the "2" include making mental trial runs. "2" is actually a *physical* number. It is intriguing to me that picturing something in your mind the way you want it to occur shows up. I find it a confirmation of the old Edgar Cayce aphorism, "Mind is the Builder, the physical is the result." In other words, making mental trial runs helps to manifest what is visualized into the physical realm.

As I thought more about this, I remembered that "University of London physicist David Bohm, a former protégé of Einstein's and one of the world's most respected quantum physicists, and Stanford neurophysiologist Karl Pribram, one of the architects of our modern understanding of the brain – believe that the universe itself may be a giant hologram."[17] A unique characteristic of the hologram is that the whole is contained within each part. By extension, our mind and its mental function cannot be localized and limited to only our brains. Rather, what we call the *mind* is distributed throughout the cellular structure of our bodies. We think as much with our bodies as we do with our brains – a provocative idea. And, whatever we think about and visualize with conscious intention helps to make it a reality.

Downside: As much as the positive side of the "2" is about relationship and how our individual lives interpenetrate with others, the shadow side of the "2" can feel like being isolated and in a vacuum. It is characterized by alienation, incompleteness, rootlessness, and loneliness. It can feel dense like a heavy burden to carry, and result in self-pity and paralysis.

The positive side looks like calm concentration, but the flip-side is rambunctiousness and irrational impulses. It is the number of the adversary, and is represented by friction, invasiveness, and social stress. At its darkest, the collective shadow of the "2" is the mob mentality which, if you think about it, is not too different from religious fanaticism, another of its dark aspects.

Mayan Connection

"2" is connected with the Mayan energy "E" (pronounced "Eh") representing the spiritual path, the sacred way. It is the path of destiny, the path that a person walks, and the road of life. It is the second step in creation, creative action, where the infinite path of time finds a space in which to manifest. "E" is the energy of travel, and of facilitators and bringers of news – especially from far away.

---

[17] Michael Talbot, *The Holographic Universe*, ISBN 0-06-092258-3 - HarperCollins, 1991

Exercise

Chant or sing *uu – iii,* the sound of the "2," when you need to enhance your ability to concentrate; or when you need to find the solution to a difficult problem. You will also find this to be physically strengthening.

Famous "2" People

Purpose (0.5%): Abba Eban, Babe Ruth, Bob Denver.

Legacy (0.5%): Claude Levi-Strauss, Sai Baba, Umberto Eco.

Drive (1.8%): Alexander Graham Bell, Grover Cleveland, James Earl Carter, Michelangelo Buonarotti, Otto von Bismarck, Theodore Roosevelt, Viktor Shauberger, Vincent van Gogh, Walter Elias Disney.

Totem Animal: bullock … squirrel … vulture.

Deities: Saturn (Roman god of agriculture and the harvest).

Power: infinite possibility.

Colors/Gemstones: Lapis Lazuli.

Science-related: epidemiological research, scientific discovery, scientific research … definitional system … astral travel, Mystical Numerology … antimatter engine, electromagnetic field, parallel universe, wave information.

Work-related Areas/Associations: civil servant, congressman, congresswoman, senator … contortionist, electronics engineer, highway contractor, hunter, professional dancer, social scientist … shamanic priest.

3 (D): Incubate, Carry, Convey, Do　　　　　Chant: uu – eh.

Medicine Wheel Path: Center/God-Source ⇒ South/Emotional

Mystical Keywords: Holographic Universe … Collective Unconscious, Joint Consciousness … Mind-Over-Matter, Transformation.

Collective Keywords: Interpersonal ... Cooperative Harmony, United, Urge for Relationship ... Holistic Intelligence; (-) Enthrallment.

Positive Keywords: Energy, Radiance, Speed ... Root, Origin, Core Belief ... Daydream, Future-Orientation, Prognostication ... Idea, Conceptual Framework ... Carry, Convey, Incubate ... Art, Science, Language ... Self-Actualization, Personal Growth ... Short-Term Goals, Purposiveness ... Creative Achievement, Creative Awakening, Imaginative Vision ... Objectify, Proof, Unlock ... True, Truth-Telling, Purify, Morally Unassailable ... Do, Try, Activities, Physical Experience ... Affluence ... Beautiful, Considerateness, Demonstrative, Hugger ... Ageless Vitality, Agility, Dancer ... Humor, Happy, Let Go.

Negative/Shadow Keywords: Mental and/or Emotional Paralysis, Immobile, Detain, Embargo ... Passive-Aggressive, Camouflage, Ignore, Cop-out ... Absent-Mindedness, Awkwardness ... Anger, Enrage, Irate, Harm ... Abuser, Cold-Blooded, Vilify ... Bad Love, Repressed Desires, Moral Corruption ... Guilt, Weep ... Egoism, Gloat, Smug ... Wild, Caprice, Off-Guard, Sudden Surprise, System Buster, Riot ... Unlucky ... Die, Ego-Death, Impoverishment.

As a Personal Number: "3" is the impulse from the God-Source outward to the emotional realm. It is the stage at which the energy puts down roots and begins to radiate outward in all directions to make connections. Note that this process of putting down roots is driven by an emotional energy.

The "3" represents the holographic universe in which everything is interconnected, and each part carries the knowledge of the whole. The vibrant emotional energy of the "3" connects us to the collective unconscious. Joint consciousness and "holistic" intelligence turn out to be a heart thing! This makes sense since it is our hearts that connect us with others. It is also our emotional power that sparks imaginative visions and fuels the power of mind-over-matter.

Everything in the physical universe is vibrating and moving, singing and dancing itself into existence. The "3" is the embodiment of this truth. It is radiance and speed. It is the dancer. It is dynamic energy that radiates outward in all directions, and so is connected to movement. It is the moving energy that has the power to carry the power of ideas, conveyed by language, art and science. When we move – walk, dance, run or exercise – we enter into the void of pure potentiality. In this space, we are able to reshape our physical reality, heal ourselves and the world around us.

All of this is to say that people who have "3" as a personal number are dynamic individuals who are enthusiastic achievers and generally like to get into action and *do* things. They are adept at getting things started and putting down roots. They are at their best when working to achieve short-term goals. Movement is important for a "3" person to stay in balance. When they feel stuck, the quickest way to get unstuck is to move – walk, run, dance, exercise, or go do something physical.

"3s" are carriers of ideas, and they may convey their ideas through the arts and sciences, and through language – both written and spoken. The "3" as a personal number bestows the power to lift others up through the energy of ideas and personality.

"3" people tend to have good social skills and like being with others. While the "2" defines the framework for human relationship and a need to share, the "3" is a more active urge for social interaction and interpersonal connection. "3" is the energy of cooperative harmony and whenever people are feeling united in a community or group, this energy is present. "3" people embody this energy. They are generally demonstrative. They are not wall flowers. They tend to be huggers.

Downside: One aspect of the shadow side for the "3" is dynamic. It can show up as a wild streak, especially when young. Or it can look like egoism. It is also the energy of anger. Anger is just a way to move energy and when expressed in the right way can be quite healthy. But, when anger crosses the line into rage, or prompts a person to become abusive, then it brings the possibility of causing harm to others. ... It is interesting to note that the words *anger* and *weep* are both "3" words. It occurs to me that to allow yourself to weep is a safety valve to keep anger from becoming rage.

The other side of the shadow stems from the dynamic "3" energy turning inward on itself. A person starts taking things too seriously. Guilt and repressed desires begin to take hold. The energy becomes passive-aggressive, or has a tendency to disconnect, ignore others and become emotionally distant. The solution is to lighten up, and remember to play a little.

Mayan Connection

The "3" is connected to "Aj" – spiritual power, the kind of power that enables one to be an authority or a person who can have social influence in the community. The symbol for Aj is *reeds* that connect heaven and earth, and are flexible but strong. The key is to be flexible and not rigid so that when you get blown over by the wind, you can stand up again.

Exercise

Chanting or singing *uu – eh*, the sound of the "3," will help to anchor a new idea in your conscious awareness, especially if you hold that as an intention. It also has a balancing effect on the emotions.

Famous "3" People

Purpose (1.7%): Alfred Edward Houseman, Boris Yeltsin, Jascha Heifetz, Rudolf Nureyev.

Path (2.6%): Albert Einstein, Alphonsus Capone, August Strindberg, Cole Porter, Esther Williams, George W. Bush, Horace Greeley, Johnny Reid Edwards, Langston Hughes, Nelson A. Rockefeller, Sandra Day O'Connor, Sylvia Plath, Tim Berners-Lee, Virginia Woolf.

Legacy (2.3%): Bill Maher, Catherine Drinker Bowen, George Halas, Jim Carrey, Pierre Cardin, Paramahansa Yogananda, Ronald Wilson Reagan.

Drive (2.6%): Beatrice Potter Webb, Donald Henry Rumsfeld, Jacques Yves Cousteau, Jean Baptiste Moliere, Johann Sebastian Bach, Lyndon Baines Johnson, Olivier Martinez, Ronald Wilson Reagan, Richard Milhous Nixon, and Thomas Jefferson.

Totem Animals: cheetah ... condor ... crocodile.

Deities: Yahweh (God of Israel) ... Apollo (god of light and the sun, truth and prophecy), Helios (god of the sun and sight).

Powers: Ageless Vitality.

Colors: blue-black, green, lemon, maize, melon, obsidian, onyx, orange.

Gemstones: obsidian, onyx.

Science-related: advanced mathematics, anthropic cosmology, atmospheric sciences, classical physics, crystallography, etiology, genealogy, science, information theory, photolithography, quantum holography, telecommunications, ultrasonography.

Work-related Areas/Associations: archaeoastronomer, astrophysicist, barber, beautician, chauffeur, chief information officer, computer animation, courier, dancer, fire chief, jailer, layman, logistics director, master of ceremonies, nanotechnologist, novice, nuclear physicist, prestidigitator, racer, real estate agent, real estate lawyer, robber, silversmith, toastmaster, ventriloquist.

4 (F): Manager, Order, Work, Freedom   Chant: uu – ah.

Medicine Wheel Path: Center/God-Source ⇒ East/Mental Dimension.

Mystical Keywords: Lightbody ... Ascend ... Mystical Brotherhood, Spiritual Master ... Expanded Awareness, Geopsyche, Higher Intellectual, Pure Consciousness, Transcendent Order, Universal Energy Field; (-) Cosmic Disenchantment ... Worldwide Collapse.

Collective Keywords: Manifested World ... Alliance, Cohesive, Civic Duty, Social Trust ... Justice, Liberty, Peacetime.

Positive Keywords: Reason, Order, Work ... Decision, Manager ... Capability, Produce, Self-Starter, Directed Intention ... Ardor,

Curious, Hopeful … Creative Intelligence, Intellectual Freedom, Mental Stability … Ego-Mind, Analyze, Compute, Factual, Measurement … Seeing, Healing, Body … Guided Imagery, Imaging, Symbology, Song … Transmitter … Bless, Forgive … Freedom … Contain, Secure, Conventional Limit.

Negative/Shadow Keywords: Unloved, Jealousy, Possessiveness … Unfeeling, Cynicism … Isolate, Lost, Recluse … Boring, Mule-Headed, Limited Viewpoint … Inaccuracy … Aggressiveness, Bossy, Dominate, Authoritarian Power … Conquer, Foe, Fight, Hothead … Curse, Loathe, Wicked … Fearful, Paranoid, Trauma, Trouble … Superstitious … Arson, Inferno, Blow Up, Horrific … Cunning, Deceit, Betray … Self-Incrimination, Shame … Romantic Rejection … Poverty Mentality, Steal … Wastefulness.

As a Personal Number: The "4" on the Medicine Wheel connects the pure potentiality of the God-Source with the mental realm and new beginnings. This connection gives rise to the manifested world and the body. The "4" teaches us that the mind is the creator, and all that we see and experience is "mind stuff." To paraphrase Edgar Cayce, the famous sleeping prophet: *spirit is the life; mind is the builder; the physical is the result.* Our minds are very powerful, indeed!

The "4" represents expanded awareness. But, it is also the number of reason, order and work. "4" people generally have a highly developed work ethic, and demonstrate the qualities of commitment, discipline, effort, practicality, and organization. They make good managers and decision-makers. The "4" energy brings capability, and people with this number are often self-starters who apply themselves to produce results.

As a personal number, the "4" suggests a strong mind and a generally ordered approach to life. It is the number of intellectual freedom. It brings the ability to measure, compute and analyze, and often a desire to use those skills. For instance, in getting ready for a meeting, event or holiday, a "4" person will put effort into planning the details, and would be uncomfortable just "winging it." Indeed, the "4" teaches the lesson of working with the power of expectations in a disciplined way to accomplish desired goals.

This ordered approach to life means that "4" people relate most strongly to life through the power of their mind and cognition. They value mental stability, and they value their personal freedom. While they are often curious and passionate about their area of interest, they may put armor around their heart and emotions to feel secure. They like to relate at an intellectual level but tend not to like people encroaching on their personal space. As a result, they may seem emotionally distant and self-contained – and may be unaware of it. This can also stem from early life and development when "4" people often have to overcome obstacles – like young seeds working their way past stones in the soil to push up into the sunlight.

"4" is the number of service. The way for the "4" person to grow emotionally and spiritually is through service. It is by giving both time and ability to help others that the "4" person can ascend to a higher level. This aspect of the "4" also builds alliances, and develops the ability to forgive themselves and others for their perceived shortcomings.

As a personal number, the "4" also brings a facility for *seeing* and *healing*. By *seeing* I mean using expanded awareness to see beyond the illusion of the sensory world and perceive the transcendent order that is the foundation for life. *Healing* means an inherent capacity for self-healing as well as healing others. "4" is also the number of "song" and "sing." It reminds us that singing is connected with this ability for seeing. Indeed, ancient teachings in the Hebrew tradition tell us that the *power of song* was considered to be one of the most direct connections with the divine, and the ability to prophesy – to see![18] This is particularly true of singing spontaneous melodies using the vowel sounds.

Downside: The "4" may feel unloved. "4" is the father energy, so it is not uncommon for the "4" person to have early childhood issues with his or her father that result in feeling unloved. This core issue can have several common results. It can create a tendency toward jealousy and possessiveness. It can also manifest as cynicism, fearfulness and being either paranoid or just shut down and unfeeling.

---

[18] Told to Jeanne White Eagle (my wife) and me by spiritual teacher, Kabalist and master jeweler David Baruch on a trip to Tsfat, Israel in 2004.

The negative "4" person can be bossy, and want to dominate others (especially in combination with a "7" Purpose or Path), so watch out for this. A "4" person will stand their ground, and generally doesn't mind having a good fight – not always a bad thing.

The way back to balance is through learning to forgive, and through service to others.

Mayan Connection

The "4" connected with "Ix" which is the "Earth Mother," her sacred sites and the guardians of those sacred sites. The totem animal is the Jaguar. It represents intelligence, the strength of Mother Earth, and the creative forces in the universe. It provides innate intuition and curiosity, and the potential to develop higher powers.

Exercise

Chanting or singing *uu – ah,* the sound of the "4," energizes the mind and expands awareness. As an aid to making a decision, hold a question in your mind while chanting uu – ah until the solution arises. It generally doesn't take very long.

Famous "4" People

Purpose (6.6%): Abraham Lincoln, Albert Einstein, Benjamin Franklin, Florence Nightingale, Henry David Thoreau, Immanuel Kant, Joseph Stalin, Julius Robert Oppenheimer, Karl Wallenda, Malcolm McLaren, Oscar de la Renta, Pierre August Renoir.

Path (7.9%): Eric Clapton, Fritz Kreisler, Gertrude Stein, Henry Kissinger, Immanuel Kant, James Dean, J. Pierpont Morgan, Max Planck, Oliver Wendell Holmes, Jr., Richard (Dick) Cheney, Sally Ride, Tommy Hilfiger, Simone de Beauvoir, William McKinley, Woodrow Wilson.

Legacy (5.2%): Betty White, Dietrich Bonhoeffer, Eartha Kitt, Garrison Keillor, Helen Keller, Jackson Pollack, J. Pierpont Morgan,

Kahlil Gibran, Somerset Maugham, Virginia Woolf, Vladimir Lenin, Wiliam Butler Yeats.

Drive (3.3%): Alexis de Tocqueville, Artur Rubenstein, Carl Friedrich Gauss, Esther Williams, Florence Nightingale, Herbert Clark Hoover, Nikita Krushchev, Paulina Porizkova, Ralph Waldo Emerson, Ray Charles Robinson, Robert Peary.

Totem Animals: impala … squid … wolf.

Deities: Atlas (the Titan that held the world on his shoulders) … Brahma (Hindu god of creation) … Mercury (the winged messenger, god of trade & travel), Uranus (god of the sky).

Powers: Air Being, Flight.[19]

Colors: copper, ivory, jonquil, linen, moccasin, wheat … white … cerise, pink, plum … bluish, blue-green … ash grey.

Science-related: agronomy, bioethics, economics, neurobiology, photographic science, symbology, particle physics, quantum particle, radiology, sociology, zero-point energy.

Work-related Areas/Associations: aquanaut, behavioral geneticist, body-builder, butler, catcher, chaplain, clown, cultural historian, deputy, environmentalist, falconer, fencer, freelance, Freudian psychologist, grip, interior designer, juggler, mailman, mechanic, neurophysiologist, neuropsychiatrist, nurse, orderly, paleoclimatologist, portraitist, preservationist, prior, Secretary of State, spiritual seeker, spiritual master, spiritual trainer, survivalist, teaching, theoretical biophysicist.

---

[19] Icarus, son of Daedalus who dared to fly too close to the sun on wings of feathers and wax, is a 31/4 energy.

5 (G): Bridge, Fluidity, Balance   Chant: oh – eh.

Medicine Wheel Path: North/Spiritual ⇒ South/Emotional

Mystical Keywords: Cosmic Leap, Promethean Quest ... Mysticism, Medium, Non-Self ... Goddess ... Precognitive Dream, Intuitive Insight ... Sacred Dance ... Non-Doing, Non-Materialistic.

Collective Keywords: Evolutionary Impulse ... Collective Thought, Mass Movement ... Underlying / Intrinsic Principle ... Social Bond, Mutual Support ... Common Cause, Common Good, Compassionate Leadership, Moral Good, Working Together ... Universal Compassion ... Limitless Supply (-) Apocalypse ... War.

Positive Keywords: Fluidity, Flux, Verb, Mental Flexibility ... Life-Transforming ... Journey ... Nature, Land, Place ... Anti-Authoritarian, Open ... Ego ... Ask, Seek, Choose ... Conceive, Create, Creative Thinker ... Develop, Bridge, Forge, Plan ... Education, Learning, Thought ... Free Expression, Words, Scribe, Telling ... Family, Friend, Couple, Caring, Fidelity, Soulmate ... Balance, Harmony, Peacekeeping, Sense of Fairness ... Female, Fertility, Bountiful ... Desire, Pleasure ... Geniality.

Negative/Shadow Keywords: Chaos, Pain, Grief ... Karma, Habit, Pitfall ... Energy Block, Lethargy, Stuck, Undemonstrative ... Covetous, Fear of Lack, One-Sided ... Addictive, Obsessiveness ... Emotional Undercurrent, Sentimentalism ... Impulsiveness, Fickle, Hurrying, Recklessness, Overeager, Immature ... Devilish, Lure, Molest, Unfaithful ... Boast ... Quarrel, Perilous, Inescapable ... Groundlessness, Mindlessness ... Disbelief, Denial, Negate ... Defeat, Self-Hate ... Racism, Slave.

As a Personal Number: The "5" on the Medicine Wheel connects the spiritual–intuitive realm with the personal, emotional dimension of the heart and feelings. It is the Goddess energy of the feminine archetype. It is mysticism and the connection with ancestral spirits. "5" is the number of intuitive insight, the bridge between the silent voice of Spirit and the open heart that hears it.

202

With the energy of the "5," Spirit reaches down to touch a person's heart, and infuse her/him with knowing and the power to conceive and create. It is the number of divine longing. It is very expansive and hard to handle at times, like drinking light from a cosmic fire hose. With the "5" energy, Spirit is in the driver's seat. Spirit takes charge, sending visions and insights that are often unbidden. And, sometimes it shakes up a person's life.

The "5" is an active verb-based reality where everything is in flux, and harmony is achieved through fluidity and flexibility. The "5" energy wants freedom, change and spontaneity. It doesn't like limitations or boundaries. "5" people are open, inquisitive, anti-authoritarian, and will push up against societal (and parental) norms to experiment with new creative approaches to life. They may tend to scatter their energy in too many directions at once. What's needed is a constructive, sustainable approach to personal creativity and freedom that results in a dynamic balance. This often requires learning the power of a focused intention to manifest needs and desires.

The "5" people are generally good communicators who express themselves easily, often with geniality and laughter. They tend to be open-minded, creative thinkers who are able to see the big picture, and can be a bridge between differing belief systems and worldviews. They can make good facilitators if they are drawn to it. Oratorical ability and a facility with the written word are also among the talents of the person with "5" as a personal number.

"5" is the number of family and friends. Its energy is the social bond that brings people together in mutual support. It is about working together, and working toward a common cause that benefits everyone. "5" people have a well-developed sense of fairness. They may be good at mediating conflicts, creating harmony and keeping the peace.

On a personal level, "5" people are innately caring and often lucky in love. In relationships, they do well as a couple and, over time, they attract their soulmate. The "5" energy can be quite erotic.

To be in balance, the "5" needs to cultivate the freedom to create, play, and pursue the beauty of life. Artistic endeavors, music, creativity, and movement are all possible ways to strengthen the spiritual-emotional connection and stay in balance. The "5" energy is about fluidity, flow, and *allowing* rather than pushing, efforting and control. This is the key.

Downside: When out of balance, "5" people may be impulsive, reckless, overeager and caught up in a swirl of chaos and hurry-worry. They lack focus and scatter their energy in too many directions at once. They may also lack appropriate boundaries and be prone to over-indulgence and having an addictive personality.

Alternately, sometimes due to childhood trauma or taking on responsibilities too early in life, the "5" person can go to the opposite extreme and repress his or her artistic/sensual/erotic sides with over-control. There may be a fear of loosening up and letting go. There can also be a fear of lack, and a feeling of not having enough. The result is being emotionally blocked, or stuck in old habits, unable to break free.

The challenge of the "5" as a personal number is to cultivate an *appropriate* and sustainable balance. This can be accomplished by channeling creative energies through a focused intention to manifest what is desired. Once this lesson is learned, the "5" person has the potential to experience unlimited supply.

Mayan Connection

The "5" is connected to "Tzikin," the "Birds" who are considered the intermediaries with the spirit realm and higher consciousness. Tzikin people are generally kind, cheerful, and are good communicators who express themselves easily. They may be intuitives and visionaries, and have a facility with dreams and divination. The "Tzikin" energy often bestows good fortune in work and love.

Exercise

Chanting or singing *oh – eh,* the sound of the "5," helps your energy to *flow,* and is particularly beneficial if you are feeling stuck. It also cultivates intuitive insights and can enhance creativity.

Famous "5" People

Purpose (12.1%): Booker T. Washington, Daniel Webster, David Bowie, Douglas MacArthur, Edwin "Buzz" Aldrin, Elvis Presley, Federico Fellini, Galileo Galilei, Hank Aaron, Howard Hughes, James Dean, Kahlil Gibran, Laura Ingalls Wilder, Oprah Winfrey, Paulina Porizkova, Ralph Waldo Emerson, Susan B. Anthony.

Path (12.1%): Adolf Hitler, Berry Gordy, Boris Yeltsin, David Livingstone, Eduoard Manet, Edgar Allan Poe, Edna Saint Vincent Millay, Elizabeth Blackwell, Frederick Douglass, George Gordon (Lord) Byron, Jimmy Carter, Johann Sebastian Bach, John Ford, Josef Stalin, Marcus Tulius Cicero, Michael Eisner, Michelangelo Buonarotti, Nikita Krushchev, Rush Limbaugh, Sylvia Pankhurst, Thomas Jefferson, Vidal Sassoon, Walter Cronkite.

Legacy (8.9%): Eric Clapton, Jesse Woodson James, Karl Wallenda, Langston Hughes, Michelle Bachmann, Oliver Hardy, Otto von Bismarck, Ralph Waldo Emerson, Robert Burns, Sarah Palin, Steve Fosset, Warren G. Harding, William James.

Drive (4.8%): Alan Alda, Anita Baker, James Joyce, Jeffrey Katzenberg, Lucretia Coffin Mott, Newton (Newt) Leroy Gingrich, Rowan Atkinson, Theodore Suess Geisel, Walt Whitman, Wolfgang Amadeus Mozart.

Totem Animals: badger ... dolphin ... hawk.

Deities: Gaia (the Great Mother of All) ... Poseidon (god of the sea, earthquakes & horses), Neptune (god of water & the sea)... Pan (god of shepherds & flocks) ... Uriel (archangel – name means "God is my light"), Raphael (archangel – name means "God heals").

Powers: Dawn, Nature, Sky, Thunder, Wind.

Colors: banana, daffodil, flame, tangelo ... creamy beige, flax ... apple-red, ruby-red, mahogany, rosewood ... blue-white, steel-blue.

Gemstones: azurite, jet, star sapphire, tiger's eye, verdite.

Science-related: acoustics, musicology ... alternative energy, cetology, cosmology, dynamics, Feng Shui, homeopathy, iconography, Kirlian photography, magnetic levitation, marine biology, microbiology, oceanography, philology, physics, psychobiology, sociobiology, string field theory, theoretical physics, toxicological research.

Work-related Areas/Associations: actor, actuary, aerobics, agent, anthropologist, apothecary, astromythologist, baker, biochemist, bookmaker, breeder, bridge builder, coroner, diplomat, docent, dowser, education, engineer, equerry, founder, friar, geologist, golfer, homeopath, husbandry, insurance salesman, intelligence operative, interior decorator, laser physicist, lawyer, medium, peddler, politician, racing, runner, sacred dance, sangoma (clairvoyant naturopathic healer), screenwriter, scribe, shamanic priestess, soldier, spiritual teacher, television producer, wayfarer.

6 (H): Influencer, Trendsetter   Chant: eh – oh.

Medicine Wheel Path: South/Emotional ⇒ North/Spiritual.

Mystical Keywords: All-Loving, Cosmic Order, Deeper Order, Governing Principle ... Causality, Formative Power ... Etheric Body, Soul, Within ... Heightened Perception ... Shaman, Prophet ... Medicine Dance.

Collective Keywords: Collective Consciousness ... People, Public, Society ... Communal, Social Cohesion, Social Tie, "We" See You ... Laws, Spiritual Principles ... Parental Authority ... Reward System; (-) Puritanical Standards.

Positive Keywords: Awakener, Originator, Influencer, Trendsetter ... Instinctual Drive, Intuitive ... Kundalini, Life-force ... Temporal Power, Personal Power ... Human Mind, Mental Stimulation ... Lateral Thinking, Predictive Certainty, Specificity: How, Who, Why, Why Not? ... Discover: Activate, Augment, Combine, Change ... Capable, Ethical, Focused, Reliable ... Coordinator, Mentor, Teach, Record ... Art of Dialogue, Communicate, Sharing ... Placement, Belonging, Unselfish ... Emotional Wellness, Individual Happiness ... Amour ... Philosophy, Poetry.

Negative/Shadow Keywords: Polarity, Imbalance, Shadow ... Negative and/or Codependent Relationship, Feeling Bad ... Fatal Flaw ... Arrogant, Prideful, Cynical, Mask, Rebel, Rule-Breaker ... Impatience ... Procrastinator, Avoidance, "If Only" ... Insecure, Indecision, Incapability ... Chronic Depression ... Lone Wolf ... Cupidity, Duplicity, Hustler ... Disrepute, Sinner, Self-Destruction ... Avarice, Self-Aggrandizement, Addict, Crave ... Abduction, Hostage, Trap ... Complicity, Traitor ... Fanatic, Nemesis ... Agitator, Abusive, Dictatorial, Domination, Tactlessness ... Revolutionary Change, Volatile, Uproot.

As a Personal Number: The "6" on the Medicine Wheel connects the personal dimension of the heart and emotions with the cosmic dimension of spirit and intuition. Note that the "6" connects the same two points on the Medicine Wheel as does the "5" but in the *opposite direction*. It is an important distinction. With the "5," spirit is in charge. The energy of the "6" is more volitional, which is to say there is more personal power to choose or determine the outcome.

People who have "6" as a personal number are drinkers of light. The "6" person has a natural, inner heart-connection with ancient wisdom that enables her/him to embrace and work with the sacred – if s/he so chooses. It provides a window to the collective consciousness and a pathway to heightened perception. The "6" is the number of the shaman, prophet, and awakener. "6" people have this inherent capability for expanded awareness, but it must be activated with intention and then cultivated.

"6" is the energy of social cohesion and is the number of the public and society. It represents the sacred marriage of masculine and feminine, and so brings balance. Maybe this is one of the reasons that "6" people have an ability to relate with others, share of themselves, and get along with most people. Indeed, the "6" enhances the ability to communicate with and influence people, be they individuals, groups, or the public at large. It is good to remember that each action we take has an effect that ripples through time for seven generations, 140–150 years. Just as great oaks grow from small acorns, small changes in the present may have a big impact in the future. I find this a very hopeful thought.

207

People who have "6" for a personal number often work with the public in some way as teachers, coordinators, healers, litigators, recruiters, salesmen, social workers and psychologists, mentors, consultants, and entertainers.

"6" is the energy of *placement* by which I mean finding one's place in the world. People with a "6" – particularly as their Life Purpose or Path – tend to be more concerned with how/where they fit in than do other numbers. And, while they do have the potential to be a lone wolf, "6" people are happier when they are not alone. As a general rule, they do better in a relationship, partnership, team or group.

The "6" is the number of cosmic order and causality; it represents the governing principles behind reality from which formative power comes. This translates into personal power and dynamism. "6" people are reliable, ethical, capable and can make things happen.

"6" is the number of discovery, and governs the questions: How, who, why and why not. "6" people like mental stimulation, and often have the ability of lateral thinking and rational mastery which they use to make discoveries. They are originators and awakeners and are adept at augmenting or combining ideas into a unique hybrid[20] or something totally new. "6s" also like to record ideas, discoveries, thoughts and experiences in journals. Once focused, which can take a while, they make good record-keepers. They can be found in a variety of business, financial, or research professions.

The "6" is the path that merges the open heart with the divine. This is why the traditional Tarot decks call the "6" *The Lovers*. Lovemaking and poetry fall under the "6" because of this inherent ability to merge with the *other* – including other people, things, and events.

"6" people may find that they have an empathic ability to pick up on the feelings of other people, or the energies of both things and events – especially if they have an "E" as the first vowel of their given name. In other words, "6s" may have the ability to vicariously experience the feelings or thoughts of another person or group, or the

---

[20] Since my Life Purpose Number is 24/6, my creation of Mystical Numerology is a good example.

energy of an event, or of a place or thing, either in the present or past, without them explicitly being communicated or explained. In fact, "6s" may sometimes have difficulty separating their feelings from the feelings of others, especially those who are close to them. This can lead to "boundary issues." In other words, "6" people may have difficulty distinguishing between where *they* stop and the *other* begins. The inherent danger that grows out of this empathic link is that "6s" may feel a need to take care of others on an emotional level – even to the point of giving their own power away. Sometimes, this represents an early challenge to work through.

The "6" person is often a sucker for people with broken wings. "6" people have often had at least one relationship in which they've been hurt badly. It seems to be the way of it in this 3-D training course called Life.

Downside: More than with all the other numbers, the "6" person tends to experience the polarities between light and dark, balance and imbalance, and so is susceptible to emotional highs and lows, and corresponding mood swings. The challenge of this number is developing a strong sense of individuality, self-confidence and balance.

"6" people can be romantics who are in love with love, and can feel they must take care of others on an emotional level. They are prone to negative relationships and, especially if there is a lack of self-confidence, creating codependent relationships. Feeling bad can lead to insecurity, indecision, incapability, or becoming an accomplished procrastinator. It can also result in passive-aggressive behavior.

Alternately, the negative "6" person can be arrogant and prideful, a real rebel, agitator and rule-breaker who acts out of impatience with people and authority. These people have the ability to be hustlers who find ways to game the system for their own self-aggrandizement and personal benefit. In positions of relative power, they can also become tactless, abusive, dictatorial and emotionally dominating. These people may also be found in the ranks of fanatics.

Whether it is through insecurity and incapability, or through avarice and/or a need for domination, the "6" person may have a fatal flaw that gets them stuck on a path to self-destruction. The way out is through finding one's place, developing appropriate emotional boundaries, and practicing love and forgiveness for both self and others.

Mayan Connection

"6" is connected with *Ajmaq*, the energy of forgiveness and reconciliation. It also represents ancient wisdom that comes from the brain in communication with the Spirit Guides. It gives spiritual strength. The energy of Ajmaq can make it possible to reconcile with others, cure illnesses, defend the dispossessed, seek justice, and achieve harmony with Mother Earth.

Exercise

Chanting or singing *eh – oh,* the sound of the "6," opens a doorway between the heart and ancient wisdom. It is the sound of drinking light. It can energize the kundalini and bring balance to empathic abilities.

Famous "6" People

Purpose (13.5%): Augustus Edwin John, Beatrice Potter Webb, Betty Friedan, Clark Gable, Esther Williams, George Washington, Giorgio Armani, John D. Rockefeller, John F. Kennedy, Josephine Hull, Lewis Carroll, Mary Tyler Moore, Mikhail Gorbachev, Sophie Tucker, Stephen Hawking, Yevgeny Zemyatin, Zachary Taylor.

Path (9.5%): Alan Ginsberg, Bridget Fonda, Charles Lindberg, Elijah Wood, Giorgio Armani, Henry Wadsworth Longfellow, Jane Horrocks, John Ashcroft, John Belushi, John L. Louis, Kevin Costner, LL Cool J, Nicolaus Copernicus, Oliver Hardy, Rod Stewart, Sathya Sai Baba, Thomas Paine, Vladimir Lenin, Warren Buffet, William Randolph Hearst, Winston Churchill.

Legacy (11.6%): A. E. Housman, Abraham Lincoln, Anne Bronte, Anthony (Tony) Blair, Benny Hill, Christopher Marlowe, David Lloyd George, Sandra Oh, John F. Kennedy, Josephine Hull, Margaret Thatcher, Vera Marie Rosenberg, Walter F. Mondale, Walter Cronkite.

Drive (7.7%): David Bowie, Diana Frances Spencer, Geena Davis, Howard Robard Hughes, Idi Amin, Lawrence J. Ellison, Martin Van Buren, Mel Gibson, Ruth Bader Ginsberg, Sally Kristen Ride, Sergey Brin, William Jefferson Clinton.

Totem Animals: dragon … hummingbird … whale.

Deities: Aphrodite (goddess of love) … Athena (goddess of wisdom, warfare and crafts) … Janus (Roman god of beginnings and transitions).

Powers: Cyclone, Thunderstorm.

Colors: almond, beige, blonde, fawn, orange peel … baby pink, brick red, Chinese red, magenta, russet, tomato … royal blue, sky-blue … violet … arsenic, charcoal, pewter … pistachio.

Gemstones: beryl, cat's eye, chalcedony, jacinth, pyrite, selenite, tourmaline.

Science-related: agriculture, atmospheric science, bioelectricity, biophysics, climatology, cultural neuroscience, cytogenics, entomology, eugenics, game theory, geography, geothermal, history, hydroelectric, magnetic field, morphic field, nanomachine, psychoneuroimmunology, reflexology, research, rheumatology, spatial relationships, synecology, telepathic communication, telepathic power, time compression, topology, x-rays, weather patterns.

Work-related Areas/Associations: acrobat, analyst, animator, auditor, cabdriver, celebrity, circus, civil litigation system, clergyman, clerk, code-breaker, communication center, computer animator, confectioner, constitutional law, coordinator, construction worker, counselor, design consultant, drummer, editor, emotional wellness, entertainment, executor, fabricator, farmer, financier, fisherman, forensic anthropologist, hustler, Jungian psychologist, litigator, lobbyist, matador, mentor, miller, mystical numerologist, nanny, painter, physical therapist, political scientist, pundit, recruiter, rebel, salesman, scout, shaman, technology forecaster, textile worker, timekeeper, wanderer, warrior, weaving.

7 (J): Idealist, Mystic, Authority

Chant: ah – uu.

Medicine Wheel Path: East/Mental ⇒ Center/God-Source

Mystical Keywords: Heaven, Center, Pure Being ... God-Like, Infinite Potential, Creation, Cocreate ... Oneness, Mystic, Oracle, Muse, Vision ... Messenger, Traveler, Path ... Contemplative Life.

Collective Keywords: Humanity ... Larger Context, Central Dogma ... Worldly Status ... Camaraderie ... Environmentalism; (-) Social Rebellion, Social Upheaval ... Ruthless Justice.

Positive Keywords: Person, Individuation, Path ... Chrysalis, Potential for Change ... Creative Thinking, Visualize, Inspire ... Memory, Past/Future ... Study, Learn, Prepare ... Linear, Logical, Precise, Accurate, Prove, Internal Consistency ... Authority, Excellence, Judgment, Expert, Purposeful Work ... Initiate, Drive, Promote, Achieve, Crusade, Industriousness, Personal Determination, Will to Survive ... Control, Nonviolence, Tact, Tolerance ... Idealist, Truth ... Trust, Trustworthy, Team Player ... Conscience, Moral Awareness, Need to Give, Sensitiveness ... Adventure, Euphoric, Genial, Joy, Joyfulness, Carefree, Playful ... Physical Ability, Physical Beauty, Sex, Propagation.

Negative/Shadow Keywords: Bigoted, Cruel, Directive, Divisive, Envious ... Irritability, Temper, Unstable, Unhappy Relationship ... Foolish, Illogical, Ignorance ... Fussy, Absentminded ... Hurry, Overdo ... Radical Change ... Humiliation, Powerlessness ... Inadequate, Inferior ... Broken Heart, Doleful, Forlorn, Psychic Distress, Turned Off ... Unaware, Uncaring ... Apathy, Fatigue, Laziness ... Blockage, Obstacle, Obstructionist ... Loner ... Immoral, Indiscreet, Disreputable, Seducer ... Lying, Shakedown, Treachery ... Decline, Death.

As a Personal Number: In Jewish Mysticism, "7" represents the Shekhinah, or feminine face of God. It is the number that connects the mind with the God-Source, and so is like a gateway to universal wisdom and infinite potential. It is this connection between the mind and the Divine Source that gives our thoughts the power of creation and each of us the ability to cocreate our own reality.

"7" is the number of humanity but also of heaven, suggesting that heaven really is within us. It is also oneness, the quality or state of mystical union with All-That-Is. Perhaps this is another way to describe heaven. "7" is the number of the mystic, the oracle, muse and messenger. It is the power of vision, the power to see clearly – on both spiritual *and* practical levels, a very powerful combination.

"7" is the number of the person, the personal, and the process of individuation. "7" people may feel that they are on a sacred path to accomplish something important in life, that there is purposeful work awaiting them. "7s" tend to be idealists who have a strong urge to find the *truth*. For them, life is a quest for fundamental knowledge linked to a passion for knowing how the world really works.

"7" people generally have a good memory. They like to study and learn, and may be adept at teaching themselves new things. Indeed, they may be happiest climbing a steep learning curve or preparing for the next challenge or adventure. As a result, they may become experts or authorities in their chosen field, especially because of their strong work ethic and desire for excellence.

"7" people have a strong will to survive and thrive. They are creative thinkers who can visualize desires, promote ideas, inspire others, initiate projects, and achieve desired results. They are generally gifted with personal determination, industriousness and a drive to achieve goals. "7s" may be overzealous in their work. Passion and idealism can combine to make achievement a personal crusade, and there can be a danger of burnout unless care is taken to not overdo it.

While there is an innate capacity to be the mystic, "7" people also have a very practical, linear side that is logical, precise, comfortable with facts, and wants to prove things for themselves. To the extent that they demand excellence of themselves, they also expect it of others. '7s" can be difficult people to live with. There is a tendency for them to feel like they know more than others. They can be impatient, judgmental, intolerant, and do not, as they say, suffer fools easily.

An important lesson for the "7" person is to learn trust. They need to learn to trust themselves, trust others and trust life, in general.

Otherwise, they can be over-controlling and shut down their capacity to experience joy, camaraderie and spontaneity.

The "7" energy is the idealist. It is also the energy of conscience and moral awareness. Even though "7s" can be sometimes difficult to be around, there is a softer side that comes from sensitiveness and the need to give to others. Scientists have recently proven that this is actually a stronger urge in humanity than the need to dominate, or the will to control.[21] The "7" also brings tolerance, good judgment and control which can be very good qualities.

Introspection and the contemplative life are also "7" qualities. Most "7s" will find themselves feeling introverted at times and drawn inwards toward periods of contemplation. These periods are linked to the potential for change, and are like going into the chrysalis as a caterpillar waiting to be reborn as a butterfly. It is important for the "7" person to periodically stop, and take time for rest, relaxation, recreation and rejuvenation. To maintain balance, "7s" periodically need alone space to think and recharge. And sometimes, recharging personal batteries looks like having an adventure, and being carefree and playful!

Downside: The shadow side of the "7" person generally comes from a lack of trust in themselves and others, and a lack of trust in life itself. It can manifest as obstacles on the path, energy blockages in the body, a broken heart, feeling inadequate or inferior, being overly fussy, or absent-minded and unaware, feeling turned-off or being just plain uncaring. These things can combine in various ways to cause psychic distress and often result in protective behaviors. These can include irritability, feeling envious, loss of temper, being directive and controlling, being divisive, and challenging authority and authority figures (not always a bad thing). Alternately, it can result in apathy, laziness, disappointment and fatigue.

---

21 Lynne McTaggart, The Bond: Connecting Through the Space Between Us, Tantor Media, 2011, ISBN-10: 1452651582.

The cure for the shadow side is learning trust and lightening up by developing a sense of joy in life. In fact, a very good practice for a "7" person is to start the day by filling the mind and body as much as possible with the feeling of joy!

Mayan Connection

"7" is connected with "Noj" which represents knowledge and wisdom that comes from the universe and the Earth. It is the energy of telepathy and "knowing" without consciously knowing how you know.

Exercise

Chanting or singing *ah – uu,* the sound of the "7," connects the mind with the Divine Source. It is the sound of creation. Chanting or singing *ah – uu* fills your being with the energy of infinite potential, increases inner knowing, and also trust.

Famous "7" People

Purpose (9.1%): Andres Segovia, Alexis de Tocqueville, Aristotle Onassis, Barack Obama, Carl Sandburg, Clare Booth Luce, Edith Wharton, Elizabeth Barrett Browning, Elizabeth Blackwell, Gertrude Stein, Harry S. Truman, Jackson Pollack, Lyndon B. Johnson, René Descartes, Samuel Langhorne Clemens, Somerset Maugham, Sandra Day O'Connor, Walt Whitman, Wolfgang Amadeus Mozart, Zora Neale Hurston.

Path (9.5%): Ayn Rand, Dolly Parton, Doris Kearns Goodwin, Florence Nightingale, George Washington, James Dickey, Jeanne-Marie Roland, Lou Diamond Phillips, Neil Diamond, Oprah Winfrey, Richard J. Daley.

Legacy (8.4%): Al Capone, Alexander Hamilton, Andrew Jackson, Andy Rooney, Betty Friedan, Christie Brinkley, Eudora Welty, George S. Patton, Hank Aaron, Joe Frazier, Karl Marx, Konstantin Stanislavsky, Max Eastman, Mikhail Gorbachev, Richard Branson, Sylvia Plath, Warren Buffet, William Shakespeare.

Drive (7.0%): Adolf Hitler, Colin Luther Powell, Elijah Wood, George Washington, Giovanni Giacomo Casanova, Lee Van Cleef, Leonardo da Vinci, Mohandas Karamchand Gandhi, Pat Benetar, Pierre Cardin, Thomas Paine, William Tecumseh Sherman, Yves Saint Laurent.

Totem Animals: barracuda ... crow ... snake.

Deities: Astarte (Greek goddess of fertility, sexuality and war), Venus (Roman goddess of love, beauty, sex, fertility, prosperity and military victory).

Powers: Full Moon ... Hailstorm, Rain.

Colors: asparagus, celadon, malachite, moss green, teal ... amber, citrine, flaxen, jasmine, umber ... alizarin crimson, barn red, burgundy, coral, crimson, flamingo pink, orchid, raspberry, red-brown, vermillion ... azure, blue violet, deep-blue, sea-blue.

Gemstones: amber, chrysoberyl, citrine, coral, fluorite, girasol, malachite, marble, peridotite, sodalite, staurolite.

Science-related: aerospace, aesthetics, architecture, audiometry, ayurveda, bioelectronics, biomedical, cybernetics, econometrics, epigenetics, ethnography, Euclidian geometry, exobiology, field theory, forensics, geochronology, geomorphology, genomics, holography, hypnology, inertial confinement, kinetics, magnetohydrodynamics, marine geoscience, military engineering, neurotheology, ornithology, phenology, phonology, phycology, phylogeny, scientific observation, solid-state physics, unified field theory, xerography, zoology ... energy body, paranormal.

Work-related Areas/Associations: angelologist, archivist, artist, auctioneer, aviation psychologist, bail bondsman, balloonist, bandmaster, banker, biographer, blogger, bookkeeper, boxer, chairman, chemical engineer, chronoastrobiologist, cocktail waitress, collector, computer programmer, concierge, critic, dentist, diver, electioneer, embryologist, engraver, epidemiologist, essayist, etiologist, expert, facilitator, fire-keeper, fundraiser, genealogist, gold miner, hagiology, helmsman, herbalist, housewife, housemaid, inspector, instrumentalist, intern, jester, maintenance, massage therapist, Mayanist, mediator, medical practice, messenger, monarch, neurologist, neurosurgeon, ophthalmic surgeon, organist, parapsychologist, parson, prioress, prodigy, proofreader, psychopharmacologist, reporter, schoolteacher, secretary, social psychologist, spiritual advisor, team leader, theater, traveler, workman, world leader, yoga teacher.

8 (K):   Love, Power, Leader, Defender   Chant: eh – uu.

Medicine Wheel Path: South/Emotional ⇒ Center/God-Source

Mystical Keywords: God, All-That-Is, Source of All, Supreme One, Giver of Life, Seed of Life, Christ, Nirvana ... Archetypal Idea ... Divine Consciousness, True Consciousness ... Faith, Pray, Spiritual Literacy ... Divine Work, Miracle ... No-Mind, Mindfulness Meditation, Doorway, Psyche ... Psychokinetic Power.

Collective Keywords: Time ... World ... Close Family Ties, Community Ties ... Social Encounter, Social Mobility ... Collective Phenomenon, Cultural Innovation ... (-) Social Contagion.

Positive Keywords: Love, Power ... Leader, Guide, Negotiator ... Imagine, Precognition, Unexpected Insight ... Causation, Beginning, Bring Forth, Key, Expectancy ... Spontaneous, Letting Go, Heart-Brain ... Ability, Competence, Purpose, Singular Passion, Singular Purpose ... Active, Alive, Achievement, Good Fortune, Successful ... Pioneering, Leap-Frog, Independent Thought ... Integrity ... Willpower, Tenacious ... Coaching, Manage, Team ... Human Being, Personal Identity ... Defender, Safety, Boundaries ... Alphabet, Symbol, Vowel, Word, Orator, Prosody, Writer ... Cheerful, Good Will, Happiness, Optimistic, Loving Compassion ... Romantic, Nurturing, Tender ... Ageless, Youthful.

Negative/Shadow Keywords: Turbulence, Conflict, Upheaval, Ordeal, Worst Case ... Abandon, Break-up ... Despair, Heartache, Helplessness, Inner Conflict, Self-Judgment, Remorse, Suffering, Worrying, Worthlessness ... Codependency, Dysfunction, Enabler ... Weak, Complain, At-Risk, Invisible, Incapable, Uneducated, Underachieve, Idleness, Freeloader ... Addiction, Debauchery, Degeneracy, Depravity ... Hysterical, Insanity ... Workaholism, Restlessness ... Self-Absorbed, Bravado, Vanity ... Insolent, Nosy ...

Fixed, Inflexible ... Coercive, Overbearing, Ruthlessness, Violent ... Soul-Shattering, Degeneracy, Evil ... Impossible, Unbridgeable.

As a Personal Number: "8" is the number that connects the heart and emotions with the Divine Source of All-That-Is. It is from this connection that the energy of love flows into the world. It is also the source of the kind of power that comes from love. It represents faith and prayer and the energy that manifests miracles. People with "8" as a personal number, especially as their Purpose or Path have an innate connection to this kind of active, generative love and power. Perhaps this is why "8" people make good leaders.

It is interesting to me that there are so many "8" words and phrases in the English language connected with the Divine Source, including: *All-That-Is, God, Source of All, Supreme One, Giver of Life, Seed of Life, Christ ... Divine Consciousness, True Consciousness ... Divine Work*. This says something important about how the God-energy interacts with us, and how miracles are made manifest. The heart is the doorway to divine consciousness. It is the feeling nature of our emotional bodies that is the fuel that drives miracles off the drawing board of our minds to manifest as a physical three-dimensional reality in the world. Indeed, "8" is also the number of both causation and of time. To cut off our feelings is to remove the possibility of miracles from our lives. (Parenthetically, this is also a comment on the rational business models that forget about incorporating feelings and emotions into the plan.)

It is also interesting to note the connection between God, love and power – all "8" vibrations. God is love. Love is God. Love is the seed of life and, ultimately, the only true generative power in the universe. God/love brings the physical world into being. It is the energy through which everything is created! This gives us a different way of looking at power and the ability to manifest things in the physical world, including prosperity, abundance, money, and other *things* in our lives. The lesson is this: everything comes from our heart-connection with God, the Source of all things. Abundance or anything else that we can manifest comes through the power of love. Fear keeps it at bay. The formula for manifesting miracles becomes: spirit is the life, mind draws the blueprint; feelings fuel the construction; the physical is the result.

Therefore, for us to have whatever we desire, we must use power in a different way. The "8" is the energy of prayer, faith and also imagination. Creating what we want is less about manipulating and controlling the people, events and things in our lives than it is about imagining what we desire, and then putting the faith, love and willpower behind it. We must be strong enough to surrender into spontaneity and let go, knowing that it is our heart connection with the Creator that brings us all good things. This idea of how things are manifested has the power to change our lives, and to change the world! (It is a very spiritual idea, but not necessarily a religious one.)

On a more practical level, "8" is the energy of power in the world and, traditionally, the number most associated with money and material mastery. It strengthens ability and competence but also loving compassion. It is the energy of the compassionate leader, guide or coach who can show the way for others. It is also the number of the team. "8" people are generally not lone wolves.

The "8" is active and oriented towards achievement. It brings good fortune and successful outcomes. As a personal number, the "8" urges a person to get into action and accomplish something. It can imbue a person with a pioneering spirit, and the willpower to follow through on dreams, goals and plans. It is connected with a strong sense of personal identity and integrity, independent thought, and a singular purpose or passion. This is a combination that has the strength to push against traditional boundaries and challenge accepted norms.

On the other hand, the "8" also represents instinctual knowing. It represents safety, so it also gives an ability to set appropriate boundaries.

It may also bestow a talent with words. It is the energy of the orator and writer, and the number associated with the alphabet, symbols, words and vowel sounds.

"8" people are generally cheerful and optimistic. They can also be tender, nurturing, compassionate and romantic. "8" people have great strength. They may act tough and be full of bluster, but they are often teddy bears inside. Because the "8" is the number that *merges* the heart and emotional self with the Divine, it is also a powerfully sensual and sexual number.

Downside: the negative qualities of a number are often the other side of the coin. Where the positive "8" is cheerful and optimistic, the negative "8" energy brings despair, heartache, helplessness, codependency, and the tendency to be fatalistic about life. The positive "8" is strong and powerful. The negative side brings weakness, idleness, being an underachiever who feels incapable and invisible.

Alternately, the negative "8" person can be coercive and overbearing, ruthless and violent. They can be full of bravado and vanity – often covers for deeply felt insecurity. The "8" energy can bring deception and misdirection. It is also the violent energy of conflict, rebellion, upheaval and the whirling vortex of the tornado.

Mayan Connection

The "8" is connected with the energy that the K'iche Mayans in Guatemala call "Tijax" (pronounced Tee-Haash), the double-edged knife. In surrendering to a Higher Power, it is often necessary to cut away and let go of that which no longer serves you – so you can step into your full power. It also symbolizes the healing and harmonizing of any of the four bodies: mental, emotional, physical and spiritual. It is the energy that guides the intelligence of doctors. It is also the power of miracles and of synchronicity.

Exercise

Chanting or singing *eh – uu,* the sound of the "8," connects you with divine consciousness and brings the energy of love into your heart center. As you fill yourself with love, you become more able to manifest whatever you desire.

Famous "8" People

Purpose (8.7%): Anthony M. Kennedy, Christie Brinkley, Donald Rumsfeld, Giovanni Giacomo Casanova, Graham Chapman, Helen Keller, Marian Wright Edelman, Rush Limbaugh, Sarah Palin, Tim Berners-Lee, Winston Churchill.

Path (11.5%): Anne Frank, Edmund Burke, Eleanor Holmes Norton, Ellen DeGeneres, Floyd Patterson, Howard Stern, Jasper Johns, John Adams, John D. Rockefeller, Ludwig van Beethoven, Paul Cezanne, Maureen Dowd, Naomi Judd, Stephen Breyer, Tenzin Gyatso (H.H. the Dalai Lama), Ulysses S. Grant, Valentina Tereshkova, Victor Hugo, William Wordsworth.

Legacy (8.9%): Albert Einstein, Angela Davis, Diane Keaton, Douglas MacArthur, Eva Cassidy, Franklin D. Roosevelt, George Gordon (Lord) Byron, Hugh Hefner, J. R. R. Tolkien, Jane Goodall, Marcus Aurelius Antonius, Mitt Romney, Susan B. Anthony, William Jennings Bryan, Zora Neale Hurston.

Drive (7.2%): Andres Segovia, Anthony Charles Linton Blair, Cary Grant, David Livingstone, Edna Saint Vincent Millay, Elvis Aaron Presley, Jesse Woodson James, John David Rockefeller, John Hancock, Laura Ingalls Wilder, Loretta Young, Nicolas Cage, Paul Newman, William Shakespeare.

Totem Animals: horse/zebra ... tiger ... spider.

Deities: Zeus (Greek god of the sky, king of the gods)... Horus (Egyptian god of the sky), Osiris (god of the underworld, fertility & resurrection – and father of Horus), Thoth (arbitrator of disputes, inventor of writing, development of science) ... Bacchus/Dionysus (god of wine, relaxation & intoxication).

Powers: Time ... Sun, Daybreak/Dusk, Evening ... Rainstorm, Rainbow, Snow, Tornado.

Colors: apricot, auburn, brown, caramel, cream, lava, magnolia, pumpkin, yellow-gold ... fire engine red, maroon, rusty red ... hazel, olive, pear, pine green ... pearl ... semi-transparent, translucency.

Gemstones: almandine, amorzonite, apatite, chrysolite, kunzite, kyanite, pearl, sardonyx.

Science-related: agroecology, alien abduction, apiculture, automation, aviation, communication, fluorescence, gastronomy, geoengineering, geoscience, greenhouse gas, harmonic motion, heliosphere, human genome, ichthyology, kinematics, mycology, nanotechnology, natural science, numeration, out-of-body travel, paleontology, precognition, radiation, scientific innovation, social sciences, solar flares, subtle energy, technology forecasting, tectonics, transportation, volcanology.

Work-related Areas/Associations: actress, agronomist, ascetic, assayer, astronomer, bagpiper, ballerina, beekeeping, bioneer, boat builder, bodywork, brakeman, bursar, caddie, calligrapher, caseworker, chancellor, channeler, clinician, clockmaker, comedian, consultant, curendera, doctor, fakir, farming, fire-tender, freeloader, frontier scientist, geisha, geophysicist, geoscientist, goatherd, grafter, grocer, high-paying job, historian, juror, liaison, lifeguard, marketing strategist, materialist, mathematician, microblogging, midwife, miner, minting, mortician, negotiator, neurobiologist, nurse practitioner, orator, painter, paladin, photographer, playwright, police chief, president, professional, professorship, psychologist, quantum physicist, quarryman, retailer, science fiction writer, shoemaker, skateboarder, sociologist, spiritual leadership, staffer, symbologist, technologist, technology forecasting, terrorism scientist, trial lawyer, unsung hero, videographer, welder, wholesaler, writer.

9 (L):   Foundation, Executive, Caretaker   Chant: iii – uu.

Medicine Wheel Path: West/Physical ⇒ Center/Source

Mystical Keywords: Mind-of-God, Holy Spirit, Intelligent Order ... Creative Principle of Life, Cocreation ... Light, Earth, Heart ... Web-of-Life ... Destiny ... Mind-Body Connection ... Psychic Ability, ESP, Intuition, Far-Sighted.

Collective Keywords: Collective Effect, Collective Psyche ... Social Cooperation, Social Identity ... Technological Progress ... Zeitgeist; (-) Historical Crisis, Mass Murder.

Positive Keywords: Earth, Foundation, Material Plane ... Drive for Wholeness, Organizing Principle ... Dream, Perceive, Believe ... Message, Story ... Music, Drum ... Artistic, Creative Personality, Fecundity ... Finish, Fruition, Fulfillment ... Human, Need to Connect: Caretaker, Compassionate, Empathic Understanding,

Emptying, Feeler, Feminine, Heart, Giver, Soft-Spoken, Sounding Board ... Diplomacy, Spoken Word ... Gratitude, Optimism ... Positive Thinking, Will, Free Will ... Fortune, Wealth Consciousness, Good Luck, Philanthropist ... Liberator, Paradigm-Buster, Record-Breaking ... Real Life, Grounded, Concrete ... Executive, Decision-Maker, Foundation-Builder, Management, Power Broker, In-Control, Bottom Line ... Knowledge, Intelligence, Enlightened Sage, Great Thinker, Self-Understanding ... Law, Codify, Judicious ... Moral Principles, Moral Transformation.

Negative/Shadow Keywords: Drama, Sentimentalize, Sensationalist ... Hubris, Narcissistic, Condescend ... Acquisitive, Domineering, Driven, Perfectionist ... Hyper-Vigilant, Psychic Tension, Overwrought ... Opportunism: Deceiver, Lie, Manipulator, Untrustworthy ... Divisiveness: Power Struggle, Us-versus-Them, Extremist, Instigate, Zealot, Martyr ... Antagonize, Denounce, Malicious, Provocation... Personal Travail, Debilitate, Dispirited, Indefensible, Punishment, Self-Deception, Superficiality ... Disempower, Personal Inadequacy, Underachievement ... High-Risk, Out of Control, Uncertain ... Abandonment, Futility, Inhibition ... Foolhardy, Impracticality, Inaccurate, Miscalculate ... Badness, Illicit, Impure, Temptation, Underworld, Wickedness ... Catastrophe, Cataclysm, Terrible.

As a Personal Number: The "9" connects the physical body and awareness with the God-Source. It represents the *mind of God* that acts to establish intelligent order in the concrete, objective reality in which we live. It is the creative principle that weaves the web-of-life by fusing the energies of light, Earth, and the heart. "9" is the foundation. People with "9" as a personal number are foundation-builders.

"9" is a physical number, and the mind-body connection. It teaches us that intuition, ESP, and far-sightedness are abilities not localized in the mental dimension. Rather, they require this mind-body connection that is the essence of our physical awareness. "9" people have an innate ability to use their intuition, and are gifted with empathic understanding.

"9" is the number of destiny. People who have the "9" as a personal number may feel pulled along by the force of destiny to accomplish a particular purpose in life. Perhaps it is this inner knowing that one's destination in life is certain that provides "9" people with a source of strength and confidence. The "9" does tend to bestow good luck, fortune and *wealth consciousness* - by which I mean that "9s" have a mindset that attracts wealth and abundance.

The "9" energy is the foundation of society, embodied in the bedrock that is the law. "9" people represent the pillars of society, and may be found as its lawgivers and executives, decision-makers and power-brokers. "9s" are generally gifted with knowledge and intelligence. They can be quite grounded, in control, and can focus on bottom line issues with single-mindedness when necessary. Yet, they are also good at multi-tasking. They often rise to become respected leaders in the community. They are often prosperous and make good philanthropists.

"9" people have the capacity to dream big dreams, and believe that they can accomplish their dreams. They have the capability to be paradigm-busters and liberators who are champions of innovative groundbreaking ideas. They can take an idea or concept and make it concrete. What they conceive, they can bring to fruition. They are blessed with the power of positive thinking. They have the ability to finish what they start. "9" people also tend to have creative personalities, and can be artistic and drawn to music.

The Zulu in South Africa say that the mark of a true leader is an open heart so that s/he can know the needs of the people. "9" people have this open heart, and it gives them the capacity to be a wise "caretaker" of the people. The reason that "9" people make good executives is perhaps because they have an empathic understanding of others. This also gives them a softer side as a *feeler*. They can make sensitive sounding boards for the ideas and feelings of others. They are often good at diplomacy.

"9" is the number of being fully human. It brings a need to connect and a need to give. "9" people achieve fulfillment through compassion, sensitivity and selfless service on behalf of others and the community. "9" is the number of social cooperation and social identity. "9s" are tapped into the collective psyche. They have an innate understanding, if not always a conscious one, that we are all interconnected in the web-of-life. Our actions and efforts, and the work we do in the world, all ultimately come back around again to our benefit or detriment.

When in balance, "9" people are generally cooperative, friendly, optimistic, tolerant, active in the community, and respected as authorities. They also tend to have a strong moral principles and a strong sense of integrity.

The overall lesson of the "9" is to open fully in gratitude to receive all that Life wants to give. The further the "9" person opens to the possibilities, the more Life will give to him or her.

The challenge of the "9" is feeling worthy to receive all that the Creator wants to give. For "9" people, *actively* practicing gratitude for all of their blessings will enable them to accept even more. Giving back to others in thanks for what life has given to them is also important. It keeps the circle of receiving and giving complete, and keeps the cycle going.

Downside: When out of balance, the "9" can be a dreamer who is detached and uncaring, foolhardy and impractical, full of inhibitions, and stuck in a cycle of chronic underachievement. These "9" people can also be selfish and bitter, depressed, grouchy and meek, with an inability or unwillingness to express feelings.

Alternately, and just as frequently, the "9" person can give so much in an effort to care for others, that she loses herself and her own sense of identity. Sometimes, this is due to early abandonment issues, and/or a deep sense of personal inadequacy. At the extreme, this person can cultivate the image of a martyr who uses caring for others as a means of control.

The aggressive shadow side of the "9" energy can be domineering, acquisitive, and driven to achieve goals. The "9" person who is caught in the shadow energy can also be driven to be a perfectionist and have the hubris of a condescending personality. They can antagonize others, and may have an *us-versus-them* attitude that sparks divisiveness and instigates power struggles. They can be untrustworthy as deceivers and manipulators. They may like drama and become enmeshed in all manner of relationship issues and experiences of personal travail. They are sometimes hyper-vigilant, overwrought and filled with psychic tension and generally out of control.

All of these negative "9" characteristics flow from something that is blocking an underlying longing for wholeness, and a deep need to connect with others. The pathway back to balance is through the feeling nature of the open heart but not in an over-caring way. Rather, balance requires a healthy love and gratitude for both self and others, and a visceral recognition of our interconnectedness in the web-of-life.

Mayan Connection

"9" is connected with "Kawoq." This is the archetype of the House, Hearth and Family around which everything revolves, and from which energy ripples outward to touch larger and larger spheres of influence. Kawoq represents anything that can be grouped: family, teams, organizations and associations, the community, society, the country, the planet, the planetary system, the galaxy, the universe and multiverse. Kawoq means the strength of unity, greater consciousness, the unfolding of the cosmic plan, growth, and fertility. Its energy brings both material and spiritual abundance.

Exercise

Chanting or singing *iii – uu,* the sound of the "9," helps to bring balance and grounding to the physical body. It will also help you discover the next steps needed to make an idea more concrete, or bring you the energy needed to finish something you started. The sound of *iii – uu* also cultivates wealth-consciousness, and helps to dispel a fear of not having enough.

Famous "9" People

Purpose (8.3%): Anita Baker, August Strindberg, Edmund Burke, Everett Dirksen, Kevin Costner, Lee Van Cleef, Lou Holtz, Julian Bond, Margot Tennant Asquith, Michael Eisner, Michel de Nostredame, Millard Fillmore, Mohandas K. Gandhi, Robert Burns, Robert E. Lee, Simone de Beauvoir, Ulysses S. Grant.

Path (11.7%): D. H. Lawrence, Clare Booth Luce, Edith Wharton, Edward M. Kennedy, Eudora Welty, Franklin D. Roosevelt, Harriet Beecher Stowe, Lucretia Coffin Mott, Malcolm McLaren, Margaret Thatcher, Mikhail Baryshnikov, Mordechai Richler, Ralph Waldo Emerson, Richard Nixon, Sri Yukteswar Giri, Viktor Shauberger, William Tecumseh Sherman.

Legacy (10.1%): Adolf Hitler, Charles Lindbergh, Diana Frances Spencer, Ernesto "Che" Guevara, Ethel Merman, Florence Nightingale, Henry David Thoreau, James Joyce, Johann Sebastian Bach, Muhammad Ali, Simone Weil, Tenzin Gyatso (H. H. the Dalai Lama), Wayne Gretzky.

Drive (11.6%): Aristotle Onassis, Booker T. Washington, Boris Yeltsin, Doris Kearns Goodwin, Edgar Allan Poe, Etty Hillesum, Elizabeth Blackwell, Fidel Castro, Gabrielle Reece, James Dickey, Janis Joplin, Jean-Marie Roland, Kahlil Gibran, Lewis Carroll, Max Eastman, Michael Bloomberg, Oliver Hardy, René Descartes, Rudolf Nureyev, Samuel Foote, Stephen Hawking.

Totem Animals: bison ... elephant ... owl.

Deities: Thor (Norse god of thunder, rain & farming) ... Hermes (the messenger god) ... Shakti (Hindu goddess representing the female divine force) ... Michael (the eldest archangel – name means "Like unto God").

Powers: Avalanche, Typhoon.

Colors: apple green, army green, arsenical green, bottle green, emerald, sea green, viridian ... canary yellow, yellow, straw, wisteria ... cinnamon, earth-tone, burnt orange, golden-brown, goldenrod, blue-brown, sepia, tan, tawny, walnut ... cerulean ... amethyst, fuchsia, lavender, mauve, periwinkle, ultraviolet ... cherry, Ferrari red, rust, salmon, sangria ... pearl gray, quartz.

Gemstones: alexandrite, amethyst, diamond, emerald, leopardite, milky quartz, moonstone, peridot, quartz, rhyolite, rubasse, selenium.

Science-related: alchemy, aromatherapy, behaviorism, biomedicine, chemistry, cognitive science, cosmochemistry, cryptography, energetics, ethnology, forestry, geometry, hydroponics, implantology, lithology, medical science, metallurgy, metallography, meteorology, mind-body medicine, neurophysiology, optics, osteology, paleobiology, paleoclimatology, prosopography, radionics, seismology, thanatology, therapeutics, tomography, virology, x-ray crystallography ... gematria, soul science.

Work-related Areas/Associations: adjudicator, admiral, aerialist, anchorman, anchorwoman, anesthesiologist, arbiter, arbitration, archer, astronaut, author, babysitter, barman, bestselling author, builder, cardiac specialist, caretaker, cetologist, chief executive officer, chief lobbyist, cinematographer, cleaner, cobbler, cognitive scientist, columnist, composer, conciliator, conservationist, constable, cosmologist, cosmonaut, couple's therapist, courtroom artist, craftsman, cytologist, depth psychologist, detective, economist, electrician, employer, epigrapher, eulogist, euthanasianist, examiner, exchequer, executive, expressionist, fabulist, firefighter, flyer, forestry, freelancer, gaffer, geochemist, gourmet, gravedigger, gynecologist, hairdresser, hotelier, hypnotherapist, journalist, labor activist, language history, intellectual, lexicographer, longshoreman, logician, mail carrier, management, mapmaker, masseur, massage, mason, marine biologist, metaphysician, military engineer, molecular biologist, music, musicologist, naturalist, neuropsychiatry, ontologist, orientalist, panelist, philanthropist, philologist, pianist, private investigator, producer, public service, research physicist, research scientist, revolutionary, runecaster, semiotician, singer, spy, spiritual activism, surgeon, theology, tinkerer, topographical engineer, tracker, underwriter, umpire, valedictorian, veterinary, vice president, voyager, watchman.

10 (M): Seeker, Pioneer, Master Builder   Chant: oh – uu.

Medicine Wheel Path: North/Spiritual-Intuitive ⇒ Center/God-Source

Mystical Keywords: Immutable Law ... Cosmic Psyche, Oversoul ... Prophecy ... Gate-Keeper, Wizard ... Ancestors, Ceremony ... Awaken, Healing Touch, Transformative Practice ... Cohesive Whole, Unseen Unity, Infinity Grid.

Collective Keywords: Manifest World, Physical Matter, Objective Reality ... Collective Intelligence, Collective Knowledge, Collective Determination, Cooperative Teamwork, Community Support, Support Network, Unified Movement ... Cultural Leadership, Cultural Values, Ubuntu (I Am Who I Am Because of / Through Other People); (-) Mass Hysteria ... Rat Race ... Criminal Underworld, Gangsterism.

Positive Keywords: Mastery, Wisdom ... Seeker, Meaning, Naming, Understand ... Conceptual Leap, Pioneer ... Thinker, Scholar, Linear Thinking, Rational Analysis ... Idealism ... Abundance, Physical Manifestation ... Aim, Direction, Movement ... New Beginning, Life Change, Launch/Outcome ... Autonomy, Ego-Consciousness, Individual Responsibility, Personal Responsibility ... Decisive, Efficient, Practical, Able ... Master Builder, Developer, Energizer, Organizer ... Policy-Maker, Rule-Maker ... Counsel ... Empathic, Emotion, Emotional Intelligence, Gentleness ... Cordial, Friendliness, Outgoing, Polite ... Intimate Relationship, Romance.

Negative/Shadow Keywords: Stupid, Irrational, False ... Careless, Naïve, Simpleton ... Anguish, Worry, Hurry Sickness, Paranoia, Personal Darkness, Struggle ... Breakdown, Crisis, Calamity, Uncontrollable ... Duality, Polarize ... Deprivation, Energetic Blockage, Emotional Numbness, Bogged-down, Entangled, Immobility, Slavery ... Pity, Pout ... Cowardly, Inhibited, Inability ... Suspicion, Defensiveness ... Envy, Ingratiate ... Arrogance, Egotism, Vain, Tactless, Ridicule, Sarcastic ... Abuse of Power, Power Grab, Acrimony, Enmity, Vehemence ... Sociopathic Behavior, Sabotage, Subterfuge, Plot ... Iniquitous, Scandalous ... Puritanical.

As a Personal Number: The "10" is the connection between the spiritual dimension of our being and the Divine God-Source or All-That-Is. It is the unseen unity of all things, the everywhere connected cosmic psyche and what some healers call the infinity grid. It is the source of prophecy and immutable law. People who have "10" as a personal number are naturally connected with this level of collective intelligence, although it may be at unconscious levels.

The "10" is the "Gate-Keeper." It is the number of wisdom, questioning and discernment. Like the ten fingers on the hands, "10" as a personal number gives you both the ability and desire to "grasp" the deeper meaning of things.

"10" people are spiritual "seekers" who want to know how things work at fundamental levels not necessarily taught in school. "10" is the number of intellectual mastery, rational analysis and the search for meaning. "10s" tend to be thinkers who are comfortable dealing with both the abstract and the practical. While "10" people can take a conceptual leap with the best of them, they are generally action-oriented and good at solving problems. The downside of this search for meaning can be a tendency to "over-process" things.

"10s" like clarity, and have difficulty with uncertainty. So, when things get chaotic and confusing, "10" people can get stuck thinking about every possibility and option, chewing each alternative over and over in their mind. The way out is through movement – take a walk, exercise, run, dance, or jump up and down.

The "10" person is the *master builder*[22] who can take a new idea and make it an objective reality. "10" people are energizers, organizers, pioneers and developers who work in cooperation with others to get things done. They are practical and able, and often adept at seeing the way forward, taking aim, and providing direction for others. "10s" are most often decisive, honest, altruistic, and egalitarian in nature. "10" people are not only good starters but also good finishers. They take personal responsibility, have the strength to follow through on ideas to make them happen, and to bring projects to completion. These are leadership qualities.

"10" is the step when creation is complete. "1" is genesis and pure potential. "10 is the outcome: the physical matter of the manifest world, objective reality. Thus, "10" is the energy of abundance, and physical manifestation. As a personal number, it suggests that things

---

[22] Traditional western numerology identifies the number 22 as the Master Builder.

will come naturally. This is the number that teaches that "nothing that is yours can be taken away." Conversely, nothing that is not yours can be had at any price or through any amount of effort – at least not in a lasting way. So, the lesson is to learn to discriminate what is really yours, and what is not.

"10" is the number of completion and outcomes. So, it is also about learning to stop, and to digest and integrate what life teaches you. It is important for the "10" person to occasionally take time to stop and reflect instead of continuing to push to get the next project done. When out of balance, the "10" may want to stay in action on a never-ending list of things to do. Alternately, the "10" person may have a tendency to hang onto things, or remain in situations longer than is desirable. These are different faces of the same avoidance strategy. Staying busy or staying stuck avoids the need to look at things that need to be processed, resolved and integrated.

"10" people not only have intellectual intelligence but also emotional intelligence. They can be empathic, and are generally cordial, outgoing, gentle and friendly. They make good friends and counselors. "10" is also the number of romance and intimate relationships, so "10" people also make good lovers!

"10" is the number of ceremony and service. It is the number of completing one thing, and then stepping up to the next level to begin something new. When this energy is prominent in a chart, it suggests that this lifetime may be, in some sense, about tying up loose ends, and coming to closure before stepping up to the next level of intensity and service.

Downside: Very often, the shadow-side qualities of the numbers are the flip-side of the coin from the positive qualities. Where the positive "10" is a thinker and a seeker after understanding and wisdom, the negative "10" can be stupid, naïve, careless and false. Where the positive "10" is decisive, the negative "10" is full of anguish, worry, self-pity, and even paranoia. The shadow of the "10" brings breakdown, crisis, and struggle.

The shadow of the "10" is about duality and things becoming polarized. As you might anticipate, there are two paths into the dark side of the "10." The first stems from an energetic blockage resulting from deprivation of some sort, and/or from becoming entangled in web of circumstances or events from which it is difficult to escape. This can lead to defensiveness, inhibitions and a puritanical mindset. It can also lead to suspicion, inability and, in the extreme, to mental and emotional immobility, and even emotional numbness.

The other pathway is more aggressive, and often a cover for deep insecurity. It presents itself as arrogance, egotism, acrimony, enmity and abuse of power. This pathway leads to calamity and often uncontrollable outcomes. It can be a gateway to iniquitous behavior and even sociopathic behavior.

The "10" person has a hardwired connection to collective knowledge and intelligence, even if it is not a conscious one. The way back to the positive side for the "10" person who is out of balance is through an understanding that we are all interconnected. It is through the recognition of what the South African Zulus call "Ubuntu." Roughly translated it means, *I am who I am because of or through other people.* It not only takes a village to raise a child, it also takes community support and a loving, supportive network to help the "10" person stay in balance. The reciprocal is also true. The more that the "10" person can be an active part of a community, the more balanced s/he will be.

Mayan Connection

"10" is "Ajpu," or Grandfather Sun, and is about clarity and mental acuity. Ajpu is the hunter who uses the breath to blow the dart through the blowgun. It is the power of breath and the voice to call to ourselves that which will nourish and support us – through both the spoken word and song. Ajpu is the spiritual warrior and soothsayer.

Ajpu brings material and spiritual certainty. It represents any work done with the hands to beautify the earth. Ajpu is transformation and mutation, and gives the power to overcome negative energy. It is also the energy of the traveler, dancer and artist.

Exercise

Chanting or singing *oh – uu,* the sound of the "10," nourishes the mind and spirit, and brings greater clarity when you are seeking answers, or making decisions. It is an aid during life-changes and periods of personal transformation including new beginnings.

Famous "10" People

Purpose (8.2%): Arnold Toynbee, Charles Lindbergh, Francis Bacon, Jacob Bronowski, Jacques Cousteau, Jesse James, Martha Carey Thomas, Milton Friedman, Nicolas Cage, Leonardo da Vinci, Nelson Mandela, Pat Benetar, Ronald Reagan, Valentina Tereshkova, William Shakespeare, Zulfikar Ali Bhutto.

Path (9.1%): Andrew Johnson, Angela Davis, Babe Ruth, Beatrice Potter Webb, Charles de Montesquieu, Donald Rumsfeld, Franklin Pierce, George Washington Carver, Grover Cleveland, Jesse James, Joan Baez, Joe E. Lewis, J. Edgar Hoover, John Henry (Doc) Holliday, Richard Branson, Sergey Brin, Stephen Hawking, Stephen Potter, Theodore Roosevelt, Yves Saint Laurent.

Legacy (9.6%): Dr. Albert Schweitzer, Andres Segovia, Anne Frank, Ayn Rand, Beautiful Painted Arrow, Charles Darwin, Dwight D. Eisenhower, Eduoard Manet, George S. Patton, Henny Youngman, Horace Greeley, Jimmy Carter, Liz Claiborne, Malcolm McLaren, Robert de Niro, Sylvia Pankhurst, Ted Kaczynski, Thomas Jefferson, Tim Berners-Lee, Ulysses S. Grant, Viktor Shauberger.

Drive (7.7%): Abraham Lincoln, Anne Bronte, Christopher Marlowe, Elizabeth Barrett Browning, Galileo Galilei, Isaac Newton, James Watt, John Belushi, Joseph Stalin, Marian Wright Edelman, Nathan Lane, Richard Joseph Daley, Sarah Palin, Sophie Tucker, Ulysses Simpson Grant, Warren Buffet.

Totem Animals: gorilla ... otter ... trout.

Deities: Artemis (goddess of the hunt) ... Hestia (goddess of home & hearth) ... Oceanus (god of the river surrounding the earth) ... Pluto (god of the underworld).

Powers: Autumn ... Storm.

Colors: bronze, champagne, coffee, copper-blonde, dandelion, golden, rose-gold, sienna, taupe, vanilla, whiskey-brown ... ... jade, mint, olivine ... ghost white, silver ... imperial blue, prune.

Gemstones: bloodstone, ebonite, garnet, jade, melanite, olivine, rhinestone.

Science-related: alternative medicine, anthropology, archaeology, arithmetic, atmosphere, atomization, biochemistry, bioinformatics, botany, calculus, chromodynamics, cognitive neuroscience, developmental psychology, electrodynamics, endocrinology, ecosystems, energy scattering, ethnopharmacology, euphenics, evolutionary biology, fringe science, genetic engineering, geomancy, geomagnetics, geophysics, global warming, hydrodynamics, hydrology, linguistics, magnetic confinement, mathematical psychology, mechanics, neuropathology, neuroscience, ophthalmology, propulsion, psychophysiology, rehabilitative science, science of immortality, space-time, solar power, solar radiation, superfluidity, theosophy, volcanism.

Work-related Areas/Associations: academician, aeronautical engineering, arbitrageur, astromythology, barmaid, biologist, broker, bouncer, bullfighter, cardiologist, cashier, cataloger, caterer, chief financial officer, choreographer, climatologist, comedienne, conventioneer, cook, costume designer, counsel, curator, deejay, deep-sea diver, demographer, dendrochronologist, developer, documentary writer, draftsman, drag queen, elder statesman, entomologist, envoy, ethicist, evangelist, executive coach, expediter, exopolitics, exterminator, farrier, filmmaker, geoengineer, goldsmith, graphologist, groundskeeper, hair stylist, harvester, headmaster, housekeeper, industrial engineer, lecturer, magician, marine ecologist, masseuse, media analyst, mind reader, mythology, neurosurgery, oceanographer, organizer, orthopedist, painting, peacemaker, pilot, plumber, poet, policy-maker, project manager, proprietor, psychophysiology, psychic surgeon, publicist, purser, radio operator, remote viewing, rheumatologist, restorer, scholar, servant, sleuth, soloist, space medicine, statistician, subcontractor, superintendent, tarot, toxicologist, trainer, treasurer, tutor, weaponeer, wizard, writing.

11 (N): Connector, Seer, Healer, Teacher   Chant: uu – yy

Medicine Wheel Path: Center / God-Source ⇒ Up Above (Higher Dimensions)

Mystical Keywords: Limitless, Beginningless, Indivisible, Pure Energy ... Universal Love, Supreme Consciousness, Cosmic Law, Divine Truth, Divinity, Higher Vision ... Avatar, Hierophant, Shamanic Priesthood ... Intuitive Consciousness, Mystical Experience, Mystical Revelation ... True Love, True Power, Highest Good ... Compassionate Meditation, Guided Meditation ... Spiritual Value.

Collective Keywords: Cooperative Venture, Cooperative Partner ... Collective Emotional Knowledge, Group Cohesion ... Collective Influence, Collective Outcome, Critical Mass ... Service-Oriented, Volunteerism, Charity, Mutual Aid, Social Capital ... Civil Liberties, Human Rights, Racial Justice ... Mass Movements. (-) Insurrection, Revolt, Collapse, Terrorism ... Environmental Collapse.

Positive Keywords: Seer, Healer, Teacher ... Futurist, Trailblazer, Entrepreneur ... Action, Change Agent, Reformer, Emancipator ... Connector, Outreach, Shepherd ... Cultivator, Shaper, Delegator ... Need to Belong, Interdependence ... Feeling, Giving, Compassion ... Diversity, Equality ... Curiosity, Creativity, Creative Breakthrough, Open Mind, Wonderment ... Playtime, Poetic Imagination ... Sound, Musician, Written Word ... Imagery, Non-Linear ... Strength, Confident, Resilient, Sure ... Masculine ... Ambition, Famous ... Manifestation, Prosperity ... Critical Reason, Ordered Thought, Practical Detail, Scientific Mind ... Individual Freedom, Individual Liberty, Personal Freedom.

Negative/Shadow Keywords: Illusory, Ego-Mind ... Shattering, Discontinuity, Unpredictable Change ... Compulsive, Excitable ... Impractical, Spacey ... Self-Centered, Self-Indulgent, Superficial, Neglectful, Unconnected ... Atheist, Godless, Soulless Vacuum ... Purposeless, Passionless, Pointlessness ... Loser, Dependent, Impotent, Inadequacy, Powerless, Self-Pity, Timid ... Angst, Foreboding, Identity Crisis, Melancholy, Mental Anguish, Pessimist ... Materialism, Power Games, Shortage ... Charlatanism, Exploitation, Underhandedness ... Antagonist, Coercion, Ego-Trip, Dominating,

Imperious Nature ... Fanatic Believer, Righteous Retribution ... Negativity, Spiteful ... Adversity, Hardship, Tragedy ... Sentimentalist ... Indecency, Naughty, Pleasure-Loving, Permissive.

As a Personal Number: The "11" connects the God-Source with the Up Above. By *Up Above*, I mean the higher dimensional realm or upper world where the qualities of universal love and supreme consciousness reside. In more modern technical terms, you can conceive of this dimension as the source field of indivisible, limitless, pure energy and perfect coherence. Out of this connection between the divinity and pure potentiality of the God-Source and this field of supreme consciousness flows cosmic law and divine truth. This is why the "11" is considered a Master Number.

"11" people are tapped into this realm of intuitive consciousness and mystical revelation that is the domain of avatars, seers and healers. "11" people have an inherent ability to receive insight, and embody inspiration in a way that it can be brought to the people. Although this may sound wonderful, the "11" is not an easy energy to have as a personal number, and it takes maturity and practice to handle its full potential. For the "11" person, inner guidance often comes unbidden in a flash of insight or an unexpected vision. It can be inner wisdom that comes in a powerful dream, and sometimes recurring dreams that show up like marching orders. At times, sudden inspiration can take the "11" person off-guard and then pull her forward, kicking and screaming to take action on what she has received.

"11" people are generally resilient, and for good reason since "11" is also the energy of sudden, unexpected events that can be totally life-changing. "11" people have to be flexible. As Charles Dubois once said, "The most important thing is this: To be able at any moment to sacrifice what we are for what we could become." If/when Life knocks the "11" person off her feet, it is telling her to open to deeper levels of inner guidance and inspiration and move forward. The alternative is to shut down and turn off.

The "11" energy is the power of manifestation. It represents the *Logos* or embodiment of divine wisdom manifest in creation, and is connected with the power of sound. When the Christian Bible says, "In beginning was the *word* ...," that *word* is the first vibration or sound from which everything that exists in objective reality was created. The aborigines of Australia say that we are "singing ourselves into existence," and this may be true. Sound carries this creative power of manifestation. Thoughts and intentions that are put into spoken words, songs, or music have the power to create – for good or ill. People that have an "11" as a personal number can use sound more effectively than most to help manifest needed money and resources, clear away obstacles, do healing, and so on.[23] In reality, "11" people often have a talent with the spoken or written word, and also may be good musicians.

"11" people have strength, confidence and tend to be action-oriented. They are futurists and trailblazers who have a high regard for personal freedom. As a result, they often push up against the limits imposed by the society in which they live. In doing so, they expand the boundaries of individual freedom for others. They are emancipators, change agents and reformers. They are teachers who, in their effort to reach out and connect with others, become cultivators of people and shapers of events. Curious, by nature, they generally have creative, open minds and the ability to make creative breakthroughs, often as a result of their inner guidance. Their ambition to realize their dreams and visions is sometimes misunderstood to be of the self-promoting kind. But, it is most often altruistic. In fact, most "11" people recognize their connectedness and interdependence with others. As a result, they tend to have an unselfish regard for the welfare of others.

While the signature quality of the "11" person may be their intuitive ability to receive insight and act on inspiration, they also have the power of critical reason and ordered thought. When they focus their intention, they can effectively manage practical details, and may even be gifted with a scientific mind – like Edward Teller and J. Robert Oppenheimer in the list of famous "11" people shown below.

Downside: All numbers have both positive sides, and negative or shadow sides. With the "11," the shadow can be dark and deep. People with an "11" as a personal number are hard-wired into a deeper level of guidance but not always conscious of it. What they are

---

[23] My wife, Jeanne White Eagle (who has an "11" Purpose *and* Path), is quite adept at doing this, and I can personally attest to its effectiveness.

receiving on an inner level can be akin to drinking from a cosmic fire hose. As a coping mechanism, the "11" person can be unfocused and spacey, and suffer from inattentional blindness – a failure to notice things that are in plain sight. They can also be excitable, compulsive, impractical, superficial and self-indulgent.

What they are receiving on an intuitive level can also create a sense of foreboding or pessimism. Alternately, it can cause a person to feel righteous and be an elitist, as if they know more or are better than someone else. All of these are actually protective behaviors in that a lack of focus, pessimism, righteousness or elitism shut down a part of the personality and insulate it from receiving and acting on inner guidance.

At its most severe, the "11 energy" can be overwhelming and shattering to the ego. This can lead to psychosis and obsessive-compulsive behaviors, but it can also cause the person to shut down and become unconnected from their source of inner insight, inspiration and guidance. As a result, they can feel like a loser who is dependent on others, impotent, powerless, and full of melancholy and self-pity. Over time, they can become passionless and adopt a mindset that everything is purposeless. This is a dark soulless vacuum where God does not exist and all actions share an equal pointlessness. It is a tough place in which to be.

The shadow side of the "11" energy can also manifest in more active ways. It can be the source of energy beneath materialism, and the power games that result around surplus and shortage, haves and have-nots. As night follows day, the fear of lack is the breeding ground for underhandedness, charlatanism and exploitation of others. The negative "11" can become the dominating antagonist who gets what s/he wants through coercion. But, in our current system, only a few can be on top of the financial pyramid. The path of materialism rarely quenches the fear of not having enough, and never fills the divine longing for connection inside one's soul. Pursuing it ultimately leads to frustration and negativity.

The shadow side of the "11" can bring hardship and adversity. But, as Benjamin Disraeli once said, "There is no education like adversity." In whichever of the guises described above that it may come, the path back to balance for the "11" person is to reclaim their inherent ability to receive inner guidance and insight - and then to be willing to act on it. Having an open mind means temporarily, and with permission, putting the ego-mind in check. Acting on guidance requires a willingness to show up, shut up, and keep saying "yes."

Mayan Connection

"11" is connected with "Imox," the energy of the *Seer, Visionary* and *Healer*. Imox represents the limbic system that deals primarily with emotion and motivation. The energy of Imox puts the mind in a receptive mode, increases spiritual strength, and helps manage the energies of change. Imox gives a natural connection to higher vision and the ability to receive inner guidance, cosmic messages and mystical revelations for oneself and others.

Exercise

The "11" is the connection between the center and the up above. Its sound is *uu – yy*. This sounds just like uu – iii, the connection between the center and the west/physical (number 2). Because of this, when you are chanting or singing *uu – yy,* the sound of the "11," visualize your own center connecting with the higher dimensional realm where the qualities of universal love and divine truth reside. Chanting or singing in this way will open you up to receive guidance on any particular question or issue that you desire.

Famous "11" People

Purpose (9.1%): Alexander Graham Bell, Anton Chekhov, Ayn Rand, Alice Paul, Barry Goldwater, Cole Porter, Edward Teller, Ellen DeGeneres, Ernesto "Che" Guevara, Hillary Rodham Clinton, Jeanne White Eagle, Jeffrey Immelt, Rosa Parks, Thomas Jefferson, Vidal Sassoon, Virginia Woolf, Wayne Gretzky.

Path (9.6%): Abraham Lincoln, Barack Obama, Booker T. Washington, Charles Darwin, Christie Brinkley, Colin Powell, Douglas MacArthur, Dwight D. Eisenhower, James Joyce, John McCain III, Mary Jane (Mae) West, Otto von Bismarck, Paul Newman, Pierre Auguste Renoir, Rudolf Nureyev, Sophie Tucker, Vincent van Gogh, Walt Disney.

Legacy (10.1%): Barack Obama, Clare Booth Luce, Daniel Webster, Elizabeth Blackwell, Frederick Douglass, Henry Wadsworth Longfellow, George Frederick Handel, John Hancock, J. Robert Oppenheimer, Nicolaus Copernicus, Oprah Winfrey, René Descartes, Samuel Langhorne Clemens, Sandra Day O'Connor, Victor Hugo, Vidal Sassoon, Walt Disney, William Tecumseh Sherman.

Drive (9.8%): Andy Kaufman, Babe Ruth, Benny Hill, Betty Friedan, Federico Fellini, George Gordon (Lord) Byron, Jackson Pollack, John Edgar Hoover, John Fitzgerald Kennedy, Margaret Hilda Thatcher, Mikhail Gorbachev Sergeevich, Susan Bromwell Anthony, Paul Cezanne, Richard Leakey.

Totem Animals: chameleon … seagull … unicorn.

Deities: Eros (god of love) … Shiva (Hindu destroyer of evil) … Gabriel (archangel messenger of God – name means "The Strength of God").

Powers: Solar … Monsoon, Water Being, Water-Fire Being.

Colors: bisque, brownish, honeydew, orange-red, sand, sinopia, … blue-gray, boysenberry, navy blue, purple … cordovan, redwood, rose, scarlet, wine … Kelly green, olive green … opalescent … pitch black.

Gemstones: andradite, cairngorm, calcite, carnelian, cyanite, descloizite, dolomite, harlequin opal, lapis lazuli, morganite, pyrope, red jasper, rose quartz, zircon.

Science-related: bioelectography, biomechanics, carbon cycle research, computing, Egyptology, ethnology, geoclimatology, heliophysics, human behavior, mathematical physics, molecular robotics, morphology, neuropsychology, non-Euclidian geometry, petrology, pulmonology, quantum biology, quantum electronics, space weather, taxonomy, thermionics, topography.

Work-related Areas/Associations: accounting, artisan, aviator, bioethicist, bookbinder, bookseller, brewer, business leader, cameraman, cardiovascular epidemiologist, cartographer, change agent, change-maker, connector, consigliore, cosmogonist, court clerk, custodian, dental hygienist, doorman, ecologist, entrepreneur, ethnomusicology, exobiologist, fishmonger, football player, forecaster, futurist, gardener, geneticist, geographer, high-priest, horseman, impersonator, impresario, internationalist, internist, laborer, linguist, marital mediator, medical anthropologist, mediumship, memoirist, modeling, musician, nursing, ornithologist, particle physicist, philosopher, photochemist, pipefitter, political leader, pontiff, porter, press, provisioner, psychiatry, pyrotechnician, radioman, radiowoman, receiver, renunciant, sailor, sentry, set dresser, shepherd, spiritual leader, surrealist, teacher, theologian, theoretician, trader, translation, trucking, whaler, writing coach, zoologist ... being "famous."

12 (P): Achiever, Pathfinder, Promoter   Chant: oh – ah.

Medicine Wheel Path: North/Spiritual-Intuitive ⇒ East/Mental

Mystical Keywords: All-Powerful, Divine Love, Divine Power, First Cause, Creative Forces, Perfect ... Spiritual/Universal Law, Spiritual Intelligence ... Extra-Terrestrial, Higher Being ... Human Spirit ... Channel, Gateway, Psychic Space, Peak Awareness ... Priest, Religion.

Collective Keywords: Global Mind ... Mass Awakening ... Connectivity, Group Coherence, Shared Meaning, Larger Whole, Social Network, Social Order, Solidarity ... Prevailing Worldview ... Social Justice ... Military Power ... World-Changing. (-) Blackmail, Witch Hunt ... Atrocity, Holocaust.

Positive Keywords: Visionary, Pathfinder, Initiator, Inspirer, Uplifting ... Innovation, Invention ... Changes, New Direction, Realign, Adaptability ... Life Purpose, Deeper Meaning, Personal Belief ... Purposeful, Dependable, Faithful ... Service, Honesty, Fair Play, Arbitrator ... Contentment, Inner Focus ... Thinking, Idea-Driven, Objective Consciousness, Systematic Investigation ... Known, Realism, Measure ... Coordination, Strategy ... Achiever, Crusader, Chief ... Business, Acquisition, Plenty ... Fearless, Uninhibited, Risk-Taker, Playfulness, Carefreeness ... Physical Body, Physical Life, Sensing, Therapy ... Alluring, Amorous, Ecstasy, Libidinous,

Procreative, Romantic Ardor … Woman, Women … Ethics, Hard Truth, Moral Principle, Morals, Moral Rectitude.

Negative/Shadow Keywords: Trial … Extremism, Workaholic, Glutton … Violence, Earthquake, Explosion, Implosion, Dangerous, Shockwave … Need for Control, Power Over, Unyielding … Manipulative, Pretentious, Self-Importance, Egocentricity … Ruthless, Tyrant … Emotional Constipation, Fixate, Obsession … Avaricious, Miser … Dishonest, Disgrace, Sinful … Moralistic, Self-Righteous … Ornery, Indignation, Resentment, Hypercritical, Vindictive … Bi-Polar Thinking, Emotional Alienation … Excessive Individuation, Outsider, Rebellious, Iconoclastic … Ignorant, Inept, Undisciplined, Narrow, Shallow … Self-Doubt, Self-Castigation, Defeatism, Hopeless.

As a Personal Number: The number "12" connects the spiritual realm with the mental dimension, infusing the mind with spiritual intelligence. Edgar Cayce, who was called The Sleeping Prophet, said, "The spirit is life; mind is the builder." The "12" connects these two archetypal energies.

Think of the "12" energy as the breath of the Creator that brings vitality to the human spirit, and connects us to the generative aspects of divine love and power. As a personal number, the "12" brings a potent constellation of potential talents that include an energetic and intuitive nature, and the ability to inspire and lead. However, the "12" energy is not entirely under our conscious control and volition. Rather, Spirit is in the driver's seat and is, therefore, in a position of dominance.

The "12" person is the visionary, pathfinder, promoter and achiever. This means that "12" people are able to help shape things on a large scale – even through small beginnings and from behind the scenes. It's helpful to remember that each action that is taken has an effect for seven generations (140-150 years). Small shifts and innovations in the present can result in big changes in the future. When the energy of the pathfinder and achiever can be harnessed for practical results, the "12" person can have an extraordinary impact on the world – for good or ill, as can be seen in the list of famous people below.

The "12" person often has a powerful sense of their own purpose in life which allows them to act with a purposeful confidence and even be fearless risk-takers when necessary. They often have strong personal beliefs, and are generally dependable and faithful. The challenge that goes with the "12" is often ego-based: either not fully accepting one's own power or, alternately, being too forceful in using it.

"12" is the energy of *woman* and *women,* and is intuitive and procreative. Yet, it is also the energy of objective consciousness and thinking. This marriage between intuition and objectivity is potent. It gives "12" people the power to create new directions through innovation and invention. They have the potential to take a creative impulse from the first intuitive spark all the way to the finished product in the real world. "12s" often make good leaders and executives. They have within themselves the ability to initiate ideas, inspire others, and then drive energetically forward to achieve the desired results. This is a truly powerful constellation of talents that the "12" person can apply in personal, social, and business arenas.

"12" is the energy of the priest and is connected with spiritual law and religion (in its most uplifting sense). It is also the energy of ethics, honesty, social justice, and service to others. So, "12s" may be found in helping professions. As "12" is also the number of physical life and the physical body, "12" people also make natural healers and good therapy providers.

"12" people can have an uninhibited nature, and be playful and carefree – all of which are wonderful, uplifting and even much-needed qualities in the right context.

"12" is the energy of ecstasy and romantic ardor. "12" people are highly creative, and the same energy that fuels their creativity may also fuel a strong sexual drive. "12" people generally make good lovers. I find it very interesting that the "12" is also the number of moral rigor and rectitude. Having a high libido doesn't necessarily conflict with moral integrity but it can strain the limits of societal norms, particularly since the "12" is a sometimes explosive and rebellious energy.

Downside: As noted above, the "12" can be an explosive energy. It often shakes things up. It gives the power to swim upstream against the current, or go against the grain. The "12" person can be rebellious and iconoclastic, a goad for societal norms to change – and this is not always a bad thing. But, the "12" is also the energy of wildfires, earthquakes, explosions, implosions and shockwaves. It can be undisciplined, ruthless, violent and dangerous.

The downside can also manifest as absolutism, extremism, obsession and a tendency to be a workaholic. Negative "12s" can be catty and ornery. They can suffer trials that come suddenly and unexpectedly into their lives. And they can be ignorant and inept, shallow and narrow-minded.

The positive and balanced "12" person is confident and purposeful. But the shadow side of the "12" energy brings self-doubt, defeatism, emotional alienation, possible cowardice and, in the extreme, a feeling that all is hopeless.

The more active energy of the dark side can be self-righteous, full of self-importance, pretentious, manipulative, and have an unyielding need for control. These "12s" can be hypercritical and vindictive, dishonest and sinful. As leaders, they can be ruthless tyrants.

Mayan Connection

"12" is connected with "Iq," the Wind, the Breath of the Creator, the element that governs ideas and change. It is inspiration, and the principle of vitality that gives life and awakens intuition. It is represented by hurricanes and tornadoes. Its energy can shake things up, but it also helps to manage the forces of change. People with this energy sometimes know when something is going to happen because they experience quakes in their body – like a twitch in the eye, or a shaking of the hands.

Exercise

Chanting or singing *oh – ah,* the sound of the "12," activates spiritual intelligence and intuition, and brings balance to inner and outer energies in uncertain times. It is especially helpful when you are making changes in your life, and need insight about what new direction to follow.

Famous "12" People

Purpose (5.3%): Adlai Stevenson, Aldo Leopold, Bridget Fonda, Calvin Coolidge, Dwight D. Eisenhower, Franklin Pierce, Humphrey Bogart, Mohammed Elbaradei, Richard M. Nixon, Theodore Seuss Geisel (Dr. Seuss), Theodore Roosevelt, Walter Elias Disney, Warren Buffet.

Path (7.3%): Christopher Marlowe, Donna Karan, Elizabeth Barrett Browning, Elvis Aron Presley, Fidel Castro, Giovanni Giacomo Casanova, Hank Aaron, Kahlil Gibran, Karl Marx, Paramahansa Yogananda, Samuel Langhorne Clemens, Sarah Palin, William James, Zora Neale Hurston, United States of America.

Legacy (7.1%): Abba Eban, Alan Alda, Arianna Huffington, Benjamin Franklin, Edgar Allan Poe, Edna Saint Vincent Millay, Edward Teller, Floyd Patterson, George Foreman, James Madison, Janis Joplin, Lewis Carroll, Pierre Auguste Renoir, Stephen Hawking, Vladimir Putin, Winston Churchill, Zachary Taylor.

Drive (9.4%): Albert Einstein, Alphonsus Capone, Ayn Rand, Eric Clapton, Helen Keller, Immanuel Kant, Muhammad Ali, Nicolaus Copernicus, Richard Bruce (Dick) Cheney, Rush Limbaugh, Sandra Day O'Connor, Sylvia Plath, Thomas Johnathan (Stonewall) Jackson, Vladimir Ilich Ulyanov Lenin.

Totem Animals: antelope … phoenix … wildcat.

Deities: Mars (god of war) … Lakshmi (Hindu goddess of good fortune & prosperity).

Powers: Mountain, Water, Women … Earthquake, Volcano … Spring.

Colors: amaranth, candy apple red, cardinal, … aquamarine, baby blue, blueberry, mulberry, powder blue, … bone, cinnabar, chestnut, cocoa brown, tangerine … emerald-green, jasper, lemon-yellow, yellow-green, raw umber, saffron, sunset, topaz … snow-white.

Gemstones: aquamarine, chrysocolla, fire opal, fulgerite, hematite, jasper, rhodolite, rutile, topaz, zirconium.

Science-related: acupuncture, astronomy, chronoastrobiology, chronobiology, computer science, digital biology, earth changes, earth science, ergonomics, fluid dynamics, free energy, personology, mathematics, nonphysical intelligence, parapsychology, psychokinesis, psychometry, psycho-pharmacology, psychotronic research, quantum memory, robotics, solar cycles, solar geomagnetic activity, superstring theory, wave genetics, world-wide-web.

Work-related Areas/Associations: adventure education, adventurer, angelology, animation, apiculturist, arbitrator, arithmetician, attorney, ayahuasquero, bio-geographer, biomedical engineer, bricklayer, butcher, calligraphy, cardiac surgeon, catering, chief, chief constable, city planner, computer scientist, conductor, contractor, copilot, cosmetology, crusader, dentistry, designer, diarist, driver, drover, electrical engineer, engineering, environmental activist, ethnographer, evolutionist, exorcist, filmmaker, fireman, folklorist, fortune teller, gambler, general, glazier, goalkeeper, guitarist, gymnast, hagiography, hypnosis therapist, ichthyologist, illustrator, importer, janitor, jeweler, journalism, managing editor, matchmaker, military leader, minister, monk, neuroanatomist, nuclear engineering, numismatist, odontologist, paleoepigrapher, paleontologist, pastor, physicist, planner, pharmacist, pollster, preacher, priest, priesthood, promoter, publisher, pugilist, puppeteer, sales, samurai, scientist, social media, staff, steganography, songwriter, sportsman, stenographer, storyteller, tailor, technician, test pilot, theoretical physicist, singer-songwriter, therapy, training, troubadour, undertaker, volcanologist, waiter, weatherman, woodsman.

13 (Q): Builder, Success, Wealth   Chant: iii – oh.

Medicine Wheel Path: West/Physical ⇒ North/Spiritual-Intuitive

Mystical Keywords: Ancestor, Guardian Angel … Causal Plane, Unknowable, Unlimited, Transcendence … Clairsentient, Revelation, Divination … Now Moment, Pure Present … Sudden Awakening, Reawakening … Mind Control, Magical Powers.

Collective Keywords: Community … Facilitation, Need to Agree, Joint Solution, Middle Ground, Partnership … Social Harmony, Social Utility, Will to Connect … Fabric of Society, Grassroots, Network, Volunteer … Human Morality, Civil Courage … Paradigm Shift. (-) Social Dilemma, Cultural Upheaval, Meltdown, Revolution.

Positive Keywords: Now Moment, Choice Point, Cycle, Personal Change, Inner Work, Realignment … Life, Build, Procreate … Natural World, Physical Plane, Physical Phenomena … Real-World, Experience … Logical Mind, Prediction, Outside-the-Box … Expectation, Readiness, Goal-Oriented, Mental Focus, Persistence … Authoritative, Independent, Bold, Self-Assurance … Adviser, Expertise … Creative, Catalyst, Dynamism … Success, Wealth … Giving Back, Goodness, Godliness, Selfless, Volunteer … Talking, Verbal Ability, Listening … Visual Imagination, Visual Ability, Aesthetic Delight, Artistic Genius … Body-Conscious, Athletic, Vitality, Youthfulness.

Negative/Shadow Keywords: Aimless, Directionless, Meaningless, Underachiever … Fail, Fool, Mistake, Blind Spot … Miserable, Moody, Pessimistic … Codependent … Disorder … Evasive, Flee, Insular, Least Sociable, Selfish, Separability, Xenophobe … Scarcity, Craving … Individualistic, Willful … Pompous, Presumptuous, Insufferable … Negative, Ill-Mannered … Antagonistic, Contempt, Disobedient, Confrontation, Hatefulness, Treacherous … Charlatan, Corrupt, Extortion, Human Greed … Seditious, Undermine, Overthrow, Fear-Monger … Unjust, Wrongdoing, Lawsuit … Over-Dramatic, Mad, Vitriolic, Fanaticism … Depraved, Malevolence, Sadist.

As a Personal Number: "13" is the energy of the physical world enfolding and embracing the fullness of the spiritual dimension. It is the causal plane from which archetypal ideas become physical phenomena. This marriage of physical and spiritual awareness allows us a connection with the spirits of our ancestors and our guardian angels. It gives us the powers of revelation, divination and clairsentience. It is the energy of transcendence and magical powers. As a personal number, "13" gives us the ability to slip into the pure present of the "now" moment and connect with the unknowable.

But, the "13" is not an airy-fairy energy. Rather, it is the energy of life and real-world experience. While "13" people are able to see into the spiritual dimension and comprehend its mysteries, they tend to be practical and goal-oriented. The "13" energy is the urge to procreate, to bring forth not only biological offspring, but also to build something material and lasting in the world.

"13" people tend to have a logical mind, and often have a kind of practical business savvy or the life experience that gives them recognizable and agreed-upon expertise in their chosen field. They are often creative, independent and bold, and go after objectives with dynamism and self-assurance. Their formula for success is: well-defined goals combined with readiness, action, persistence, and an expectation of success brings accomplishment and produces prosperity. In truth, "13" is the number of wealth, and its qualities can be a clue to creating greater abundance in your life.

Over time, "13" people gain expertise and become authoritative in their chosen field of work. They make good advisers, facilitators who often have an ability to see another way, and can help people find a middle ground that leads to joint solutions. "13" people help hold the fabric of society together.

"13" people are also catalysts for change because they can think outside-the-box. *Paradigm shift* is a "13" energy, and "13" people are sometimes creators of whole new ways of seeing the world!

"13s" may be good listeners as well as being gifted with verbal ability. "13" is also the number of visual imagination and ability, which most "13" people may possess but some use in artistic ways. Some are artistic geniuses, as you can see from the list of famous people below.

"13" is the number that represents the will to connect with others. It is community and the urge to form networks. It is social harmony and the need to agree. It is the energy of partnership. "13" people make great friends, and good partners in relationship. They also make good grassroots supporters of the communities they feel drawn to, often becoming volunteers to help with local projects. They have an innate understanding that giving and receiving are intimately connected. In giving back something of themselves to the community, the wheel of life keeps turning, and they become open to receive its fruits.

Downside: Every number has both positive aspects and not-so-positive ones. The downside of the 13-energy can bring disorder, failure, meltdowns, and a feeling that life is meaningless and all pursuits are aimless. It can cause a person to become insular, standoffish, selfish, codependent and moody. These "13" people tend to be underachievers who experience the glass "half-empty," and see the scarcity in life. As a reaction to this belief in scarcity and the meaningless of life, the negative "13" can seek personal aggrandizement at the expense of others.

The more active shadow side of the "13" is willful and individualistic, antagonistic, negative and disobedient. These people can be confrontational, presumptuous, overdramatic, unjust, and insufferable to be around. They become charlatans who are corrupt and feed off of human greed. At the extreme, "13" is the energy of fanaticism. It can cause a person to be hateful, treacherous and even sadistic and depraved. "13" is the number of lawsuits, and these people deserve them!

The path back to balance for a "13" is twofold. First, it is to return to the pure present of the "now" moment. Most of the stuff that moves us off-center is due to regrets about the past or fears of the future. Second, the "13" person has a need to connect. Balance is restored when he or she can connect with individuals in the community and begin to give of their time, energy and talents for the good of the whole.

Mayan Connection

"13" is connected to "Aqabal" (Aq'ab'al), the dawn and the dusk. It is the time just before the sun has risen when the sky is red, the first rays of the sun – the aurora. It is also dusk and sunset, the last rays of the sun. It represents light and dark, two sides of the same coin, two opposing yet harmonious energies. It is the energy of polarity: beginnings and endings, starting new things and letting go of others, breaking through old barriers and limitations and cleaning up what's out of balance, taking a break from the routine.

More generally, Aqabal represents the ongoing process of personal rejuvenation and renewal. It also signifies sons and daughters, and the life of children and their development. It also represents plants in their growing phase.

Exercise

Chanting or singing *iii – oh,* the sound of the "13," is particularly helpful in letting go of the old and shifting into something new. It restores balance by bringing you back to the pure present of the "now moment," and gives you a platform from which to peer into the future. The sound of *iii – oh* connects with the ancestors and the powers of prediction and divination. It helps you think outside-the-box and adapt to new possibilities and potentials.

Famous "13" People

Purpose (1.8%): Catherine Drinker Bowen, Cecil Robert, Christopher Marlowe, Ernestine Ulmer, Estelle Winwood, Langston Hughes, Potter Stewart, Tenzin Gyatso (H. H. the Dalai Lama), Victor Hugo, Victor Borge.

Path (1.6%): Anthony (Tony) Charles Lynton Blair, Diana Frances Spencer, Hugh Hefner, Ivor Novello, James Schoolcraft Sherman, Martin Luther King, Jr., Michele Bachman, Vera Maria Rosenberg.

Legacy (4.9%): Adlai E. Stevenson, Carl Sandburg, Etty Hillesum, Harriet Beecher Stowe, Hillary Rodham Clinton, James Dickey, Kevin Costner, Leona Helmsley, Michael Bloomberg, Michelangelo Buonarotti, Naomi Judd, Rosa Parks, Valentina Tereshkova, Bill Clinton.

Drive (8.4%): Alan Watts, Barry Goldwater, Bill Maher, Diane Keaton, Douglas MacArthur, Eartha Kitt, Ethel Merman, Franklin Pierce, Gertrude Stein, Graham Nash, James Monroe, James P. Hoffa, Jascha Heifetz, John Galliano, Michael Eisner, Vidal Sassoon.

Totem Animals: duck … narwhal … praying mantis.

Deities: Buddha (one who is awake) … Quetzalcoatl (Aztec/Toltec creator sky god) … Vishnu (Hindu Supreme Being).

Powers: Dryness, summer, sunshine … sundown.

Colors: aqua, blue topaz, turquoise … cyan, gray-green, lemon lime, myrtle, shamrock green … burnt umber, carrot, orange, mustard, sand, sunglow … eggplant, purple-black … redness, reddish-gold … battleship grey, platinum … translucent … calico, pastels.

Gemstones: blue topaz, mother-of-pearl.

Science-related: ballistics, bioengineering, chromatography, conflictology, cryogenics, cryptology, epistemology, healing arts, hydraulics, lexicography, materials science, metaphysics, mineralogy, numerology, onomastics, paleoanthropology, palmistry, pharmacology, psychology, vibrational medicine.

Work-related Areas/Associations: adviser, alchemist, ambassador, announcer, appraiser, apprentice, archaeologist, barkeeper, biophysicist, body-worker, campaign worker, chemist, chief operating officer, chief technology officer, civil engineering, civil litigation, cosmochemist, cryptoanalysis, decorator, director, exotic dancer, family doctor, financial planner, florist, fumigator, gamekeeper, hair colorist, healing arts, hitchhiker, hostess, humanities, investigator, Jungian analyst, kabalist, landlord, leatherwork, librarian, logistician, magistrate, marine geologist, metasystems analyst, meteorologist, modern nursing, money lender, national security, number cruncher, oncologist, pacifist, paleobiologist, paralegal, pediatrician, phlebotomist, photographer, podiatrist, printer, production, prospector, psychoanalysis, public arena, pulmonologist, satirist, self-promoter, seismologist, shopkeeper, sommelier, speaker, sponsor, technical service, thanatologist, technocrat, theorist, think-tank, ufologist, veteran, virologist, war historian, warlord, weaver.

14 (R): Humanitarian, Harvest, Leadership   Chant: eh – iii.

Medicine Wheel Path: South/Emotional ⇒ West/Physical

Mystical Keywords: Consciousness, Higher Self, Superconsciousness, Observing Consciousness … Ancient Wisdom, World Mind, World

Soul ... Cellular Memory, Genetic Memory ... Prophecy, Telepathy, Psychic Experience, Remote Influence ... Mind-Body Healing.

Collective Keywords: Connectedness, Cooperativity, Deep Connection, Deep-Empathy ... Internet ... Prevailing Ideas ... Civil Liberty, Utopian Equality, Social Support ... Organization, Societal Norm; (-) Parochialism ... Otherness ... Societal Conflict ... Wealth Incumbency.

Positive Keywords: Affirmation, Belief, Conviction ... Harvest ... Creative Impulse, Fertility, Growth, Propagate ... Objective Judgment, Pragmatic, Organization, Structure, Matrix ... Goal, Planning, Concreteness, Groundedness ... Performed Action, Physical Labor ... Leadership, Fame, Individuality, Individual Excellence, Individual Gain ... Articulation, Conversation, Meditator, Negotiation ... Life-Enhancing, Fairness, Supportive, Nurturance, Maternal Love, Protective ... Vibrant, Wonderful ... Glee ... Humanitarian, Moral Stance, Peace.

Negative/Shadow Keywords: Separation, Heartbreak, Pessimism ... Inferiority, Needy, Social Isolation, Withdrawn, Unknown ... Slow-Witted, Dumb, Incorrect ... Feeble, Exhausted, Actionless ... Do Without, Impoverished, Poverty ... Disharmony, Disparagement, Incompatibility, Marital Discord ... Compulsion, Drivenness ... Craziness, Overexcite ... Obstinate, Controlling, Manipulative Relationship ... Dogmatism, Judgmentalism ... Aggressor, Instigator, One-Upmanship ... Ungrateful, Ugly ... Hazardous, Tight Spot ... Surveillance, Arrest.

As a Personal Number: The "14" fuses together the emotional and physical realms. It is the heart merging with physical awareness, the emotional part of our being that reaches out and embraces the physical world. This is what Obiwan Kenobe was talking about when he says to Luke Skywalker in the 1977 *Star Wars* movie, "Stretch out your feelings! Use the force, Luke!"

"14" is the energy of superconsciousness, the world mind – an aspect of the unconscious mind that is shared by a society, a people, or all humankind that is a product of ancestral experience. It is the genetic memory that is carried in our cells. People who have the "14" as a personal number have an innate connection with the Higher Self, the observing consciousness that provides access to ancient wisdom and may bestow the powers of telepathy, prophecy and remote influence. Everyone has the ability to influence nonlocal events to some degree. This is a now scientifically proven fact.[24] However, in "14" people the ability is intrinsic and, therefore, often stronger.

It is also interesting to note that these abilities – telepathy, prophecy, remote influence, even consciousness itself – are not mental functions, per se, although the intellectual mind may be in the driver's seat. Instead, they flow from the emotional heart connection with the physical world. It is also interesting that what is known as mind-body healing is a "14" energy. This teaches us that while the healing impulse may originate as a mental intention, it is the heart-body connection that fuels the process and makes healing possible.

The "14" represents a life-enhancing energetic matrix that connects all things. It is, quite simply, the power of connectedness. The Internet is an example of this "14" energy that allows us to connect, interact and network globally. On a collective level, this power of connectedness and cooperativity is the energy that binds organizations and structures together, the energy that undergirds societal norms, and is the activating energy of social support. It is our connectedness with one another that is also the foundation of our civil liberties.

"14" is the number of the humanitarian and of peace because "14" people have this inherent ability for deep connection, empathy, and cooperativity with others. This bestows a natural, if not always fully conscious, understanding of how energetically interconnected we all are. My wife, Jeanne White Eagle, who has a "14" Legacy Number, is fond of saying, "The time of separation is over." This is because she understands that no matter how geographically far apart we are, our energies are intertwined, and there is really no separation between you and me. We are invisibly connected. And that means if I hurt you, I hurt me. So, with this understanding, anything *but* peace becomes masochistic!

---

[24] See Lynn McTaggart's book, *The Field,* 2008, Harper-Collins.

"14s" tend to have a heightened sense of fairness, and have the strength of their convictions to take a moral stance even if it is unpopular. They tend to be articulate, have good conversation skills, and make good mediators and negotiators. They are generally supportive of family, friends and coworkers, and can be quite protective, perhaps because "14" is also the energy of maternal love. The common thread between all of these qualities is an ability to connect. Because of this, "14s" make good networkers, and are often well-suited for Internet marketing and Internet businesses.

"14" is the energy of "belief," and having the "14" as a personal number can give a talent for translating beliefs into reality – personal beliefs or other people's beliefs, as well. It is the ability to harvest, by which I mean the ability to attract whatever is needed or strongly desired – an ability that is linked to the generative power of belief and supported by affirmation.

"14" people tend to have a creative impulse that spurs their own growth. They take new ideas and fertilize them, and help to extend and propagate existing ones. They are generally good at planning and setting goals, perhaps due to a talent for seeing probable future outcomes and plotting a course to achieve them by setting achievable goals. Having a "14" as a personal number brings groundedness, concreteness and objective judgment. It can be a very pragmatic energy that gives the ability to stay in the present moment, deal with the "here and now," and to work within established structures and organizations.

Being objective and grounded doesn't mean being without a certain flair. On the contrary, "14s" can have a strong, vibrant individuality and a wonderful personality. They tend to have a drive for individual excellence and individual gain. They often have leadership qualities and may even achieve fame.

Downside: The positive side of the "14" is the life-enhancing energy of connectedness and the qualities that flow from it. The shadow side is its opposite – separation from this energy and all that proceeds from it. Examples include: social isolation, feeling unknown, and dealing with a sense of inferiority. Living these shadow qualities can lead to being withdrawn and actionless, and feeling exhausted, slow-witted and feeble.

The positive "14" energy bestows the power to draw to oneself the people and resources needed at any given time. Separation from this energy, or a lack of awareness of this ability to harvest abundance, can create its opposite: poverty and doing without the material and financial resources or people needed to accomplish life goals – or even to live.

This is often coupled with a tendency to get tangled up in a web of manipulative relationship dramas that can create disharmony, incompatibility, marital discord and heartbreak. Controlling behaviors, judgmentalism, and dogmatism ("It's my way or the highway!") live in the dark shadow of the "14" energy, as do compulsion and drivenness. Once an instigator starts the negative cycle spinning, it can create a trauma vortex and a tit-for-tat mentality. The "14" person can become the aggressor and get ensnared in one-upmanship, feeling compelled to give an equal or better hurtful retaliation for any they receive. Around and around it goes, creating a feeling of no escape. But, there is always a way out.

The path back to balance is first to recognize that this is craziness, and then resolve whole-heartedly to do something about it. The source of the shadow of the "14" is disconnecting from the power to:

a) connect with others at very deep levels and,
b) to attract all that is needed in the moment.

The "14" person need only understand that they have this power. It is intrinsic to their nature. Awareness and acceptance of this gift can allow them to relax, let go of judgmentalism and fear, and begin to create the life they desire.

Mayan Connection

"14" is "Kat," the Web, the energy matrix that connects all things. It is symbolized by the spider that sits in the middle of her web and is able to sense her connection with everything. "Kat" people have this power of connection. It enables them to unite people and draw to themselves the resources and help required to do whatever is needed to accomplish their desired goals.

The net is also used to store what we will need in the future, and not only physical or material things. It is the power to store memories, knowledge, life experience, as well as spiritual or mystical visions, guidance or wisdom – aspects of consciousness which may get passed on from one generation to another through cellular and genetic memory.

Kat is not only about the positive magnetic power of connection to attract what is needed or desired, it is also the not-so-positive energy of nets and entanglements. The same power to draw people and things to ourselves can also tangle us up in the web that we, ourselves, have spun. It is akin to a fisherman throwing out a net but getting caught up in it himself. Kat is the state of being trapped. It symbolizes the problems of our own making that entrap or ensnare us in order to teach us. It is that sinking feeling of confusion or emotional paralysis that results when things in our lives get tangled and there seems to be no way out. But, there is *always* a way out – as symbolized by the lizard that escapes the trap by losing its own tail. Therefore, Kat not only represents difficult problems in our lives – such as doubt, envy, jealousy, resentment, and so on – but also the energy to escape, transform or transcend them.

Exercise

Chanting or singing *eh – iii,* the sound of the "14," connects you with ancient wisdom carried in the world mind, and genetic memory carried in your cellular structure. This is also the sound of connectedness and brings the power to draw to you the people and resources needed to accomplish life goals.

Famous "14" People

Purpose (3.7%): Alphonsus Capone, Andy Rooney, Claude Levi-Strauss, Diana Frances Spencer, Diane Keaton, Edna Saint Vincent Millay, Giulio Andreotti, Margaret Storm Jameson, Margaret Thatcher, Paramahansa Yogananda, Ray Charles Robinson.

Path (0.5%): Anne Bronte, Richard Leakey, Robert Edward (Ted) Turner, III. (Interestingly, this turns out to be a fairly uncommon path!)

Legacy (2.9%): Alan Greenspan, Artur Rubenstein, Francis Bacon, Henry Kissinger, James Dean, Jeanne White Eagle, Jimmy Hoffa, Mikhail Gorbachev Sergeevich, Nikita Krushchev, Savielly Tartakower.

Drive (6.0%): Abba Eban, Anne Frank, Anton Chekhov, Clare Booth Luce, David Lloyd George, Edward Moore (Ted) Kennedy, Ellen DeGeneres, George Walker Bush, Giorgio Armani, Isaac Asimov, Jane Bryant Quinn, Joe Frazier, Josef Stalin, Konstantin Stanislavsky, Malcolm MacLaren, Robert Burns.

Totem Animals: eagle … mountain lion, panther.

Deities/Powers: Diana (goddess of nature, childbirth, hunting and the protector of the weak) … Odin (Norse – father of all gods & men) … Ra (Egyptian sun god, king of the gods).

Powers: Cold, Winter.

Colors: banana yellow, chrome yellow, corn silk, yellowness … sapphire … fern green, sea foam green … puce, red-violet … slate-gray.

Gemstones: chalcanthite, lazurite, nephrite, prehnite, sapphire, sunstone.

Science-related: anesthesiology, astrophysics, behavioral science, chaos theory, choreography, conspirology, depth psychology, eutrophication, geochemistry, horticulture, lithography, molecular biology, neurocybernetics, new science, noetic science, optometry, quantum optics, quantum theory, statistics, superconsciousness, superconduction, trigonometry.

Work-related Areas/Associations: anatomist, anesthetist, annotator, astrology, bartender, board of advisors, board of directors, botanist, choirmaster, choreography, computer engineer, connoisseur, contracting, criminalist, dispatcher, excavator, explorer, film producer, film star, geopolitics, gospel music, governess, hydrologist, law enforcement, leadership, legislator, life-saver, marksman, mathematical psychologist, meditator, mentalist, merchant, money-changer, novelist, performer, planning, psychoanalyst, public defender, receptionist, reductionist, reinsurer, sculptor, soccer player, sorcerer, sound technician, translator, superstar, telepath, translator, trapper, urologist, vocalist.

15 (S): Optimist, Businessman, Judge — Chant: ah – eh.

Medicine Wheel Path: East/Mental ⇒ South/Emotional

Mystical Keywords: Centeredness ... Clairvoyant, See ... Mother Goddess, Mother Nature ... Illuminator ... Psychic Abilities, Spiritual Energy, Vision Quest, Mystery School, Spiritual Science.

Collective Keywords: Sense of Belonging, Social Interaction, Social Contract, Tight-Knit, Consensus, Indaba ... Cultural Influence.

Positive Keywords: Turning Point ... Heal ... Will to Power: Fixity of Purpose, Follow-Through, Self-Disciplining, Unbending Intent, Unbending Will ... Steadfast, Support, Consensus Builder ... Businessman, Businesswoman, Judge ... Traditional, Reputation ... Aptness, Pattern, Functionality, Practical Utility, Tangible Result ... Visualization, Materialization ... Pregnant, Procreation ... Creative Doubt ... Mental Plane/Emotional Plane, Visual Thinker/Verbal Thinker ... Innovator ... Grassroots Philosopher, Plainspoken, Politeness ... Extravert, Optimist ... Fun, Game, Impetuosity, Joke, Comedy ... Literature.

Negative/Shadow Keywords: Bore, Overly Analytical ... Creative Block, Dumbstruck, Impossibility, Pointless, Unresolved, Unsustainable ... Spiritless, Inattentive, Wishy-Washy ... Apprehension, Angst-Ridden, Social Pressure ... Exasperation, High-Strung, Rambunctious ... Bluntness, Crassness ... Cynic, Resentful ... Socially Isolated, Bunker-Mentality, Long-Suffering, Morbidness ... Corruption, Delude, Rob, Suspicious, Underclass, Unscrupulous ... Indictment, Interrogation ... Vengefulness, Assassinate, Grim Reaper.

As a Personal Number: The "15" links the mental plane with the emotional plane. It is mental energy that fuses itself with the power of emotions. It is the integration of head and heart – with the head still in the driver's seat.

"15" is the energy of Mother Nature, the instinctual, fully conscious and alive natural world. People who have "15" as a personal number often have an innate connection with nature and the power of instinctive knowing that it bestows. They may also have psychic abilities and the gift of clairvoyance. They have a facility for achieving centeredness when they need it, even in the midst of chaos and confusion.

One of the important characteristics of the "15" person is the *will to power* which I will define as the striving to become fully realized; the ambition to become all that one can be. This may not always be congruent with material or financial success, power and fame. Rather, it may be a drive to become fully realized on a spiritual level, or to be the best one can be in a particular area of expertise. This "will to power" does bring with it a constellation of other formidable qualities, including: fixity of purpose, follow-through and unbending intent. This is linked to the quality that the "15" person has of being steadfast in their personal and business relationships. "15s" make great friends who are supportive and optimistic.

"15" people have the ability to be both visual and verbal thinkers. This means that they are good at visualization and can think in pictures. But they can also think through words. They tend to be extroverts and expressives who may talk to think. This means that they may open their mouths without a clue about what they are going to say, and clarify their views on the fly as they put them into words. It is a talent that most people do not possess. But, "15s" can also be plainspoken and say what they are thinking or feeling without a lot of filtering. Their visual-verbal thinking style can make them innovators who are quite creative and spontaneous in what they do. They are often fun to be around. In fact, "15s" can be naturals at comedy.

"15" represents the implicit social contract that we have with one another. It is the energy of "indaba," a South African Zulu term for getting together to have serious discussions, generally among the principal leaders and elders. "15" is the active energy that enables the "15" person to connect with others, build consensus on the issues and solutions at hand and, over time, have a cultural influence. Accordingly, "15s" generally enjoy social interaction and a sense of belonging to a community especially in tightly-knit groups.

259

"15" is the power to work selflessly for the collective good of the people. "15s" generally make good businessmen and women, and good administrators who are able to work within the framework of what is traditional – even though they may see beyond the normal boundaries. They are good at recognizing patterns, and are generally pragmatic. They look for the functionality or practical utility in things, and how to apply something. This can make them good with their hands, or in creating things that have a lot of practical value. They may be involved with literature, and may make good writers, bloggers, commentators, and so forth.

Many people whose names begin with "S/15" or who have the "15" energy as a prominent personal number are healers, or are involved in the helping or healing professions. An ability for instinctive knowing also allows the "15" person to be a good judge of character, or a good judge in the courtroom.

Downside: The positive side of the "15" is practical and has an unbending will. The shadow side of the "15" person is spiritless and wishy-washy, and feels fragmented and displaced. The positive side is upbeat, expressive and fun to be around. The shadow side can be overly analytical and boring. The positive "15" is an innovator and procreator, the negative "15" tells herself that the goal is either pointless or an impossibility, and moves forward in unsustainable ways.

The positive "15" person is extroverted. The negative "15" person can be socially isolated, suspicious and resentful of others, and adopt a long-suffering attitude. The positive "15" person is plainspoken, but the negative "15" takes this to a level of bluntness that is objectionable and even crass.

In the penumbra of the "15's" shadow lies apprehension and timidity on one side, and exasperation and rambunctious action on the other. At the extreme, the negative "15" person can become unscrupulous, corrupt and vengeful.

Mayan Connection

The "15" is connected to "Kan," the serpent, the kundalini energy or inner fire which begins at the base of the spine. Kan represents the Creator of the universe. It is the energy behind human evolution, spiritual development, and every kind of growth. Kan represents the energy behind cyclic patterns such as the orbit of planets, the double-helix of DNA, and the cycles of time and change.

Kan gives the power to continue to move forward even in the face of adversity. It is the ability to act, and the agility of action. It is the energy of athletes, all kinds of games and high energy things, and the energy in the nervous system. Kan makes a person strong and fast. Indeed, people with this energy can be suddenly fiery and ferocious when angered. Kan also fuels sexual energy and drive.

The energy of Kan not only makes a person strong and fast, it also feeds mental ability, intelligence, knowledge, and its transmutation into wisdom.

Exercise

Chanting or singing *ah – eh,* the sound of the "15," connects the head and heart. It activates the life force, provides increased energy and focus for practical action, and may help accelerate healing. It may also bring clairvoyance and the ability to "see" what others may not be able to see.

Famous "15" People

Purpose (0.4%): Hal Holbrook, Hal Roach, Meg Ryan, Rob Lowe, Rob Roy MacGregor, Sai Baba, Sue Mehrtens.

Path (0.7%): Alan Carney (AKA David Boughal), Hortense Calisher, Maxwell (Max) Alan Lerner, Sidney Hook.

Legacy (1.1%): Alexis de Tocqueville, Clark Gable, Francis Picabia, Julian Bond, Lee Van Cleef, Michele de Nostredame.

Drive (4.6%): Anthony M. Kennedy, Charles Osgood, Christie Brinkley, Edwin (Buzz) Aldrin, Gerald Rudolph Ford, Henry Wadsworth Longfellow, Jasper Johns, John Quincy Adams, John Sidney McCain III, Leona Helmsley, Rod Stewart, Rosa Parks, Virginia Woolf, William James.

Totem Animals: bear ... wolverine ... lightning bug.

Deities: Eos (goddess of the dawn)... Proserpina (goddess of springtime) ... Saraswati (goddess of knowledge, music, arts and science).

Powers: Ability to heal.

Colors: ruby, sapphire-blue.

Gemstones: aventurine, chrysoprase, ruby, smoky quartz.

Science-related: behavioral genetics, cartography, data storage, dream symbolism, electronics, levitation, optical camouflage, space flight, dendrochronology, dream research, otolaryngology (ENT), plasma dynamics, political science, psi research, internal medicine, psychic phenomena, psychic warfare, quantum mechanics, refrigeration, scientism, semantics, spiritual science, thermodynamics, wave holography, vector equilibrium.

Work-related Areas/Associations: authorship, bacteriologist, behaviorist, businessman, businesswoman, carpenter, civil engineer, construction, contestant, ecological activism, Egyptologist, empiricist, equestrian, esotericist, ethnologist, experimenter, funeral director, geoclimatologist, graphic designer, illuminator, jack-of-all-trades, judicial activist, narrator, physiologist, princess, priestess, psychiatrist, pulmonologist, registrar, religious leader, security guard, specialist, steeplejack, stock broker, stonemason, supervisor, tarot card reader, taxonomist, tort lawyer, TV producer, TV star, waitress, woodcutter, world authority.

16 (T): **Mastermind, Shapeshifter, Instinctive**   Chant: ah – iii.

Medicine Wheel Path: East/Mental ⇒ West/Physical.

Mystical Keywords: Shapeshifter ... Direct Knowing, Inner Vision, Infinite Wisdom ... Ancient Ritual, Spiritual Life ... Grandmother ... Reincarnation ... Retrocausation.

Collective Keywords: Collective Mind, Interdependent, Relational Space, Social Well-Being ... Impenetrable Bond, Total Agreement ... Inequity Aversion. (-) Ethnic Cleansing, Murderousness, Serial Murder.

Positive Keywords: Mastermind, Grandmaster ... Coherent Energy, Mental Push, Positive Thought Pattern, Propulsive ... New Frontier, New Possibility, Fundamental Change, Impregnation, New Growth ... Synthesizer, Interpreter, Strategist ... Liberal Thinker, Culturally Mobile, Unconventional ... Logic, Pragmatist, Observed Action ... ... Lucrative Career, Philanthropic, Legacy ... Emptiness, Introspection, Tranquility, Introvert ... Instinctive, Natural Aptitude, Subjective Reality Home, Paternal Love ... Authentic Self, Courteous, Good Intentions, Unassuming Grace ... Gain, Hardworking, Long-Term Goal ... Cure, Eat.

Negative/Shadow Keywords: Constricted, Closed-Mindedness, Limitedness, Self-Limiting, Stinginess ... Stranglehold, Frustrate, Sternness, Oppression ... Unanswerable, Irresolvable, Supersecret ... Introvert, Emptiness, Listless, Uncommunicative ... Thoughtlessness, Defocused Attention, Inconsistent, Inconvenient ... Dunce, Kook, Narcissist ... Distrust, Negative Energy ... Mismanagement ... Intemperate, Abuse, Bitterness, Nag, Surliness ... Embezzlement, Subversive, Dirty Tricks ... Difficult Times ... Agony, Cry.

As a Personal Number: The "16" is the number that connects the energy of the mental and physical realms, the power of the mind fusing with physical awareness and the body. "16" is matter in service to the higher mind. It is the mental push that puts the physical world in motion.

For instance, adding the suffix "ing" (a "16" energy) to a noun puts it into motion.[25] Try it with your name. For instance, I am "John-ing" myself into existence. The table is table-ing, the chair is chair-ing, and my computer is computer-ing. Get it? They are vibrating and singing themselves into existence.

Verb forms in English offer another example because they include another "16" energy, the word "to" – as in to fly, to swim, to sleep, to

---

[25] As Joseph Rael, Beautiful Arrow teaches.

run, to dream, and so on. The "16" puts whatever it is coupled with into motion.

The "16" energy gives the power to be a shapeshifter, at least metaphorically. A shapeshifter is a being that can change shape at will to assume different forms. For our purposes, this translates into the ability to transform oneself in whatever manner necessary. "16" people have a natural talent for adapting to any physical circumstances that are encountered. They are what can be called culturally mobile.

In its essence, "16" is the energy of the Master Mind. It is the potential to achieve expertise akin to that of a grandmaster in a chosen field. This is because "16" people inherently have a direct link to all the accumulated perennial wisdom of the ages – particularly to Grandmother wisdom – even if they are not fully conscious of the connection. The "16" person can bring this wisdom through in dreams, inner visions, and with the power of direct knowing – i.e., knowing something without knowing how you know it. "16 people are often quite instinctive because of this unconscious link to the collective mind.

As the famous "sleeping prophet," Edgar Cayce, was fond of saying, "Mind is the builder." In other words, by holding an intention in your mind and giving it adequate focus, you can manifest or create what you intend. This is especially true with the coherent energy of positive thought patterns that are both propulsive and generative (and thank goodness that positive thought patterns are more powerful than negative ones). When your "mind" connects with the physical world it puts the energy into motion that manifests your intention in the physical world – in a split second, or over time. This is the key to the ability to cure or heal, or make significant shifts in the physical world. It is the power of impregnation, or planting seeds that will grow over time. "16" is the number of new frontiers, new possibilities and fundamental change.

The "16" is logic, and so gives the "16" person a strong logical mind and the ability to sort things through in an orderly manner. The positive "16" energy inclines a person toward discipline and hard work, a grounded wisdom, and an underlying trust in life. "16s" are often liberal thinkers, but they are also generally pragmatists. They make good strategists, as well as synthesizers and interpreters of information. They are self-assured, introspective and calm, courteous and well-intentioned, and may carry themselves with an unassuming grace. They have natural aptitude for success that can lead to a lucrative career – if that is their chosen path. Successful "16" people tend to be philanthropic and be promoters of human welfare.

Downside: While the positive side of the "16" is extremely powerful, the shadow can be deep and difficult to handle. The "16" provides a direct connection with the ancestors and ancient wisdom. This can sometimes feel like an energy overload. It can blow the ego apart. The natural protective strategies are either to shut down and turn off completely, or to restrict the flow of energy through over-control. Both are unhealthy.

Shutting down and turning off can include having defocused attention, or acting in inconsistent, thoughtless and even kooky ways. The negative "16" person can be close-minded, introverted, uncommunicative, empty and even listless. Limitedness becomes the prominent self-limiting mindset. Life's questions become unanswerable. Its issues and problems become inconvenient and irresolvable. The answers are available but when Spirit calls, the "16" shadow cuts the connection and hangs up the phone.

Restricting the inner access to spiritual guidance can also be achieved through an unhealthy over-control. The "16" people who adopt this strategy can use sternness as a weapon. They put a stranglehold on the channels that might open them up to inner knowing. In doing so, they become abusers and agents for the oppression of themselves and others around them. They sow seeds of distrust, and are prone to surliness, testiness and thoughtless, unsympathetic, biting remarks, and even dirty tricks. In the extreme, drunkenness can be a problem as a way to anesthetize the feelings of emptiness and downtrodden uselessness.

Alternately, these people may focus totally on themselves and become narcissists. This is another creative way to constrict the flow of spiritual wisdom, but is a path that leads to a hollow, self-absorbed existence.

In its most general sense, when the shadow of the "16" energy rises, it can throw a shroud of negative energy over people and events. It is the harbinger of difficult times.

The cure from all of the above has two parts. The first step is to recognize the creative power of the mind to manifest physical results, substitute positive thoughts for negative ones, and cultivate positive mental patterns. The second step is to release the fear of being overwhelmed by the direct access to spiritual wisdom. The "16" person needs to ask for spiritual insights to come in gentle ways, and for their spirit guardians to protect them.

Mayan Connection

"16" is called "Kemé." It represents the great cycle of death, reincarnation and rebirth. The Owl is its *nawal*, or medicine animal. In the Mayan world, death is viewed as a beneficial energy because it frees our spirit to go to the place where our ancestors dwell, a place of true peace and harmony. Still, Kemé also symbolizes the opposite qualities that mark our journey from this life into the spirit world: the fear of death, darkness, night, and ignorance.

Kemé is also the power and strength of our ancestors and invisible guardians who advise and protect us throughout our earthly incarnation. Its energy is beneficial for connecting with the ancestors and entities from other dimensions to seek guidance and call for help from these beings with great knowledge and wisdom. When we do, they will send us answers through dreams and visions, or through intuitive flashes of insight.

This connection is particularly powerful for asking if we need to let something go in our lives — such as relationships, material things, resentments, jealousies, and so on. The energy of Kemé can also be used to ask our invisible guardians for protection whenever we feel threatened.

People with this energy often live a long time, perhaps because they see the good side of life. They see beauty and love all around them.

Exercise

Chanting or singing *ah – iii,* the sound of the "16," puts the energy of the mind in motion to manifest desired intentions. Hold an intention or mental image of the desired result as you chant or sing *ah – iii* to manifest it more quickly.

Famous "16" People

Purpose (1.3%): Adolf Hitler, Cary Grant, Eric Clapton, Fidel Castro, Floyd Patterson, Geena Davis, Gene Siskel, Ingo Douglas Swann, Joel Benjamin, Julia Bond, Konstantin Stanislavsky.

Path (0.1%): Susan Bromwell Anthony. [This is the rarest of all the paths.]

Legacy (1.6%): August Strindberg, Gabrielle Reece, Hugo von Hofmannsthal, Loretta Young, Mikhail Khodorkovsky, Potter Stewart, Rod Stewart.

Drive (3.8%): Alan Greenspan, Benjamin Franklin, Daniel Webster, Earl Scruggs, Edgar Dean Mitchell, Emily Watson, Howard Stern, James Earl Jones, Milton Friedman, Pedro Calderon de la Barca, Richard Whately, Samuel Palmer, Susan Sontag.

Totem Animals: ibis … iguana … orca.

Deities: genie (guardian spirit).

Powers: … Agni (fire) … shapeshifter.

Colors: forest green, myrtle green … chocolate-brown … reddish-purple … pearlescent.

Gemstones: quartzite, travertine.

Science-related: aging process, archaeoastronomy, brain activation, cell growth, coherent energy, compression, deforestation, distillation, electrocardiography, endocrine system, evolutionary leap, gravitation/antigravity, holographic memory, interference field, magnetic resonance, material science, medical anthropology, mitrogenic radiation, morphic resonance, obstetrics, orthodox science, polymorphism, probability wave, quantum vacuum, randomness, retrocausation, scientific inquiry, spectroscopy, string theory, subatomic level, subatomic particle, vacuum physics, wave resonance.

Work-related Areas/Associations: assistant, bio-prospecting, cognitive biologist, caricaturist, chronobiologist, commentator, cosmetologist, dental work, digital marketing, econophysicist, ethnobiologist, general manager, historiography, holistic healing, instructor, interpreter, law student, legal system, numismatics, obstetrics, online strategy, pathologist, primatologist, procurement, programmer, propagandist, radiology technician, revivalist, science advisor, secret agent, spiritualist, spiritual life, stenography, strategist, synthesize, tantrist, therapist, travel agent, truck driver, unskilled labor, wedding planner, weight lifter, working-class.

17 (V): Transformer, Doer, Understanding   Chant: iii – ah.

Medicine Wheel Path: West/Physical ⇒ East/Mental

Mystical Keywords: Godhead, Godly, Unconditional Love ... Zero-Point Field, Energy Matrix ... Being, Cause, Pure Intelligence ... Altered State, Expanded Sense, Spiritual Plane, Otherworldly ... Illuminated Adept, Psychokinetic Ability ... Magic, Miracle Worker, Titanic Power, Vastness ... Superconductor, Entrainment ... Kundalini Meditation.

Collective Keywords: Dialogue, Group Process, Public Relations, Togetherness ... Collective Memory, Collective Vision ...Civic Organization, Societal System, World Politics ... Material World;
(-) Dangerous Times, Deluge, Popular Hysteria, Supreme Test, Time of Purification ... Environmental Stressor.

Positive Keywords: Transformer, Metamorphosis, Modify ... Healing Process ... Enterprising, Dare, Doer, Positive Action ... Peak Intensity, ... Business Plan, Ideology, Efficient Control, Empirical Research, Quantitative ... Individual Identity, Personal Autonomy, Self-Realization ... Artistic Ability, Intuitive Imagery, Verbal Thinking/Visual Thinking ... Understanding, Read ... Agape, Beauty, Deepest Truth, Altruistic Love, Mahaba ... Sensual Ecstasy.

Negative/Shadow Keywords: Narrowness, Shallowness, Fundamentalism … Negative Thought … Erode, Estrangement, Marital Strife, Possessive, Separateness … Grief-Stricken, Mournfulness … Dour, Relentless … Entanglement, Enslavement, Subservient … Nervousness, Temperamental … Argumentative, Controversial, Rebelliousness, Rude … Assassin, Terrorist, Perpetrator, Rid … Dire, Starvation … Opportunistic, Prevaricator … Dandy, Ostentatious … Binge, Sensory Overload … Taboo, Negotiable Virtue.

As a Personal Number: Like the "16", the number "17" connects the physical and mental dimensions, but in the opposite direction – and this is a powerful difference. "17" is the body-mind connection; it is the material world infusing the mind with sensible power so that it becomes like a superconductor of physical awareness. It is unconditional love. It represents the energy matrix scientists call the zero point field, the ground state of being out of which the material world unfolds – the explicate order. This invisible energy matrix is also the source of causal and psychokinetic ability that enables one to work magic and miracles. "17" is the power of metamorphosis like the caterpillar becoming the butterfly. Thus, the "17" person is the *transformer* who has the power to transform the world around her/him.

The "17" is the number of the expanded sense that comes from altered states of consciousness. It brings the ability to connect with Higher Wisdom and pure intelligence. It often ignites a quest for understanding. Indeed, the "17" person has the potential to become an illumined adept such as Sai Baba or Yogananda.

The connection with Higher Wisdom often happens in a kinesthetic way, using body-knowing – call it the belly brain, or gut instinct. Physical exercise and conditioning is usually important for "17" people, who generally enjoy movement. They tend to be comfortable hiking in the wild, or even as an adventure guide. It's not so much that the physicality is important in itself. It is more that moving the body is a way for the "17" person to quiet the mind, connect with Higher Wisdom, and access the collective memory.

"17" is the energy of togetherness, so "17s" also tend to be good with public relations and enjoy dialogue processes (e.g., dia logos being the exchange of ideas). They can also be adept at helping groups arrive at a collective vision of the future.

"17s" may also be drawn to sitting meditation and quieting the mind as a way of tapping into the "zero-point field" of all knowledge. However they do it, through physical exertion or meditation, the "17" is often on a quest for understanding. They have a natural ability to shape things around them, and have often the power to create material abundance and success.

"17s" tend to be doers who are enterprising. They affect the world around them by taking positive action. "17s" have a drive toward personal autonomy and self-realization. They dare to be all they can be, and are familiar with operating at peak intensity to accomplish goals. They are generally good with business plans, empirical research and quantitative analysis.

For all of this action-orientation and practical intensity, "17" people can also have artistic ability and be good with their hands. They have an innate sense for beauty and an connection with deepest truth. They are, like "15s," good with both verbal and visual thinking, and may also have a flair for intuitive imagery.[26]

Downside: The negative "17" person can be dour and relentless. They can exhibit shallowness and narrowness of thinking. They can be drawn to fundamentalism because it offers a strict but comfortable structure free of questioning. This is not to be disparaging of fundamentalist thinking. Rather it is an observation that the strict discipline of fundamentalism is the polar opposite of a deeply questioning approach to life.

The negative "17" may feel misunderstood, and feel a need to be ostentatious and showy in order to be accepted or seen. Negative "17" people can be also be nervous, temperamental and argumentative. They may feel defensive or possessive, and can be controversial, rebellious, and rude. They can lie to others and be marked as prevaricators. The out-of-balance "17" person can binge on food, alcohol, or other sensory indulgences – even ones that are taboo. They may overstep

---

[26] See *Intuitive Imagery: A Resource At Work* by John B. Pehrson and Susan E. Mehrtens, 1997, Butterworth-Heinemann.

traditional boundaries in sexuality, and get caught up in entanglements that can lead to marital strife, estrangement in relationships and separateness.

In the extreme, this sense of separateness and disconnection can lead to becoming an assassin or terrorist.

The path back to balance for the negative "17" person is to get in touch with their inherent ability to connect with the Source of all knowledge. Renewing this connection brings not only balance, but the power to move forward in a positive way. Movement is also important for the "17" person to maintain balance.

Mayan Connection

"17" is connected with "Kej," the Deer. It combines the powers of swiftness, balance and sure-footedness. Kej is the bringer of harmony because the deer has one leg in each of the four cardinal directions (east, south, west and north), the four elements (water, fire, earth and air), and the four aspects of the psyche (mental, emotional, physical and spiritual).

Kej is the guardian of forests and nature, and safeguards the balance between humans and Mother Earth.

Exercise

Chanting or singing *iii – ah,* the sound of the "17," helps one to slip into an altered state and connect with Higher Wisdom. It also brings balance, inner harmony, and understanding.

Famous "17" People

Purpose (1.5%): Eudora Alice Welty, Eva Cassidy, Hugh Hefner, Isaac Newton, Jack London, Jim Bakker, Jim Carrey, Rod Stewart.

Path (0.6%): Austin Dobson, Benjamin Franklin, Betty White, Don Zimmer, James Earl Jones.

Legacy (1.3%): Charles Peguy, David Lodge, Donna Reed, Jimmy Page, Lara Adair, Richard Leakey, Rudolf Bing, Sally Ride.

Drive (1.8%): Andrew Jackson, Arthur Hugh Clough, Helen Gurley Brown, George Frederick Handel, Lisa Marie Presley, Mary Elizabeth Todd, Paramhansa Yogananda, Robert Nathan, Sai Baba, Stephen Breyer, Steve Fosset.

Totem Animals: bat ... deer, elk.

Deities: Cupid (god of love) ... Kali (Hindu Goddess who removes the ego and liberates the soul from the cycle of birth and death) ... Loki (Norse god who is the Trickster, challenges the structure and order of things to bring about needed change).

Powers: Agape, Unconditional Love ... Dry.

Colors: gold, red.

Element: gold.

Science-related: astrophysical, brain chemistry, empirical research, frontier, science, lasing material, magnetization, magnetosphere, military technology, periodic rhythms, photovoltaic cell, solar activity, solar magnetic field, solar photons, superconductor, Tantric science, troposphere, zero-point field.

Work-related Areas/Associations: academic, biblical archaeologist, busboy, business planning, civic organizations, conservator, correspondent, cryptologist, healing processes, hospice worker, illuminated adept, jockey, medical researcher, pharmacologist, power politics, production manager, prostitute, remote viewer, retail merchant, slick marketing, world politics.

18 (W): **Way-Shower, Seed, Hope, Ideas**   Chant: eh – ah.

Medicine Wheel Path: South/Emotional ⇒ East/Mental

Mystical Keywords: Creative World, Above, All-Encompassing, Transcendent ... Elemental Power ... Awe ... Virtual Creation.

Collective Keywords: Establishment, Substantiality ... Communitarianism, Social Integration, Interbeingness ... Women's Issues ... Information Society, Feedback, Newsletter ... Stewardship: Environmental Preservation ... Scientific Community; (-) Moral Absolutism ... Greatest Danger.

Positive Keywords: Seed, Hope, Ideas ... Unified, Centralization, Superordinate Goal ... Acuity, Conceptualization, Define, Way, Find ... Act, Accrue, Breed, Make ... Expansionist, Broad, All ... Wealth Accumulation ... Free, Fair ... Basic, Persistent, Resourcefulness, Self-Assertion ... Insatiable Curiosity / Non-Attachment ... Emotional Well-Being/Mental Well-Being, Long-Term Memory ... Affable, Enjoy, Fond, Wholesomeness ... Humanist Values ... Ally, Decency, Loyal ... Meek, Pacify ... Administrator, Board, Establishment.

Negative/Shadow Keywords: Fear, Frightfulness, Meek, Mistrustful ... Superstition ... Stubbornness, Intransigent ... Dogma, Moral Absolutism ... Self-Justification ... Coerce, Territoriality, Odious ... Imprisonment ... Bluff, Hype Cajole, Bilk ... Explicitness ... Fiery, Fury, Fray, Rabid, Yell ... Abrade, Cut, Damage, Defile, Flog, Kick ... Bleak, Brood, Drab, Sad, Woe.

As a Personal Number: "18" is the number that connects the heart with the head. "15" and "18" are complementary energies. Both merge the energies of emotional and mental realms. But, with the "18," the heart is directing the show.

"18" is the elemental power of "fire," the energy of hope, and the ability to inspire awe in others. It is the transcendent archetypal creative world where the seeds of new ideas are born. These seeds represent the virtual creation that precedes the actual objective creation in physical reality – the fully realized thing already inherent in the seed. The "18" teaches us that the *power of seeding* is accomplished by emotions that energize our intentions and thought patterns. The "18" person has the power of conceptualization and the ability to seed new ideas and create new things.

"18s" are way-showers. They have the ability to show the way for others to follow. They have the talent to formulate superordinate goals that unify people and purposes. This is one way in which they can define the path to follow and/or help people find their way. In doing this they influence others, bring hope for new growth, and have a broad impact within their sphere of influence. Sometimes, they may even change the world.

In carrying the "seed" energy, they also have the ability to cultivate and expand things – ideas, children, plants, animals, relationships, projects, businesses, networks, intangibles such as love or respect, and so on. "18" people can be extremely curious, as you might expect from those who are good at creating new ideas. But, they also want to act on their ideas, and make something tangible out of them. They are generally gifted with the resourcefulness to accomplish what they set their heart and mind to do, and can be quite persistent in their drive to accomplish goals. As a result, "18" people can have the ability to accrue material and financial prosperity even though they also have the capability for non-attachment to material things. They work well within the establishment although they have the strength and self-assertiveness to swim upstream or buck the tide. They make good administrators and may sit on the boards of organizations.

When in balance, "18" people tend to be affable, relationship-oriented, loyal and fair toward others. They make good friends and allies, and can soothe, pacify or allay the anger and agitation of others. "18s" may have an altruistic streak that gives them an unselfish regard for the health and well-being of others. They usually have keen perceptions, strong mental acuity and good long-term memory. They can also be wise, self-assured, and have a strong will that allows them independence of thought and action, and patience in the face of criticism and injury.

Downside: The downside or shadow side of the "18" is fear and stubbornness. "18" people can become fearful and mistrustful. They may be superstitious, but this is just another face of fear. And they may be meek, or sad, and brood over things that don't go their way, or over imagined slights. And, as an extension of fear-based thinking, territoriality can be an issue – i.e., this is mine, not yours!

Alternately, the negative "18" may become stubborn, intransigent, and set in their opinions and ways. In the extreme, they may adopt a mindset of moral absolutism in which there are absolute and inflexible standards of morality. If this is the case, they are likely to be bigoted and coercive. In fact, they have the potential to be fiery, furious adversaries in disagreements.

The negative or unbalanced "18" person can also be a huckster who is good at hype, and can bluff and cajole his or her way to frustrate, bilk and cheat others out of whatever they put their hearts and minds to: possessions, credit for successful endeavors, ideas not their own, and so on.

The way back to balance for the negative "18" person is to get in touch with their inherent creative power that comes from seeding new ideas into the collective consciousness. Their salvation rests in the realization that they are being carried along by something much larger than themselves. If they will just let go and let God, they will find that there is nowhere to fall. This realization brings hope and renewed balance.

Mayan Connection

"18" is connected to "Qanil" (pronounced Kah-neel)." Qanil means germ, seed, semen, life, and creation. Humans are bearers of the spiritual seed. Qanil carries all of the codes for potential life. It is the energy of creation that gives birth to the vastness of the multiverse and all life in it, of which our own physical universe is a part. Qanil is also the energy of constant regeneration. In particular, Qanil is Mother Nature, and is also about cycles of agriculture; nurturing children, relationships, ideas, and so on.

Exercise

Chanting or singing *eh – ah,* the sound of the "18," infuses you with the energy of creation and regeneration. It can give a boost to new ideas, and provide energy to assist you in the beginning phases of most anything.

Famous "18" People

Purpose (2.0%): Chuck Noll, Jane Bryant Quinn, Jane Goodall, Jean Baptiste Moliere, Jean Chretien, Joan Baez, LL Cool J.

275

Path (0.9%): Anton Chekhov, Cary Grant, Danny Kaye, Douglas L. Wilder, Federico Fellini, Irving Beecher, Ken S. Keyes, Jr.

Legacy (0.6%): Bridget Fonda, Katie Couric, Kirstie Alley, Marcus Tulius Cicero.

Drive (1.3%): Hugo von Hofmannsthal, Edward H. Harriman, Estelle Winwood, Garrison Keillor, James Knox Polk, John Dos Passos, Langston Hughes, Louis Gerstner, Michel de Nostredame.

Totem Animals: buffalo ... coyote ... honeybee.

Deities: Juno (Queen of the gods – Roman counterpart to the Greek goddess Hera).

Powers: Seed, Fire.

Colors: drab.

Gemstones/Elements: white sapphire ... Alloys.

Science-related: cell differentiation, degenerative diseases, gamma ray burster, interferometer, long-term memory, magnetic storms, neurological disorders, photochromatics, plate tectonics, ufology, vibratory motion.

Work-related Areas/Associations: administrator, advertising agency, bailiff, bard, congressional page, conspirologist, industrialist, mental/emotional well-being, nutritionist, plastic surgeon, political history, scientific advisor, scientific community, street musician.

19 (X): Guru, Official, Duty   Chant: iii – eh.

Medicine Wheel Path: West/Physical ⇒ South/Emotional

Mystical Keywords: Deity ... Guru, Lama ... Sufi ... Augury ... Augur, Behold.

Collective Keywords: Web, Loom ... Mail, E-mail ... Cadre.

Positive Keywords: Duty, Creed ... Official, Bona Fide ... Decree ... Doing: Agenda, Eager, Keen ... Urge, Nudge, Dote ... Fuse, Labile ... Male ... Voice, Agree, Candid ... Audit, Edit, Egghead, Data, Label ... Mail, E-mail ... Safe, Subdue ... Behold, Body Image ... Décor, Gear, Nook, Tidy.

Negative/Shadow Keywords: Disobey, Rogue ... Rig ... Argue, Accuse, Bully ... Acerbic, Acrid ... Rage, Melee, Maul, Nuke, Cudgel, Axe ... Dubious ... Phobia ... Evacuee, Subdue ... Lack, Recede ... Biased, Decry, Libel ... Cloak, Lock ... Liable ... Idiot, Lame, Toady ... Vice: Debase, Defiled, Orgy ... Crud, Dung.

As a Personal Number: "19" and "14" are complementary numbers. Both connect the physical and emotional realms but in opposite directions, and with distinctly different results. The "19" is the energy of physical awareness infusing emotions with physicality – not an easy concept to understand. Think of it as the power of the inner urges that can be felt in the body. Now go one step further to recognize that it is the body that is in the driver's seat, and it gives rise to impulses that are experienced emotionally. A crude example might be sexual stimulation being a physical cause that gives rise to an emotional response. Another example might be the body's ability to know something the mind does not and can induce a sense of uncertainty, angst or a protective, fight-or-flight sense of fear. These are physically engendered emotional responses. This kind of physical "urge" may also be closely linked to concepts such as duty – duty to God, country, loved ones, and so on – a physically engendered emotional commitment.

People who have "19" as a personal number often have a strong sense of duty. They tend to be earnest, thoughtful, no-nonsense individuals who are focused in the present and have a natural disposition for doing practical things. This is true even if they are a guru like Yukteswar Giri, or a comedian like Bill Maher (see the list of famous "19" people below). That is to say, Bill Maher is *serious* about his comedy, and takes on serious issues. Yukteswar Giri, a yogavatar and Paramahansa Yogananda's guru, could bridge the miraculous with the practical.

277

"19s" also tend to be candid – even in agreement. They make good officials because of a deep sense of duty, a keen mind, and strong inclination to keep others safe.

The "19" energy activates *power issues* between the one/self ("1") and the many ("9"). It is about the choice of power <u>with</u> others (dominion) versus power <u>over</u> others (domination). As a personal number, the "19" energy presents a choice. Where does your power come from? Whom will you serve? Do you choose fear or faith?

Power issues are often connected with the labels that we place on things, and how we give voice to our opinions and ideas. The "voice" is also a physical means of conveying emotions via the voice box or larynx. "19" people have an innate understanding of how the voice creates meaning and power. It is one of the reasons they make good officials, politicians, or holders of the public trust in some way.

The "19" is also the power of giving voice to a creed that summarizes a set of strongly held beliefs – such as a religious creed (like the Apostle's Creed), a medical creed (such as the Hippocratic Oath), or the guiding principle of a political creed (such as "all men are created equal"). The creed, properly used, allows us to experience dominion. Misapplied, it can create domination. Thus, the connection back to power issues described above. There is something about a structured path that appeals to a "19" person such as following a particular creed, and living with a sense of duty. "19" people may also be creators of creeds that offer guidance for others to live by.

The "19" is also about the physical web of connections we have with others and, by extension, mail, e-mail and other means of conveying information and data. "19" people may be adept at networking or marketing on the Internet. They are also generally good at gleaning information from an array of disparate sources.

"19" is the energy of the Deity and its physical embodiment in a guru or spiritual teacher or augur who is able to connect with higher wisdom and divine future events. The "19" person can have the qualities that make them a teacher for others. They may also have the ability to see into the future, or foretell events by omens. Even if this is so, the "19" person will generally want to apply this future knowledge for practical purposes in the here-and-now.

Downside: The shadow side of the "19" is misuse of one's personal power. Negative "19s" can argue with an acerbic wit. They can libel and/or bully others, projecting their inner problems outward onto others. They may be prone to fits of irrationality and rage.

Negative "19" people can avoid duty, disobey authority, and be dishonest scoundrels and rogues. They may even debase themselves and others through pursuing a variety of personal vices.

The "19" shadow can also manifest in a more subdued way. The "19" person can be hamstrung with phobias, and/or the fear of lack. Or, they can just be a simple idiot.

Remember, the "19" energy is about physical urges and impulses driving emotional experiences. The shadow side of the energy comes from an imbalance in one's bodily urges. When they become too strong, the outcome is a lack of conscious awareness.

The path back to the positive "19" energy requires balancing the physical and emotional energies. This can be done through the voice: singing or chanting the sound of the "19," *eh – iii*. It can also be done through a reconnection to a sense of duty or creed, and/or a recommitment to having generative power with others instead of degenerative power over others.

<u>Mayan Connection</u>

"19" is connected with "Toj," and is symbolized by the sacred ceremonial fire. It represents gratitude, the clearing of debts. It is karma, and the law of cause and effect that repays us for the actions we have taken in life, both positive and not-so-positive. Toj is the sign of payment and atonement to the Creator and to Mother Earth. It teaches us that having sincere gratitude and saying thank you to the Creator for all of our blessings is a necessary step to keep abundance flowing into our lives.

Exercise

Chanting or singing *iii – eh,* the sound of the "19," helps to bring balance to physical and emotional energies, and is especially helpful to alleviate and calm feelings of uncertainty, anxiety, insecurity, or fear.

Famous "19" People

Purpose (0.5%): Bill Maher, Emily Watson, Ken S. Keyes, Jr., Mel Gibson, Ted Kaczynski (the Unabomber).

Path (0.9%): Augustine Birrell, Edwin "Buzz" Aldrin, Jeffrey Katzenberg, Marcus Aurelius Antonius, Muhammad Ali.

Legacy (0.6%): Alexander Graham Bell, Calvin Coolidge, David Bowie, Richard Bruce (Dick) Cheney, Yukteswar Giri.

Totem Animals: bull, mule, ox ... mole.

Deities: Phoebe (goddess of the bright intellect).

Powers: Ocean tides ... rage ... the voice.

Colors: cedar, gray, indigo, lime, rouge.

Gemstones: cedar beads.

Science-related: biofeedback, dying, geology.

Work-related Areas/Associations: daycare, gigolo, guru, lama, official, voice teacher.

20 (Z): Sage, Hero, Fate ... Accuracy   Chant: oh – iii.

Medicine Wheel Path: North/Spiritual ⇒ West/Spiritual

Mystical Keywords: Void ... Auric Body.

Collective Keywords: Bank, Barcode ... Debate; (-) Siege.

Positive Keywords: Sage, Hero, Fate … Accuracy, Cogency … Audacious, Force, Head-On … Avid, Aficionado … Bloom, Fecund … Debut, Diva … Fit, Honed … Call, Hear, Memo … Debate, Mime … Chop, Cull, Lean … Keep … Local, Here … Mobile, Amble … Abiding, Amiable, Balm … Child, Joyful, Laugh, Yummy, Fete … Good Deal … Heir, Hire, Loan, Debt … Pay Off.

Negative/Shadow Keywords: Doubt, Alone, Limbo, Lone … Denuded … Alien … Anal … Avoid, Evade, Guise … Ego-Bound … Block, Bondage, Box, Cell, Dead End … Brag, Buffoon, Busybody … Loony, Farce … Cheap … Audacious, Defiance, Fierce, Obduracy … Grab, Maim, Poach, Poke … Suicide … Muck … Blame, Mock, Deride … Befuddle, Boggle.

As a Personal Number: "20" and "13" are complementary numbers. Both connect the spiritual dimension with the physical realm. But, they connect in opposite directions, and this creates distinct differences. "20" is spiritual wisdom that merges with physical awareness, like Spirit taking you by the hand to guide your physical actions. It is less volitional than the "13" because with the number "20" spiritual awareness is the driver.

It is the energy of the "sage," and "20" people often have a combination of intellect, inner knowing and wisdom that gives them the potential to become the sage. "20" bestows the power to enter the void of all potential possibilities and hear the call to do something. The awareness that comes is not entirely volitional, and is consequently connected with "Fate." "20" people may feel this call. They may also feel in touch with larger forces and pulled along by fate.

"20" is the energy of the hero. It brings a sense of independence, the capability to confront issues head-on, and the urge to push the limits. It is the "force" in the same context as Obiwan Kenobe from the 1977 *Star Wars* movie entreating his young student, "Use the force, Luke!" It is this spiritually guided physical force that gives the power to clear away obstacles and blockages. But, of course, this is not always an enjoyable process, as one's own inner obstacles must first be cleared away. "20" represents the "Hero's Path," something that must be walked alone. The Chinese sage, Lao Tsu, provided an apt summary of this path when he wrote: "Be first the master of yourself, then lord over all you see." "20" people have this capacity.

There is an interesting connection between the sage, the hero, and use of the ever-present force. What links them all is the ability to slip into the void of all potential possibilities from which come inner knowing, the confidence to be heroic, and also childlike innocence. "20" people have an intrinsic capacity to be a child at heart, to be joyful and laugh. It is a good personal number for comedians as you can see from the list of famous people shown below.

"20s" are generally amiable, kind and cheerful. They are mostly good, just and balanced. They believe in social justice, peace and tend to have a strong *spiritual* faith – although not always a religious one.

"20" people make good detectives and can be discoverers of great secrets. They often have a need to be accurate, sometimes to the point of being a bit too linear and meticulous (that some might call "tight-assed," "anal-retentive" or just simply "anal"). This tendency to be thorough can be a positive thing – especially in research professions, banking, accounting, detective work, etc. – unless, of course, it is taken to extremes. "20" people have a talent for cogency, which is to say that they can appeal to the mind and reason in ways that are astute, relevant and convincing. The need to be accurate is also connected with the number "20" representing things like barcodes, banks, loans and debts.

Downside: The downside or shadow side of the "20" is that the hero's path is a lone one. Even if others are supportive, the path and the growth it engenders must be experienced alone. So it is that the shadow of this personal number puts one in touch with the feeling of being alone, even in a crowd. It can cause the "20" person to feel like he is in limbo, an alien in society and, sometimes, alien even to himself. Doubt and uncertainty can seem to block the way forward, or lead down dead end paths.

It is difficult to get outside the box in which we or society or our job or our various roles put us. The hero's path is, in part, about breaking free from this self-imposed bondage to grow beyond limitations. It is about finally realizing that we, ultimately, are our own jailers. The cell we are in is unlocked and the door is open. We need only step through into freedom and a larger life. But, coming to this realization and stepping through the door is tough work.

This ability that the "20" person has to enter the void and work with force can be stimulating but sometimes overpowering and destabilizing. It can engender certain protective behaviors. It can cause a person to become ego-bound by which I mean acting out in self-serving ways to gratify their own ego needs. They can brag and play the buffoon or the busybody to redirect attention away from inner insecurities. What is really going on is that the "20" person is using farce, or pretentious behaviors to evade their own inner work, and their own loneliness. Alternately, they can put on guises and masks to hide themselves and avoid working through the muck of their own inner issues. At its most severe, the "20" person may entertain thoughts of suicide.

There is also a more active shadow-side energy for the "20" that can make a person fiercely defiant and audacious, with a tendency to blame, deride or mock others. A certain amount of fierceness and audacity is a healthy thing, especially in walking the hero's path. But, it is unhealthy when it crosses the line into hardened feelings and obdurate actions. The result is a stubborn persistence in hurtful or wrongful actions – often as a perceived defense for uncertainty and insecurity.

The path back to balance for the "20" person is to redirect their substantial abilities to benefit others – friends, family, coworkers, and society at large. In this context, being fierce and audacious can make them an ideal guardian of both individuals and social justice, in general.

Mayan Connection

"20" is connected with "Tzi," the guardian of the family and community. It is the law that cannot be bought or sold, and also spiritual authority. Tzi people can handle both material and spiritual laws. It is connected with justice and is the best energy for dealing with legal issues.

The nawal, or medicine animal, is the dog, because he will give his life to protect the home against threats and thieves, insuring that nothing gets damaged.

Exercise

Chanting or singing *oh–iii,* the sound of the "20," infuses the body with spiritual energy and is very helpful in dealing with feelings of doubt, and in overcoming obstacles on your path.

Famous "20" People

Purpose (2.0%): Alan Alda, Alan Greenspan, Dave Chappelle, Eduoard Manet, Leon Jaworski, Leon Mirsky, Leona Helmsley, Mack Sennett, Mick Taylor, Neil Armstrong, Neil Diamond.

Path (0.6%): Lord George Lyttelton, Isaac Newton, Mack Sennett, Michael R. Bloomberg, Richard Lester.

Legacy (1.7%): Beatrice Potter Webb, Billings Learned Hand, Donald Fagen, Nathan Lane, Orlando Bloom, Patricia Neal, Samuel Foote, Victor Borge.

Totem Animals: lion … lamb … goose.

Deities: Hera (Greek queen of the gods – counterpart to the Roman goddess Juno), Rhea (mother of the gods).

Colors: black … lion, peach … lilac, ruddy … sage.

Gemstones: None …

Science-related: Auric body.

Work-related Areas/Associations: bank, bellboy, heir, mime, sage, voodoo.

21: Guidance, Grace, Money   Chant: ah – oh.

Medicine Wheel Path: East/Mental ⇒ North/Spiritual

Mystical Keywords: Guidance, Gate, Grace ... Moon ... Omen ... Name.

Collective Keywords: Elope, Wed, Nubile ... Allied ... Judicial, Jury, Plea, Edict ... Many, Wide; (-) Gang ... Genocide.

Positive Keywords: Audacity, Leap, Chance ... Money, Get, Play ... Apex, Noble, Homage ... Anima ... Coax, Engage ... Man: Courage, Defend, Defray ... Accord, Affiance, Allied ... Educate, Eidetic ... Beeline, Focus, Main ... House ... Beautify, Calm, Feel Good, Gaiety, Good Life ... Aging.

Negative/Shadow Keywords: No Choice, Unable ... Enemy, Mean, Gang ... Besiege, Fiasco, Malice ... Afraid, Baffled, Quake, Shy ... Banal, Dull ... Defer, Behind ... Bumble, Flake, Gibber ... Mania ... Bogus, Fraud, Deceit, Ploy ... Abhor, Jeer ... Booze, Decadence, Weed ... Homicide.

As a Personal Number: The "21" is the power of the mind embracing the spiritual realm. It is a complementary number with the "12." Both connect mind and spirit but in opposite ways, and with different results. With the "21," the mental functions are in a position of authority and dominance, making its energy more volitional than the sometimes explosive "12."

House is a "21" energy. One of my mentors, Joseph Rael, Beautiful Painted Arrow, defines our perceptual reality as the "house of shattering light."[27] He says that our objective reality exists only for the soul's purpose of continuing its own livelihood. The "21" as a personal number puts one in touch with the vastness of the soul's purpose because it links the mind and spirit.

In that respect, it is a gate to spiritual insight and, therefore, the energy of guidance. It is also the gateway to receiving grace, or unmerited divine assistance given for our regeneration and growth. "21" people have an innate ability to open this gate between the mind and spirit to receive both guidance and grace.

---

[27] See also *House of Shattering Light* by Joseph Rael, Council Oak Books, 2003.

With a little practice and confidence in themselves, they are also able to see in natural phenomena the omens and portents for future events. In truth, "21" is the number of man, as in humanity and human potential, perhaps because we all have the capacity for guidance and grace.

"21" people tend to be intuitive in a deep knowing-something-in-your-gut kind of way but without being able to explain how it is known. They are able to think "outside the box," see things in a larger perspective, and take chances and leaps of faith because of their intuitive sense. This not always conscious inner knowing also brings them courage in the face of uncertainty, and the audacity to stand up and defend themselves when necessary.

"21" people have the power to attract money because *money* is a "21" energy. Howard Hughes is a powerful example (see below). Isn't it interesting that the power to gain or get money is not a physical one? Instead, it flows from the connection between mind and spirit – as in setting a mental intention with a spiritual focus. This, in itself, is a great teaching about how to create more abundance in life. Yet, there is more.

"Play" is also a "21" energy in the sense of letting go of worries and totally losing oneself in the moment. This ability to play, which "21" people also tend to have, is linked with money. It teaches us that to have more money in our lives, we must learn to give up worry, give up the attachment to money and the fear of lack, allow ourselves to become lost in the moment and play! If we can see the adventure of life as a game, if we can adopt an attitude of play as we go about our work – or only choose work that feels like play to us – then we will make ourselves naturally magnetic to money.

Closely connected with this ability to play and make money, "21s" are able to approach life with a sense of purpose. They have the power to help others feel good about themselves, and can exert a calming influence on people and situations in their sphere of influence.

"21" people also are gifted with an innate talent to beautify their surroundings, if they put their mind to it. Indeed, "21" is the energy of the good life, and teaches us something about the elements that go into such a life. The formula includes not only enough money, but also an ability to let go of worry, lose oneself in the moment and play. Add to this the courage to stand for one's convictions while finding accord with others, and a capacity to face life with calmness and you've got the good life! If they desire it, "21" people have the ability to create this good life.

The way "21" people are wired gives them an inherent connection between their mind and spirit, and the power to focus their attention on what they desire. They have an ability to sift through data and information to identify the main points. When confronted with a variety of choices or alternative paths, the "21" person has a natural aptitude to see the principal path, perhaps by an inherent sense for which one has the most energy.

"21" is also the power to educate. It teaches us that the true power to educate comes from this mind–spirit connection. This connection is also the source of having the extraordinarily accurate and vivid recall – especially of visual images – that is known as an eidetic or photographic memory. "21" people often have a good memory, and tend to have a gift for educating others, sometimes just through personal example, yet often through their work, music or teaching ability. They can have a world-changing impact, as did Galileo or Sir Francis Bacon who are included in the list of famous "21" people below.

On a collective level, the "21" energy has to do with judicial processes. It is the number of the jury and represents the power of discrimination that a group of people has to give their verdict on a body of evidence, or for judging and awarding prizes in a contest. Alternately, it is the plea that the jury hears in a lawsuit, as well as the power to make a plea – an earnest entreaty for understanding. "21" people may find themselves connected with the legal system and can make excellent lawyers, judges or jurors. But, they may also wind up as plaintiffs or defendants.

Aging is also a "21" energy, and connected with the merging of mind and spirit. Maybe this tells us that when we get older and get gray hair, we are moving closer to spirit and become more open to guidance. Perhaps that is the secret to becoming friends with the aging process – to be aware that the gateway to a deeper connection with Spirit is opening. And, even at 63, I can confess that this transition is not for sissies. It takes courage. "21" people have an inherent ability to make this passage with grace.

Downside: The shadow side of the "21" is a result of something going awry with the mind-spirit connection. Sometimes, the connection shuts down or gets constricted. When it does, it can sever or severely inhibit the flow of inner guidance and source of courage. This can be frightening and cause the unbalanced "21" person to pull back from life. She can feel shy or baffled by life and unable to make her way. Alternately, it can feel as if she is trudging through a life without choices that is banal and oppressively dull. This is an out-picturing of an inner disconnect.

The more active impact of the constricted or severed mind-spirit connection can manifest as a deceit, fraud, malice and being just plain mean – either as inner qualities or ones that the "21" person confronts on an outer level. Outwardly this can also manifest as confronting a gang, or enemy. Under the influence of the shadow energy, the "21" person can feel besieged and afraid, and quake in her boots as if a fiasco is waiting just around the corner.

When the mind-spirit connection gets too revved up, there can be too much inner guidance akin to drinking from a cosmic fire hose. This can result in mania – as in the excitement manifested by mental and physical hyperactivity, disorganization of behavior, and elevation of mood. As a result, the unbalanced "21" person can turn to substance abuse such as with booze, weed, or other drugs. From this point, she can get easily pulled into a life of decadence and deterioration.

The path back to the positive side is in restoring balance to the mind-spirit connection. This requires either opening back up to inner guidance, or working with intention to establish appropriate boundaries to the flow of insight – perhaps through a spiritual discipline, or help of a spiritual teacher. This is the key to renewing the courage to face life, and to open oneself up to grace.

Exercise: Chanting or singing *ah–oh,* the sound of the "21," activates the mind-spirit connection and opens the gate to guidance and grace. The knowingness that can come as a result can reduce uncertainty and provide the courage to make choices and take leaps of faith.

Famous "21" People

Purpose (1.3%): Dolly Parton, Naomi Judd, Nick Carter, Paul Cezanne, Paul Newman.

Path (1.5%): Alfred North Whitehead, David Lloyd George, Francis Bacon, Howard Hughes, Galileo Galilei, James Madison, John Henry Newman, Konstantin Stanislavsky, Robert E. Lee.

Legacy (1.3%): Alice Paul, Elijah Wood, George Pal, Gerald R. Ford, Idi Amin, Henry Ford, Joan Baez, Ron Paul, Rutherford B. Hayes.

Totem Animals: camel ... cougar ... goat.

Deities: Yeshua (Hebrew name of Jesus).

Power: Money.

Colors: camel, ice-gray, opal, pale.

Gemstones: agate, opal ... wood.

Science-related: aging, genes, G-field, GUT (grand unified theory), tobacco.

Work-related Areas/Associations: cowboy, housing industry, judicial system, tobacco industry, yeoman.

22: Union,   Succeed, Guard   Chant: uu – yy.

Medicine Wheel Path: Center/Source ⇒ Down Below

Mystical Keywords: Buddhahood ... Kriya.

Collective Keywords: Union, Ark ... Wife.

Positive Keywords: Nuclei, Cohere, Grid, Meld, Mold ... Equal ... Guard, Heroic, Limbic ... Noun, Fact, Map ... Oath ... Reach, Climb, Voyage ... Succeed, Rich, Beget, Fill, Full, Enough ... Medal ... Give, Offer, Kind ... Advice, Beckon, Defuse ... Youth ... Poem ... Amicable, Cozy ... Cheer, Hoot, Joyous ... Clean, Hygiene.

Negative/Shadow Keywords: Imbecile, Inane, Lunacy ... Greed ... Deceive, Folly ... Few, None ... Numb, Ennui, Subdued, Vague ... Undecided, Myopia ... Deficiency, Malady ... Oddity ... Offend ... Rigid ... Hate, Bigot ... Bemoan, Dirge, Mope ... Abdicate, Abduct, Fall ... Playboy, Bawdy, Affair.

As a Personal Number: The "22" connects the Center of the Medicine Wheel and the Down Below. The center is the zero-point and represents all potential possibilities that flow from the Higher Power. The Down Below represents the Earth. Therefore, the "22" represents the sacred union between the Source of infinite possibilities and the Earth. It is Divinity anchoring itself into the very ground upon which we walk and live. It teaches us that every step we take upon the Earth is holy because we are walking on holy ground. People who have the "22" as a personal number have an innate inner knowing about this truth even if it is not entirely conscious.

"22" is a complementary number with the "11" that connects the Center and Up Above. Both are considered Master Numbers by most numerology traditions but most, if not all, never say why. Or, if they do, they say it's because of the power of doubling the same number i.e., two "1s" in the "11," two "2s" in the "22," etc. What I've found is that the 11, 22 and other double numbers can be considered sacred, master numbers because they share an intimate connection with the Source or Higher Power that is the font of all potential possibilities. The other numbers do not have this unique characteristic. Only the zero and double numbers have this special quality – e.g., 0, 11, 22, 33, 44, 55 ... and so on.

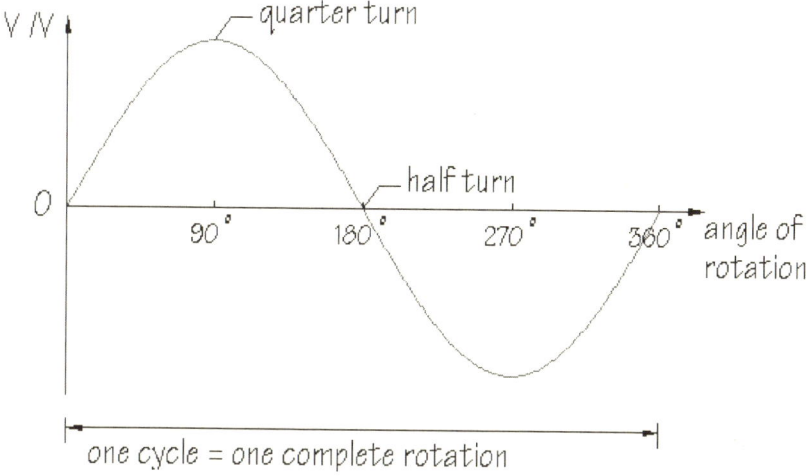

one cycle = one complete rotation

In the picture of the sine wave above, the straight line extending horizontally through the center of each wave is the zero-point line. The numbers 1 – 22 fall on this wave, starting at the beginning zero-point. Number "11" falls at the half turn where the wave crosses the center/zero line on the downswing. "22" is where the wave crosses the center/zero line on the upswing. Successive waves cross this center/zero line at 33, 44, 55, 66 ... and so on. This is why all the double numbers are considered Master Numbers. They all carry the qualities of the zero-point energy, and the power of the Divine Source! And so, people who have the "11" or "22" or other double numbers as a personal number also carry this connection with the God-Source.

The "22" represents the energy that merges Divine power with the Earth. On a mystical level, it represents the potential for Buddhahood, the state of perfect enlightenment. Kriya yoga, brought to the west by Paramahansa Yogananda also carries this "22" energy.

On a practical level, "22" is the glue that causes things to cohere. It is the energy of union. More specifically, it is the invisible energy grid underlying physical creation holding the nuclei of all atomic structures together in our perceptual reality.

The "22" is love energy in service to the greater whole. As a personal number, it carries this very practical, grounded energy of creating a sense of union, being the glue, holding things together, and selflessly serving others and the community. Interestingly, the "22" is the energy of the "wife"[28] who often provides this same function in the family!

The "22" combines a grounded physical connection to objective reality with the ability to receive inspiration and inspire others. It is the energy to reach beyond one's grasp, to climb and succeed. It brings the ability to mold and give shape to ideas, things, projects, music, movements, and so on, especially those which will have an impact on the community, society and the world. "22" is the energy that fills things up and makes them full. So, "22" people often attract prosperity that is more than sufficient to their needs, and may become rich.

The 22 person is often someone who is like a guard watching over the community, giving what is needed unobtrusively and without fanfare, sometimes doing heroic things. "22s" tend to be grounded in the here-and-now, and generally have a pragmatic, "get it done" approach to life. They are generally cheerful, amicable and kind in their relationships with others. "22" people make good advisors and poets. In ceremony, they make good fire-keepers.

Downside: The downside of the "22" is a tendency toward "lunacy" in the sense of being totally ungrounded (e.g., the "lunar" in "lunacy" referring to the power of the moon to pull one off-center). The negative "22" can be an imbecile, or a playboy (or playgirl) who deceives himself through affairs of the heart, pursuing follies, and being blithely unaware of offending others through his words and actions. When caught in the shadow energy, "22" people can abdicate their roles and responsibilities and allow themselves to fall, becoming numb to what's going on around them.

"22" people have the inherent ability to attract to themselves whatever resources or people are needed to accomplish their purpose. When they forget this, they can become greedy and act to deceive others for personal gain. They can become myopic, rigid and adopt

---

[28] Husband is a "9" energy – the foundation. In a mystical sense, the husband builds the foundation. But, the wife holds things together.

controlling behaviors. In the extreme, they can become bigots and act in hateful, hurtful ways.

The path back to balance is in remembering their natural power to attract abundance, and also their role in the family and community. They are the guardians and the glue that holds everything together.

Exercise

Chanting or singing *uu – yy,* the sound of the "22" (sounds like uuu – iii), must be done with an intention to connect the center/Source with the Earth because it is the same sound as the "11." Visualizing the connection between your Higher Self and the Earth, and chanting or singing *uu – yy* is very helpful for getting yourself grounded and centered in the here and now. It can also help anchor inspiration in your body so that you are able to act on it in practical ways.

Famous "22" People

Purpose (2.2%): Anna Pavlova, Anne Frank, Colin Powell, Edgar Allan Poe, Edgar Dean Mitchell, Elijah Wood, Horace Greeley, Jose Ferrar.

Path (1.6%): Daniel Webster, Eartha Kitt, Helen Gurley Brown, Jacob Bronowski, James Watt, Janis Joplin, Karl Wallenda, Leodardo da Vinci, Paul Keating, Ruth Bader Ginsberg, Thomas Johnathan (Stonewall) Jackson.

Legacy (1.1%): Authur Hugh Clough, Berry Gordy, George W. Bush, Hal Roach, J. Danforth (Dan) Quayle, Mary Elizabeth Todd, Max Roach.

Totem Animals: bumblebee … puma.

Deities: Theia (the Titan goddess of sight; she was also the goddess who endowed gold, silver and gems with their brilliance and intrinsic value).

Powers: Heat.

Colors: ochre, iceberg, khaki.

<u>Science-related</u>: Kriya yoga, Reiki.

<u>Work-related Areas/Associations</u>: guard, guardian, houseboy, model, nun, playboy, Reiki practitioner, selfless service.

Chapter Eleven:

Putting It All Together

When you have mastered the numbers,
you will no longer be reading numbers, any
more than you read words when reading a
book. You will be reading meanings.

~Harold Geneen~

We've actually covered a lot of ground together. You have learned quite a bit, perhaps more than you know. What is left to do is to put it all together into a complete reading. Doing this will also help you see how powerful Mystical Numerology is as a tool for understanding people. You will also get a more comprehensive feel for just how much information can be developed from just the name and birth date of a person.

At the very beginning of this book, I introduced the idea that sounds and numbers have the power to shape our individual and collective reality. The sound of our names, the numbers of our birth dates, and the sound of the words we speak carry the vibrations that shape our reality. This is the foundation upon which I have built this entire system of Mystical Numerology.

Here's what else we've covered:

- In Chapter 1, we started our journey together with the vowel sounds, and introduced the concept that they are the fundamental energies of creation. We learned about the meaning of each vowel sound, and their association with directional energies, elements, and archangels.

- In Chapter 2, we learned that we can actually do a respectable reading for someone just by looking at the vowel sounds in her or his name. This included a special look at the meaning of the first vowel, the first name vowel progression, and the missing vowels.

- In Chapter 3, we visited the consonants and learned how to convert them into numbers. I introduced the Medicine Wheel map of the numbers, and we learned the basic, simplified meanings for the numbers 1 – 22, the fundamental, archetypal numbers of creation.

- In Chapter 4, we learned about the First Letter and how it relates to the Personality of a person.

- In Chapter 5, we went deeper in working with names, learning how to calculate and interpret the Life Purpose, Inner Urge, Legacy and Drive Numbers.

- In Chapter 6, we learned about a new 13-month calendar that could help transform how we experience reality. I introduced two versions of the 13-month Mystical Numerology Calendar – one for a normal year, and one for leap years. We learned how to convert normal Gregorian Calendar dates into the 13-month calendar dates using the calendar conversion charts.

- In Chapter 7, we learned how to calculate and interpret numbers based on converted 13-month calendar dates: Life Path, Attainment Cycles, and the Personal and Universal Year, Month and Day.

- Chapter 8 gave you a reference on the meanings of the numbers 1-22 when applied to time-dependent cycles such as days, months, years and multi-year cycles.

- In Chapter 9, we learned how to calculate Life Challenges, and I gave you a handy reference to help interpret the numbers 1-22 as challenges.

- In Chapter 10 I presented a deeper look into the multi-layer meanings of the numbers 1 – 22, and their association with energies from the K'iche Mayan tradition.

All that is really left to do is to put it all together. And, for that we need to pick an interesting historical figure to demonstrate the potential in what we have learned. We need someone with universal appeal that can captivate our interest. For this task, I have chosen Leonardo da Vinci, born 15-April-1452 and who died at age 67 on 2-May-1519. He was a genius of unquenchable curiosity and is often is considered to be the archetype of the Renaissance Man.[29]

Leonardo da Vinci is one of the most diversely talented people ever to have lived. He is widely considered to be one of the greatest painters of all time, with works such as the *Mona Lisa,* and *The Last Supper,* and his iconic drawing of the *Vitruvian Man.* Yet, the scope and depth of his interests were without precedent. He was also a sculptor, architect, musician, scientist, mathematician, engineer, inventor, anatomist, geologist, cartographer and botanist!

For all of his genius and inventiveness, he was difficult to know as a person. Art historian Helen Gardner writes that Leonardo da Vinci's "mind and personality seem to us superhuman, the man himself mysterious and remote." Perhaps, Mystical Numerology will be able to shed a little light on the man.

He was born out of wedlock to a wealthy notary, Piero Fruosino di Antonio da Vinci, and a peasant woman, Caterina, in the Tuscan hill town of Vinci near Florence, Italy. His full name would be *Leonardo di ser Piero da Vinci,* so right away we must make a decision about what name to use. For our purposes, let us use the name by which he is most known, the shortened version: Leonardo da Vinci.

---

[29] See Wikipedia.

After choosing the name to use – something that is not always easy, especially with married women – the next step in doing a reading is to prepare the Mystical Numerology chart:

LEONARDO DA VINCI

9   11 14 3   3   17 11 2

37/10   +   33/6   =   70/7

(Purpose)   (Legacy)   (Drive)

Note: If we use the name, *Leonardo di ser Piero da Vinci,* the Drive = 128/11

Vowel Distribution in the Name: Leonardo da Vinci

- Mental/East: **A, A**
- Emotional/South: **E** (1ˢᵗ **Vowel**)
- Source/Center: *missing*
- Physical/West: **I, I**
- Spiritual/North: **O, O**
- Other Dimensions: *missing*

First Vowel: E

First Name Vowel Progression: E ⇒ O ⇒ A ⇒ O

Missing Vowels: U, Y

First Letter: L/9

Gregorian Calendar Birthday: 15 – April – 1452 (a leap year)

13-Month Calendar Birthday (Day–Month–Year): **5 – 5 – 1452/12**

Life Path = 5 + 5 + 1+4+5+2 = 5 + 5 + 12 = **22**

Attainment Cycles

17 (Ages 29 – 57)

(Ages 0 – 29)   10   17   (Ages 58 – 86)

5 – 5 – 12 (Birth Date D–M–Y)

(Ages 0 – 29)   0   7   (Ages 58 – 86)

7 (Ages 29 – 57)

Life Challenges

From the information developed in the chart, we can use the reference material in this book to do a reading. The first place we start is with the vowel sounds because they represent the fundamental creative energies in the name.

First Vowel (E)

Looking up the description of "E" as First Vowel on page 45, we can glean the pertinent information. There we are reminded that the "E" is concerned with issues of the heart, relationship, growth and finding one's place in the world. Indeed, finding his place in the world must have been an early issue with Leonardo da Vinci, especially since he was born an illegitimate child in the mid-1400s to a peasant woman in, perhaps, the most Catholic of all countries.

As a first vowel, the "E" helped Leonardo to be expressive, and provided the fuel and motivation for his amazingly prolific imagination and inventiveness. Very likely, he was able to receive information and insight on the emotional level through feelings. He may have had an empathic ability to feel what others around him were feeling, as well as to connect with the natural world.

Remember, the "E" as first vowel also indicates that a person is naturally "clairsentient." In other words, Leonardo may have an ability to receive precognitive information through his feelings.

Vowel Distribution

The name Leonardo da Vinci has 1-E, 2-As, 2-Is, and 2-Os: 7 vowels in total. And, we note that his Drive Number is also a "70/7," and two of his life challenges are "7s," giving us a clue that the "7" is an important energy. Other than this, the balanced distribution of vowel sound energies gives him the ability to move in many different directions.

First Name Vowel Progression: E ⇒ O ⇒ A ⇒ O

This gives us a picture of how the energy in Leonardo da Vinci's life flows, and gives us insight into his creative process. Energy and information is received through the heart and emotions, and maybe by way of clairsentience. The information and input gets processed in the spiritual-intuitive realm and sent to stimulate the mind and cognitive abilities. The information is digested, organized and sent back to the intuitive mind to activate the imagination. All of this happens in a nanosecond.

First Letter (L/9)

Other than his prodigious creativity, not much is known of Leonardo's personality. From the description of the L/9 as a *first letter* (chapter 4), we get a hint. It shows him to be a caretaker personality. It was likely that he was a diplomatic person with altruistic and philanthropic motivations. He had the power to lift others up. His amazing talent brought him many connections in the community of his day. His genius has provided illumination through the ages. With as many projects as he was working on, he probably had executive ability. We do know that he certainly did attract good fortune, a signature "9" quality.

Total Number of Letters (17)

I didn't cover it in the book until now, but I want to mention that I have noticed that the total number of letters in a person's name often seems relevant. The name *Leonardo da Vinci* has "17" letters, in total. If you look at the simplified meaning of the "17" (chapter 3), you will find words like *transformer … miracle-worker, magic … beauty, unconditional love, artistic ability … enterprising, doer.* If you go deeper, and look at the keywords for "17" in chapter 10, you will also find descriptors such as *pure intelligence, illuminated adept* and *titanic power*. All of these qualities seem to fit what we know of Leonardo da Vinci.

Working with the number values for the consonants give us the Purpose, Legacy, and Drive Numbers. The numbers of the 13-month calendar birth date will give us the Life Path number, Attainment cycles and Life Challenges.

Purpose (37/10)

The Purpose Number represents WHY Leonardo was born and WHAT he came to accomplish. In other words, the Purpose Number tells us about Leonardo's mission in life. It is the most important number in his chart.

In the basic meanings chart in chapter 3, we find descriptors for Leonardo's "10" Purpose that include: seeker, thinker, meaning … wisdom, mastery and understand. The keywords for the deeper meaning of the "10" (from chapter 10) add qualities like: cosmic psyche … prophecy … wizard … collective intelligence … Master Builder … intellectual Mastery, linear thinking … emotional intelligence, empathic. These qualities give a glimpse into why Leonardo was born and what he was here to do. We can use them to write a description of his purpose that would look much like what I have written on pages 229–232.

We also find that the Mayan Connection with his "10" Purpose is called *Ajpu,* and it is about mental acuity. It also represents work done to beautify the earth, and is the energy of the artist. What a nice fit!

Path (22)

The Purpose Number describes Leonardo's mission, which is akin to defining his destination in life. The Path Number represents "how" to best get there. It is the <u>second</u> <u>most</u> <u>important</u> number in his chart.

The "22" represents the sacred union between the Source of infinite possibilities and the Earth. It is the energy of Divinity anchoring itself into our objective reality. It confers Buddhahood upon those who are open to it, and able to handle its power. Leonardo da Vinci was one of these individuals.

Looking in the chart of basic meanings in chapter 3, we find keywords for Leonardo's "22" Path that include: *Union ... Nuclei, Cohere ... Advice, Mold ... Reach, Climb ... Succeed, Rich ... Give*. Many of these descriptors fit the Leonardo that comes down to us through history. He was certainly successful, climbing up from a humble illegitimate birth to become rich through his extraordinary abilities. In doing so, he demonstrated the power that can be brought into the world through union with the divine. More than perhaps any other individual of his time, Leonardo da Vinci embodied the humanist values of the Renaissance period. Through his genius and prodigious accomplishment, he became a focal point or nucleus around which future learning and development could cohere. He was a gift to the world that kept on giving.

Inner Urge (58/13)

The name Leonardo da Vinci has no "middle name" to give us an Inner Urge Number. If we used his full name, *Leonardo di ser Piero da Vinci*, we could use the middle part – *di ser Piero* – to calculate an Inner Urge. This would give us "58/13." This is the energy of the builder, and the number of creating a paradigm shift – in this case the movement to a new worldview with a new philosophical and theoretical framework. Leonardo da Vinci, as much as any other person, gave energy to the Renaissance which was the transition from the medieval world into the modern world.

Legacy (33/6)

The legacy is what lives on after a person has returned to Spirit. It often has to do with one's livelihood or vocation, and the body of work that is left behind. For the the simplified meaning of the number 6 in chapter 3, we see words like: *influencer, trendsetter ... awakener, intuitive ... discover, research ... teach, record ... sharing, communicate ... people, public, society*. The keywords for the "6" from chapter 10 add: *prophet ... collective consciousness ... originator ... teach, mentor* and *record*. We also have to remember that "33" is a master number. It is 3 x 11, "11" being the number of the seer and avatar.

The Mayan connection to the "6" is Ajmaq, the energy that represents ancient wisdom that comes from the brain in communication with Spirit Guides, and that gives spiritual strength. It also is about forgiveness and reconciliation. Although little is known of Leonardo's early life and relationships, growing up as a child out of wedlock in 15th century Italy probably provided ample opportunities to practice forgiveness, and may have fueled his desire to be successful and make a place for himself in the world (very much a "6" quality).

We could again take the keywords shown above and write a description of Leonardo's legacy that would incorporate many of the key elements described for the "6" in chapter 10.

The "6" is a good fit for Leonardo's legacy. His ingenuity and imagination not only influenced individual people, such as his own students, peers and benefactors, but also had an impact on society down through the ages. His paintings together with his notebooks, which contain drawings, scientific diagrams, and his thoughts on the nature of painting, taught many generations of artists. His discoveries were prophetic in the sense of that his technological ingenuity was way, way ahead of his own time. He conceptualized such things as the helicopter, the modern military tank, concentrated solar power, a calculator, double-hulled ships, and outlined a basic theory of plate tectonics.[30]

Drive (70/7)

The Drive Number is the fuel or motivation that *drives* Leonardo along his Path (22) to accomplish his Purpose (37/10). The basic meaning for the "7" shows Leonardo's Drive to include: being a *messenger,* having *vision,* being able to *visualize* and *inspire,* becoming an *expert* and an *authority* in his work. He also had the ability to *study* and *learn.* The "7" has the ability to connect metaphysical oneness and be able to translate visions into reality with the very practical capacity to be linear, logical and precise. It imbues a person with *industriousness* and *personal determination* to do *purposeful work* and *achieve excellence.* "7" is also the number of *physical ability* and *physical beauty,* qualities that certainly show up in his paintings.

---

[30] Ibid.

70/7 Drive as a Double-Digit

I haven't yet taught you about the power of the double-digit numbers. Actually, writing about the double-digit number meanings would be beyond the scope of this introductory book simply because it would make it too long.

For now, it is sufficient to say that there are different ways to arrive at a "7." Most frequently, it will be by reducing a number to a "7." For instance, the numbers 25, 34, 43, 52, 61 and 70 all have a reduced value of "7." Although each of these numbers share the general interpretation for the "7," each of these double-digit numbers also has a slightly different meaning.

"70" is about the absolute and unlimited oneness and potentiality of the Divine (0) that merges with the energy of the mystic. It is the vibration that bridges heaven and humanity. The result is the prescience and realization of a *metaphysical messenger*. It also brings *brainpower* and the power to use one's "attention" and *physical ability* to make breakthroughs and create and *disseminate* prototypical ideas and discoveries.

The preceding paragraph is a passage that I wrote for my "master readings file" three years ago before I even started this book, but it fits Leonardo da Vinci's "70/7" Drive Number perfectly. (Note: the words in italics are "70/7" words. *Prototype* is also a "70/7" word. In the text I used prototypical, instead).

OK, now let's do some more work with the birth date.

Birth Year

1452 is a "12" year (1+4+5+2 = 12). You carry the energy of your birth year throughout life. It is like an imprint. Leonardo, being born in a "12" year, carried this energy. The "12" bestows a link with the *global mind*. It is the energy of *creative forces, innovation* and *invention* – all qualities that Leonardo manifested in his work. Further, it is the number of the *visionary, pathfinder* and *initiator*.

Birth Month & Day

It is also true that the birth month and day imprint their energies on an individual, and can give us added insight. What is significant about Leonardo da Vinci's birth day and month is that they are both "5s," on the 13-month Mystical Numerology calendar. "5" is the number that connects the intuitive and emotional realms (see Appendix A), bringing the power to *conceive* and *create* – which Leonardo did so extraordinarily well!

Attainment Cycles

Leonardo's early Attainment Cycle was a "10" (Ages 0–28). His Purpose Number is also a "10." This was a time of seeking understanding and wisdom, and a time of achieving mastery. At 14, his father apprenticed Leonardo to the artist Andrea di Cione, known as Verrocchio, whose workshop was one of the finest in Florence. There, he associated with other famous painters studying under Verrocchio. He was also exposed to a vast range of technical skills including drafting, chemistry, metallurgy, metal working, plaster casting, leather working, mechanics and carpentry as well as the artistic skills of drawing, painting, sculpting and modeling.

While in Verrochio's workshop, he collaborated with his master on a commission to paint *The Baptism of Christ*. But even then, when he was still developing his own skills, Leonardo's technique was already so far superior to his master that Verrochio's is said to have put down his paint brush and never painted again.[31] Such was the mastery of Leonardo da Vinci – a "10" quality.

At 20 years of age, Leonardo qualified as a master in the Guild of St. Luke, the local guild of artists and doctors of medicine. He received his first independent commissions in 1478 at the age of 26, when he finally left Verrochio's workshop.

---

[31] Ibid.

The Attainments for ages 29 – 57, and age 58 until his death at age 67, were both "17" cycles. Remember, the name *Leonardo da Vinci* also has 17 letters.

If you will refer back to the description of the "17" cycle in chapter 8, you will see that this period in Leonardo's life was about achieving the power of balance and sure-footedness. It was a time to be enterprising, and move forward to achieve his desired goals. The "17" cycle is a good time to explore new ideologies, and can be used to peer into the future.

"17" is the number of metamorphosis. And while it is about individual identity, personal autonomy and self-realization, it is also about shifting the energy in the surrounding world. It makes titanic power available to individuals who are open to it. In the case of Leonardo da Vinci, this energy enabled him to have a transforming influence on both people and events during his lifetime, and long afterward.

A "17" period highlights the quest for understanding, including the search for the deepest truths that undergird our objective reality. The combined effect of Leonardo's "10" Purpose with the "17" attainment cycles was to spur his ingenuity and inventiveness. And, of course, "17" is also the number of artistic abilities … and miracle workers! Indeed, during these "17" attainment cycles that spanned his mature life, Leonardo had access to the ground state of pure being, and the psychokinetic abilities that can flow from it. I wonder if this was partly the basis for Leonardo da Vinci's amazing accomplishments.

Challenges

From birth through age 28, Leonardo's challenge was the "0." The zero-point is the center, the God Source or Higher Power. As a *challenge* number, it represents the need to stay centered, and the importance of connecting with one's Higher Power.

Not a lot is known about Leonardo's early life. It is known that he lived with his mother in the small village of Anchiano until he was 5 years old. From ages 5 through 13, he lived with his father, grandparents and uncle in Vinci. He had at least two stepmothers in succession (one died). At 14, he was apprenticed to Verrochio in Florence. At 26, he left his master's workshop, left home, and was ready to be independent.

For a young man, rubbing shoulders with the talented artists of his day, being exposed to new ideas and ideologies, exploring the range of his own talents, and getting connected with powerful families in the community was certainly exciting. But, it was also sometimes destabilizing. At age 24, Leonardo and three other young men were charged and acquitted of sodomy with a male prostitute. The acquittal came probably because the Medici family exerted its influence to have the charges dropped. Perhaps this indiscretion was an indication of Leonardo's struggle to maintain balance and stay connected with his Higher Power.

The Challenges for ages 29 – 57, and ages 58 until his death at age 67, were both "7s," the challenge of *knowledge, trust* and the ability to find *joy* in one's life.

The description of the "7" Life Challenge in chapter 9 fits what we know about Leonardo da Vinci pretty well:

The "7" challenge deals with being overly serious, idealistic and driven to become successful by worldly standards. It brings a tendency to be a little too linear, logical and precise. Balancing these tendencies is the major challenge of the "7." There is a need to lighten up and allow joy into one's life. There is also the need to learn to trust – trust in oneself, trust in others, and trust in life. Ultimately, this kind of trust must come from developing a reverence for life, cultivating the innocence of "beginners mind," and the "teachability" that results. This leads to greater tolerance and respect for others and, ultimately, a more egalitarian worldview.

Leonardo was a genius of monumental proportions whose range of talents was breathtaking, but it doesn't take much to imagine that he was also driven by his genius. He must have been on a treadmill of constant achievement that allowed little time for relaxation and true enjoyment.

"7" is also the number of sex (34/7) and sexuality (43/7). There is speculation that Leonardo da Vinci was a homosexual, partly because of his indiscretion with a male prostitute when he was 24. In addition, he had no known heterosexual relationships. If it were true that he was gay, this certainly could have engendered substantial trust and safety issues, assuming that living a gay lifestyle within the religious constraints of 15th century Italy would be significantly more difficult than today.

There is also another dimension to the "7" challenge that lies in the quest for knowledge. The "7" challenge brings a desire to explore the world and learn how things work at a fundamental level. The challenge is not only the exploration and acquisition of knowledge – that's the fun part. The deeper challenge is to become a teacher and share with others the life experience and wisdom that is gained. The Lao Tsu quote referred to earlier in this book is very apt for da Vinci: "Seek first to be the master of yourself, then Lord over all you see." Leonardo da Vinci certainly embodied this quest for knowledge and mastery. He became a teacher and had students in his own lifetime, but has also taught generations of artists and engineers through his work, and the notebooks that he left behind.

Take just a minute to look back over the reading we just completed for Leonardo da Vinci.

Wow! That is a *lot* of information! In fact, when you survey the amount of information that comes from just his name and birth date, you will have to agree that it is truly amazing.

Here's the best part. You can use the Mystical Numerology techniques that you have learned in this book for deeper introspection and understanding of your own mission, abilities, challenges and turning points. You can also use it to gain deeper understanding of family members, friends, coworkers, acquaintances, bosses, clients, politicians, celebrities, and historical figures. You can also use it to understand businesses, organizations … and even countries!

It is a truly powerful set of tools. My hope is that you will have fun with it, and that the knowledge you gain by using it will be both gratifying and an enrichment to your life – as it has been for mine.

Chapter Twelve:

Conclusion

> We shall not cease from exploration. And the end of all our exploring will be to arrive where we started and know the place for the first time.

> ~T. S. Eliot~

I hope you have had fun learning Mystical Numerology. You have learned a lot! Pat yourself on the back. Take a little time to celebrate coming to a stopping point. We have reached the end of our journey together. And yet, it is also a beginning.

Now, take a breath. There is more.

There are other tools that I could not include in this introductory book because it would make this single work too long, cumbersome and maybe also a bit overwhelming. I decided to teach you the basics, and leave the rest for a second book.

What is left to teach are things like:

- How the Purpose and Path Numbers work together to create an Opportunity.

- How the Drive and Path Numbers combine to create your fully mature Power.

- How to do forecasting or retrospectives – for yourself or other individuals. For instance, what energies are you working with this year and next? What energies were present when you had that accident, or got married, or broke up with someone, or started to work for your present employer? What's the best day to start that business?

- How to analyze your name to find how your energy is distributed among the 5 modes of perception: intuiting, thinking, feeling, sensing and centering. The resulting profile tells something important about how you interact with the world.

- How individual consonant values of the name and the numbers in the birth date combine to show early life lessons, and how the distribution of the energies provide insight into a person's passion in life.

- How to use Mystical Numerology to look at your relationship with another person. What kind of "fit" do you have? What are the potential obstacles?

- How to interpret double digit or triple digit numbers – e.g., 43/7 or 115/7. These are both "7s," and both share the overall general meaning of the "7." But, each also has a slightly different meaning that adds nuances that can be important. What does the "43" or "115" mean more specifically? How do you interpret double or triple-digit numbers in general? As we've seen in the example with Leonardo da Vinci's 70/7 Drive number (chapter 11), this can sometimes give brilliantly clear insights.

My hope is that as you understand the basics of this new system of Mystical Numerology, it will build a foundation of understanding for a second book that will take you even deeper.

That said, the tools that you have already acquired will give you tremendous insight if you use them. As with all things, using Mystical

Numerology will become easier with practice until it becomes second nature and begins to reshape how you see the world.

The best way to learn this process is to have fun with it. Approach your practice with Mystical Numerology like a child playing with a new toy. Play with it. Be open to being amazed! If and when you get tired or frustrated, set whatever you are working on aside. Come back to it later.

My hope is that you will get many hours of enjoyment from practicing the techniques in this book, and that Mystical Numerology will become a good companion, and a good advisor.

Enjoy!

Appendix A

The laws of nature are but the mathematical thoughts of God.

~Euclid~

Medicine Wheel Map

What I am going to show you here is a diagram of how the numbers fit onto the Native American Medicine wheel. To anyone that is familiar with the Medicine Wheel and/or ceremonial work using the Medicine Wheel, I am giving fair warning. What I discovered is counter-intuitive and not what you will expect. This is because the logical and even intuitive expectation is that the number paths will start in the east and proceed clockwise to the south, west and north. Truthfully, when I initially started to "map" the numbers onto the Medicine Wheel, this is how I started. But, it didn't work.

It took me three years to finally figure out how all the 22 archetypal numbers fit in the right places. The hardest shift to make was when I finally discovered that the numbers actually start in the north and *not* in the east, and then proceed counter-clockwise around to the west, south and east.

The Medicine Wheel represents the psyche and also the world. Finding the correct progression of the 22 energy pathways on the Medicine Wheel is also discovering something important about how reality works. A full discussion of this will be saved for a future book.

When you study the Medicine Wheel Map, you will see that the numbers 1, 2, 3 and 4 start in the center and connect the four cardinal directions. They are the initial emanations from the God-Source and the building blocks of reality:

- 1 connects the Center/God-Source with the North/Spiritual-Intuitive. It is a spiritual-intuitive number.

315

- 2 connects the Center/God-Source with the West/Physical. It is a physical number.

- 3 connects the Center/God-Source with the South/Emotional. It is an emotional number.

- 4 connects the Center/God-Source with the East/Mental. It is a mental number.

The numbers 5 and 6 are the connectors between the Spiritual and Emotional realms but in opposite directions:

- 5 connects the North/Spiritual-Intuitive with the South/Emotional. It is a spiritual-intuitive number.

- 6 connects the South/Emotional with the North/Spiritual-Intuitive. It is an emotional number.

In the Medicine Wheel map of the numbers, the directionality of connection is important. You might think that since these two numbers connect the same two points on the Medicine Wheel that their energies would be the same or similar. While there are some similarities, the 5 and 6 are actually quite different. The 5 is the energy of the spiritual realm enfolding the heart/emotions. Spirit is in charge, and it is less volitional than the 6. The 6 is the energy of the emotional realm reaching up to embrace the spiritual, and this makes it quite a bit different from the 5. The heart is in charge with the 6, and it is more volitional, more within one's power to direct the energy.

The numbers 7, 8, 9 and 10 are the reflections of the numbers 4, 3, 2 and 1, respectively. They start in the east and proceed clockwise around to the north:

- 7 is a reflection of the 4, it connects the East/Mental with the Center. Like the 4, it is a mental number.

- 8 is a reflection of the 3, it connects the South/Emotions with the Center. Like the 3, it is an emotional number.

- 9 is a reflection of the 2, it connects the West/Physical with the Center. Like the 2, it is a physical number.

- 10 is a reflection of the 1, it connects the North/Spiritual-Intuitive with the Center. Like the 1, it is a spiritual-intuitive number.

Most numerology systems stop here. But, as with the Jewish Kabalah, there are 22 sacred pathways along which energy flows in the Mystical Numerology Medicine Wheel Map. The 22 archetypal numbers representing these pathways are the fundamental building blocks of creation.

The numbers 11 and 22 are Master Numbers. They connect the Center/Source with the "up above" and "down below," respectively. The "11" draws in inspiration and guidance from higher realms and other dimensions. The "22" grounds this energy deep into the earth so it will grow.

The numbers 12, 13, 14 and 15 each connect two cardinal points on the Medicine Wheel around the outside of the circle. And now, hold onto your knickers because this is *very* counter-intuitive. It was only through an epiphany while riding an overnight train from Frankfurt to Venice that I was given a flash of insight that finally, after three years of searching, allowed me to put all the numbers together on the Medicine Wheel map in a way that made sense. Even so, it blew my mind the first time I looked at it because I was shown that the numbers 12 – 15 proceed counter-clockwise around the circle – and counter to the direction of the connection they make! Here's what I discovered on that train ride:

- 12 connects the North/Spiritual-Intuitive with the East/Mental. It is a spiritual-intuitive number.

- 13 connects the West/Physical with the North/Spiritual-Intuitive. It is a physical number.

- 14 connects the South/Emotional with the West/Physical. It is an emotional number.

- 15 connects the East/Mental with the South/Emotional. It is a mental number.

This brings us to the numbers 16 and 17. They are reflections of each other, and connect the Mental and Physical realms. Again, the directionality is important and gives the two numbers very different energies:

- 16 connects the East/Mental with the West/Physical. It is a mental number.

- 17 connects the West/Physical with the Mental/East. It is a physical number.

The numbers 18, 19, 20 and 21 are the reflections of the numbers 15, 14, 13 and 12, respectively:

- 18 is a reflection of the number 15. It connects the South/Emotional with the East/Mental. It is an emotional number.

- 19 is a reflection of the number 14. It connects the West/Physical with the South/Emotional. It is a physical number.

- 20 is a reflection of the number 13. It connects the North/Spiritual-Intuitive with the West/Physical. It is a spiritual-intuitive number.

- 21 is a reflection of the number 12. It connects the East/Mental with the North/Spiritual-Intuitive. It is a mental number.

Here, then, is the Map that puts it all together:

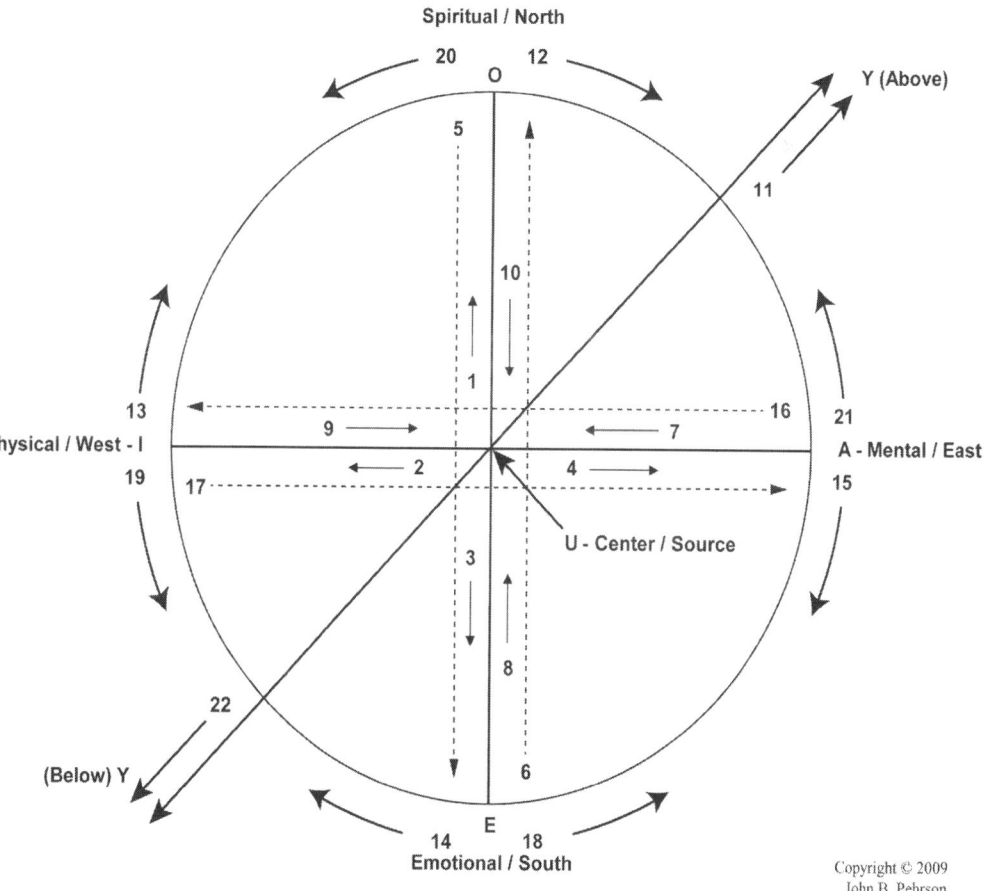

Appendix B

Traditional Systems of Numerology

Numerology has ancient roots that have grown up in the fertile soil of many civilizations over thousands of years. It is generally accepted that the ancient cultures of Babylon, China, Egypt, India and Japan were familiar with numerology long before the Greeks and Romans began using it.

Pythagoras, a great mathematician, philosopher and teacher in Ancient Greece (569–470 B.C.), once said "God Geometrizes." He taught that reality is mathematical, and that numbers are alive and are the creation tools of the Universe. His teachings were later adopted by Socrates and Plato, and studied by early Christian scholars, including St. Augustine. This laid the foundation for numerology in the western world.

Types of Numerology

Different systems of numerology have been developed through the ages. These include Chinese numerology, Indian/Tamil numerology, Chaldean numerology, Abracadabra numerology and the two most widely used systems of today: Kabbalah numerology, and Pythagorean or Agrippan (Western) numerology. The way I view these different systems is that they are each the product of their time and culture, arising to address the needs of the day. Each is valid within the context of the historical and social energies of the time. Each new system, such as Mystical Numerology, arises to replace an older one as the consciousness shifts, and a more comprehensive view of reality is needed. This doesn't necessarily negate previous, more traditional forms of numerology. Rather, a new system has the potential to draw a larger circle of understanding within which the older forms of numerology exist. This is what I believe Mystical Numerology offers: a more complete worldview for the new age of enlightenment we are entering.

If you wish to investigate any of these various traditional systems of numerology, plenty of information is available in bookstores and on the Internet. I will only comment on one or two as they relate to my system of Mystical Numerology.

Pythagorean or Agrippan (Western) System

This is the most popular and widely-used numerology system today. It uses a number system that assigns the number values of 1–9 to the English/Latin alphabet by the sequence of the letters as follows:

Pythagorean System

1	2	3	4	5	6	7	8	9
A	B	C	D	E	F	G	H	I
J	K	L	M	N	O	P	Q	R
S	T	U	V	W	X	Y	Z	

Based on these values, the value for a person's name is calculated. If the result is greater than 9, the values of the digits in the number are added up until it is reduced to a single-digit number.

This number system is often called "Pythagorean," but is not really connected to Pythagoras. It was Heinrich Cornelius Agrippa that first applied this number concept to the Latin alphabet in the 16th century (although considering the letters "U" and "V," and the letters "I" and "J" to be separate was not common until the 18th century).

You will note that in this number system, all letters in the alphabet are assigned numbers in sequence, including the vowel sounds. Also any number greater than 9 is reduced to a single digit, and this is true whether calculating the number values for names or for birth dates. For instance, in this system the name "JOHN" would be $J/1 + O/6 + H/8 + N/5 = 1 + 6 + 8 + 5 = 20$. But since "20" is greater than "9" it is reduced to a single digit as follows: $20 = 2 + 0 = 2$.

In my system of Mystical Numerology, the vowel sounds, A, E, I, O, U and Y do *not* get assigned numbers. Also, since there are 22 primary paths on the Medicine Wheel, only numbers greater than 22 are reduced. These differences are covered more specifically in chapters 1–3.

Kabbalah Numerology

Kabbalah (or Kabala) in Hebrew (קַבָּלָה) literally means "receiving." It means knowledge that comes through the mind and soul rather than through a flesh and blood teacher. This system originated in Hebrew mysticism. The basic belief is that everything in the world consists of energy, and this energy is the source of all life and power. People and names possess energy. The energy in a name can shape and guide your experience. In fact, Kabbalah numerology *only* analyzes the name of a person, and from this a reading can address an individual's future, the natural cycles in his or her life, and their probable interactions and fit with others.

There are two similarities between this system and Mystical Numerology. It is helpful to recognize that the Jews invented alphabetic writing, and the word "alphabet" itself stems from the Hebrew, "aleph-bet." The Hebrew alphabet has 22 letters, not including the vowel sounds that are written with a system of dots over or under the letters. In Kabbalistic numerology, numbers are assigned to the 22 letter vibrations ranging from 1 to 400. Later, this system of numbers was adapted to the Greek alphabet, and later to the Roman alphabet.

It is an interesting synchronicity to me that the Hebrew alphabet has 22 letters (consonants). There are 22 pathways connecting the 10 Sephirot in the Kabbalah or "Tree of Life." There are also 22 pathways connecting the cardinal directions on the Native American Medicine Wheel that is the basis for Mystical Numerology.

A second similarity between Kabbalah numerology and Mystical Numerology is in the treatment of the vowel sounds as fundamental energies. Hebrew, even today, is most often written without the vowel sounds delineated. Vowels sounds are also not assigned numbers. This is not because they are dismissed as unimportant. To the contrary, the vowel sounds (ah, eh, iii, oh, uu) are viewed as sacred and formative energies that have the power to create and manifest. Mystical Numerology also considers the vowel sounds to be the fundamental energies of creation that are given shape and direction by the consonants.

Acknowledgments

Many people have been involved in the process of discovery which resulted in developing this new system of Mystical Numerology. Some of them are aware of their participation and some are not.

I would first like to thank my lovely and accomplished wife, Jeanne White Eagle, who has who has been my inspiration, my sounding-board, and my friend throughout the years of developing, researching, teaching and finally writing about this new system of Mystical Numerology. From the first eureka moment all the way to the completion of the writing, Jeanne has been a constant support. She was also my first reader and editor. Words are insufficient to express my love and gratitude.

Many teachers and writers have influenced my thinking over the years, but not even I can remember all of their names and how their work creates subtle echoes here and there in the text of this book. I do know that there are a few that have opened the doors to new horizons and potential possibilities. These shining individuals and wisdom keepers have my everlasting thanks.

The foremost of these teachers is my mentor and friend, Joseph Rael, Beautiful Painted Arrow. He taught me about the creative power of the vowel sounds and was the catalyst for seeing the ancient study of numerology in an entirely new (or perhaps ancient) way. Joseph once told me that it was his job to open the door, but my job to step through it. Perhaps the greatest thanks I can give to him is to have stepped through the door ... and never retreated.

I would also like to thank Don Alejandro Cirilo Perez Oxlaj, a K'iche Mayan Priest who taught me about the Mayan Day Lord energies that have become a part of my system of Mystical Numerology. Even with Don Alejandro's teachings, I would still have been lost without Cynthia Walker, who is also a Mayan Priestess, and a good friend. Cynthia helped me deepen my understanding of these Mayan archetypal energies, and has kept me on-track with my count of the Mayan calendar days. Thank you, my dear!

Other teachers have been more peripheral but important. David Baruch, a holy man in Israel; and Wirimu, a Maori wisdom keeper in New Zealand; independently confirmed the creative power and sacredness of the vowel sounds in the ongoing process of singing our reality into existence. They both gave me confidence in the validity of my new system, and I am thankful.

I am thankful to Spirit for all the sudden epiphanies and eureka moments that have moved this work forward, and for all the blessings it has already given to me and others.

I offer a special thank to my middle son, Sean Pehrson, a talented artist and whiz with computer graphics. He designed the cover for this book to convey the connection between Mystical Numerology and the Native American Medicine Wheel. Sean, you have my love and appreciation.

Finally, my whole-hearted and full-throated thanks go to Joe Nusbaum and Cathy Ryan at Eltanin Publishing for their expertise, guidance and friendship. Joe and Cathy are a writer's dream team, and the best in the business!

About the Author

John Pehrson is the creator of a new 13-month calendar and a numerological system called Mystical Numerology. With an educational background as a chemical engineer, he has translated his love of numbers and understanding of the power of sound into a fascinating and potentially life-changing look at the ancient science of numerology.

Pehrson is also co-author of Intuitive Imagery, A Resource at Work, and is one of the foremost teachers on applied intuition in both business and personal life. He is a published author on community and learning in business, and co-creator of the Pathway to the Open Heart process. With an international career spanning more than 30 years, his workshops and seminars have guided organizations, groups, and individuals, promoting creativity and connectedness in multicultural environments. With his wife, Jeanne White Eagle, he travels the world teaching, counseling and working to create expanded awareness through sacred dance, deep dialogue, the practice of applied intuition, and the transformative power of sound and numbers.

8560761R00192

Printed in Great Britain
by Amazon.co.uk, Ltd.,
Marston Gate.